KU-706-529

THE WORLD'S GREATEST
COMIC MAGAZINE

WITHDRAWN
FROM
STOCK

WRITER: **JONATHAN HICKMAN**

ARTIST: **DALE EAGLESHAM** [ISSUES 570-572] AND **NEIL EDWARDS** [ISSUES 573-574]

INKER: **ANDREW CURRIE** [ISSUES 573-574]
COLOR ARTIST: **PAUL MOUNTS**
LETTERER: **VIRTUAL CALLIGRAPHY'S RUS WOOTON**
COVER ARTISTS: **ALAN DAVIS, MARK FARMER & DAVE MCCAIG** WITH **JOHN RAUCH** AND **JAVIER RODRIGUEZ**
ASSOCIATE EDITOR: **LAUREN SANKOVITCH**
EDITOR: **TOM BREVOORT**

COLLECTION EDITOR: **JENNIFER GRÜNWALD**
ASSISTANT EDITORS: **ALEX STARBUCK & NELSON RIBEIRO**
EDITOR, SPECIAL PROJECTS: **MARK D. BEAZLEY**
SENIOR EDITOR, SPECIAL PROJECTS: **JEFF YOUNGQUIST**
SENIOR VICE PRESIDENT OF SALES: **DAVID GABRIEL**
SVP OF BRAND PLANNING & COMMUNICATIONS: **MICHAEL PASCIULLO**

EDITOR IN CHIEF: **AXEL ALONSO**
CHIEF CREATIVE OFFICER: **JOE QUESADA**
PUBLISHER: **DAN BUCKLEY**
EXECUTIVE PRODUCER: **ALAN FINE**

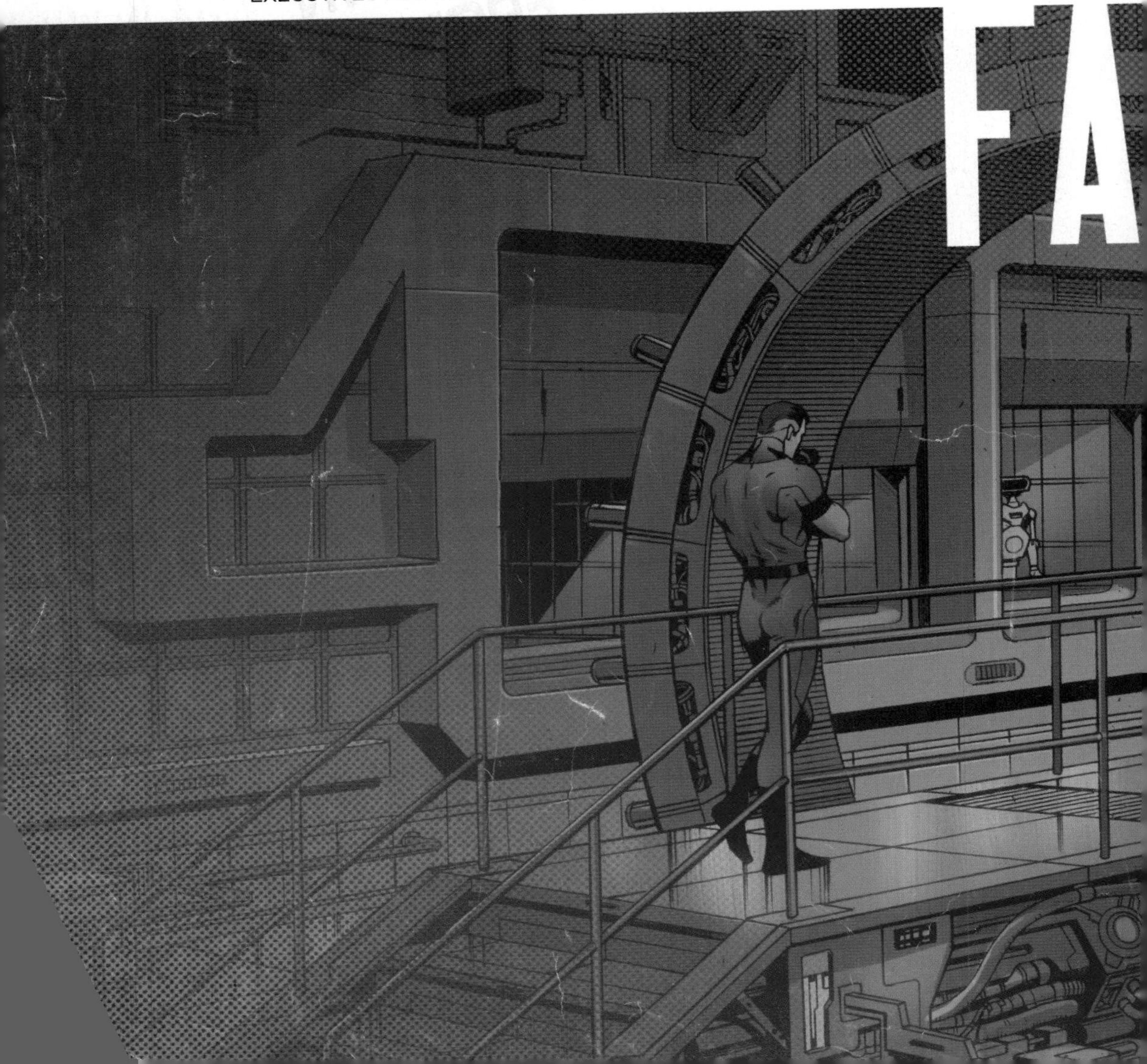
FA

NTASTIC FOUR

UNIFIED FIELD THEORY: STAN LEE & JACK KIRBY

NTASTIC FOUR BY JONATHAN HICKMAN VOL. 1. Contains material originally published in magazine form as FANTASTIC FOUR #570-574. Third printing 2012. ISBN# 978-0-7851-3688-0. Published by MARVEL ORLDWIDE, INC., a subsidiary of MARVEL ENTERTAINMENT, LLC. OFFICE OF PUBLICATION: 135 West 50th Street, New York, NY 10020. Copyright © 2009 and 2010 Marvel Characters, Inc. All rights reserved. $15.99 per opy in the U.S. and $17.99 in Canada (GST #R127032852); Canadian Agreement #40668537. All characters featured in this issue and the distinctive names and likenesses thereof, and all related indicia are trademarks Marvel Characters, Inc. No similarity between any of the names, characters, persons, and/or institutions in this magazine with those of any living or dead person or institution is intended, and any such similarity which ay exist is purely coincidental. **Printed in the U.S.A.** ALAN FINE, EVP - Office of the President, Marvel Worldwide, Inc. and EVP & CMO Marvel Characters B.V.; DAN BUCKLEY, Publisher & President - Print, Animation & igital Divisions; JOE QUESADA, Chief Creative Officer; TOM BREVOORT, SVP of Publishing; DAVID BOGART, SVP of Operations & Procurement, Publishing; RUWAN JAYATILLEKE, SVP & Associate Publisher, Publishing; C.B. EBULSKI, SVP of Creator & Content Development; DAVID GABRIEL, SVP of Publishing Sales & Circulation; MICHAEL PASCIULLO, SVP of Brand Planning & Communications; JIM O'KEEFE, VP of Operations & Logistics; DAN ARR, Executive Director of Publishing Technology; SUSAN CRESPI, Editorial Operations Manager; ALEX MORALES, Publishing Operations Manager; STAN LEE, Chairman Emeritus. For information regarding advertising Marvel Comics or on Marvel.com, please contact John Dokes, SVP Integrated Sales and Marketing, at jdokes@marvel.com. For Marvel subscription inquiries, please call 800-217-9158. **Manufactured between** 2/2012 and 5/21/2012 by R.R. DONNELLEY, INC., SALEM, VA, USA.

09876543

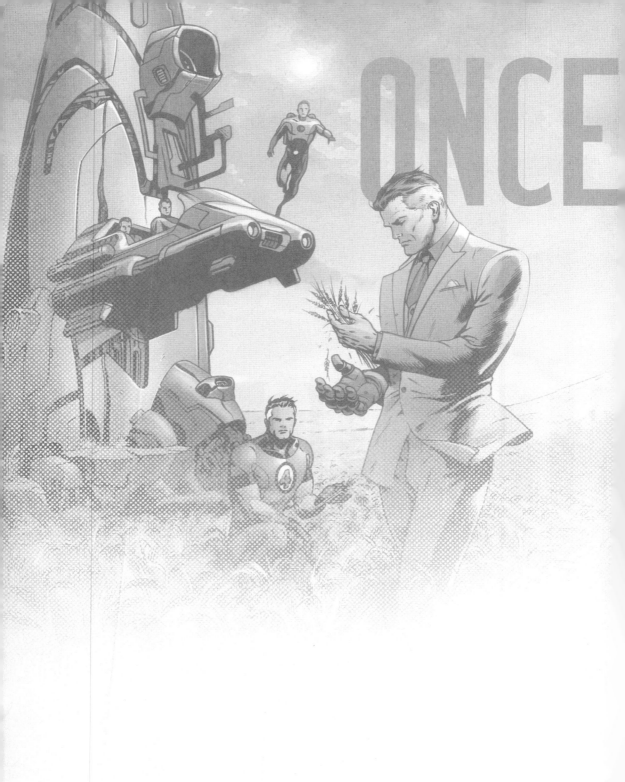

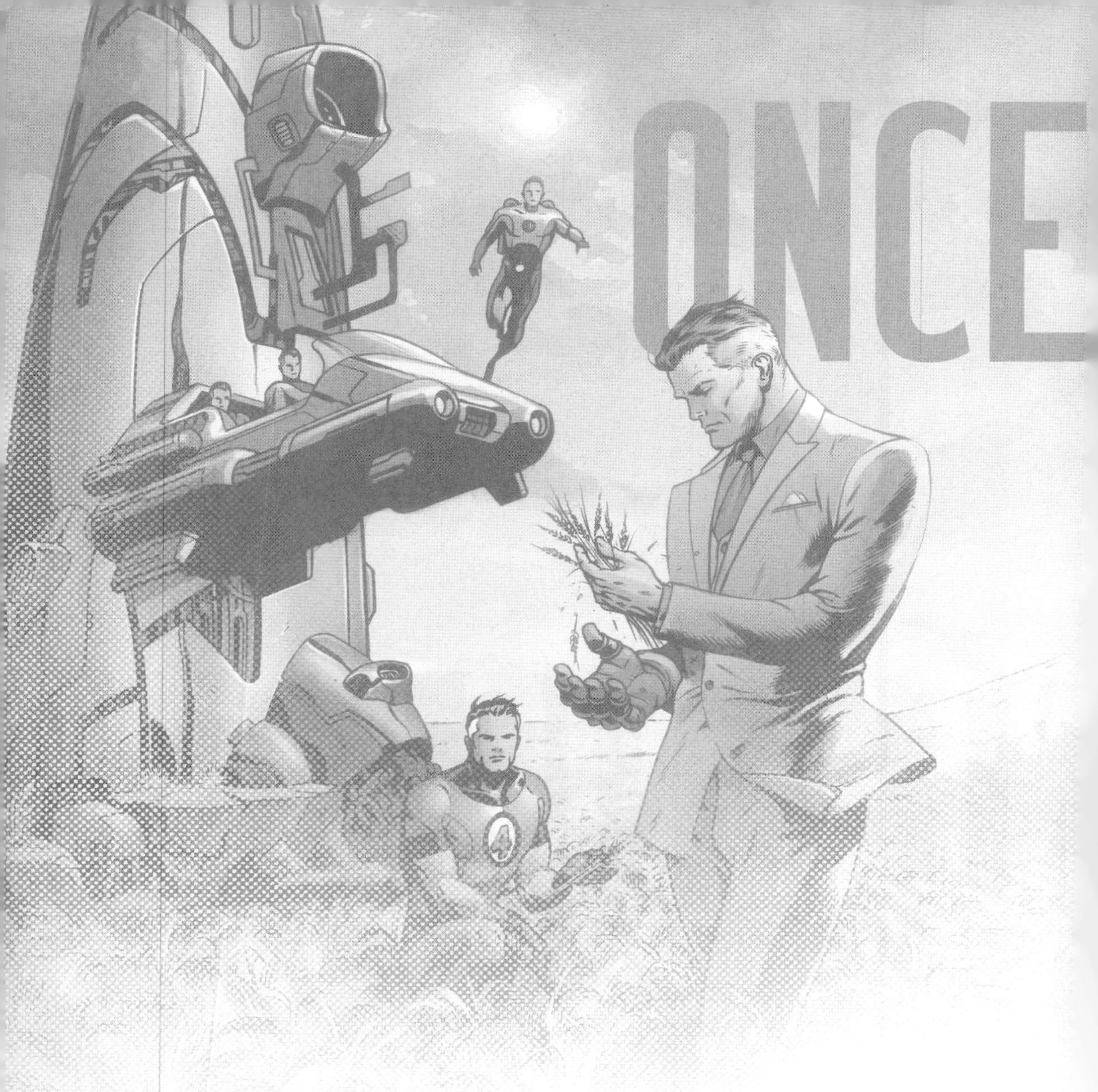
ONCE

I BUILT A
GREAT MACHINE

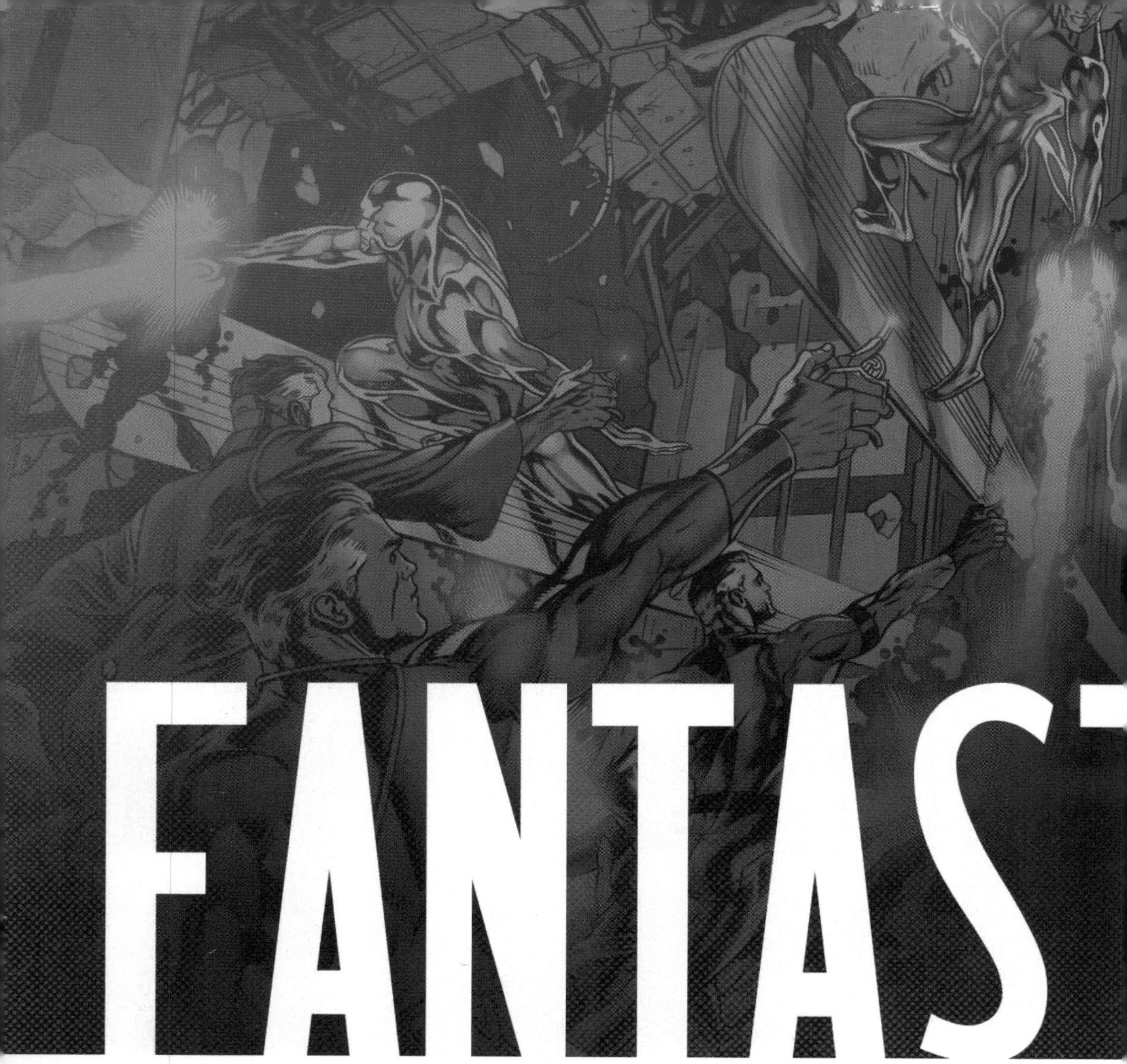
FANTAS

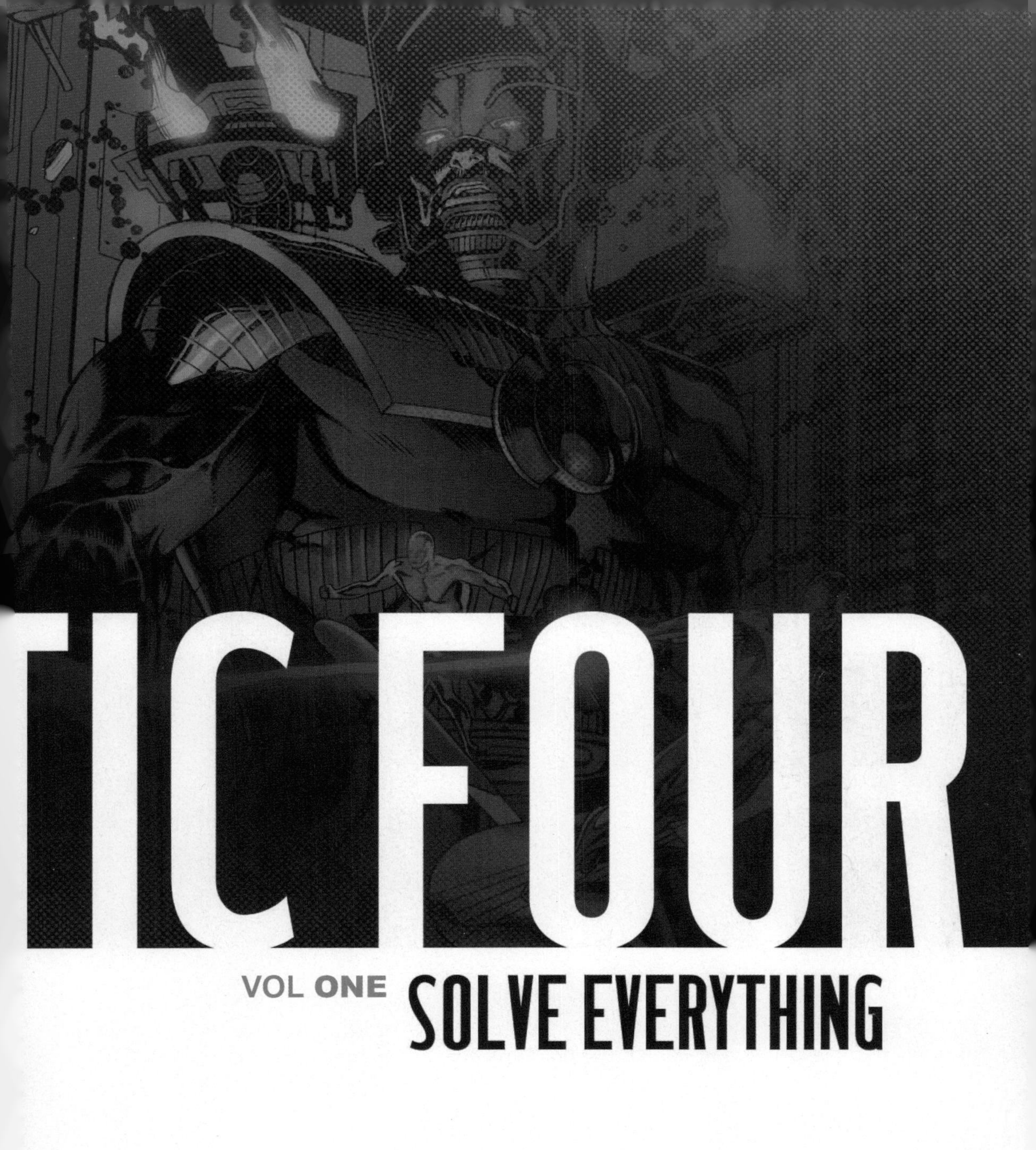
TIC FOUR

VOL **ONE**

SOLVE EVERYTHING

IS IT PLAYING GOD

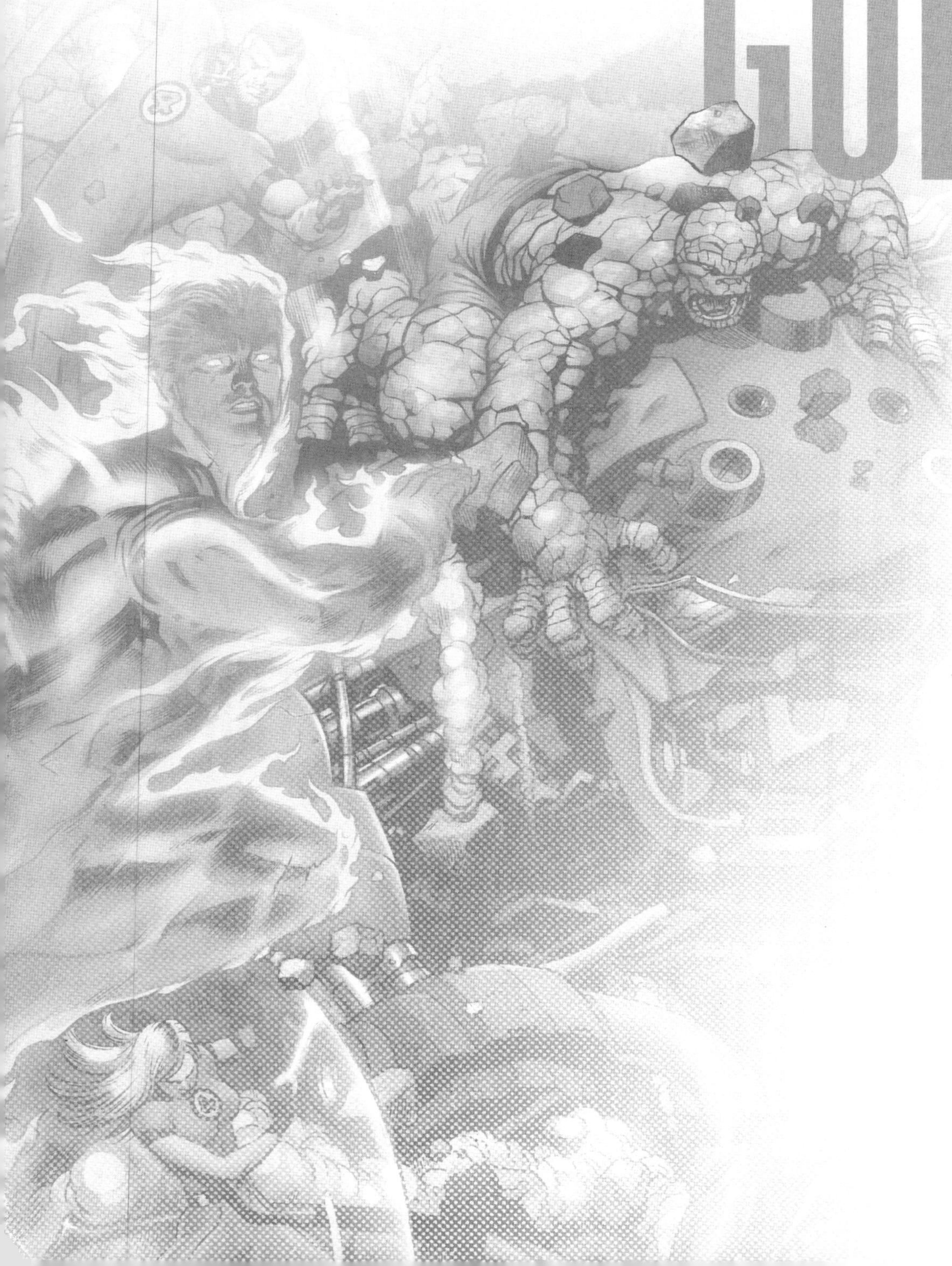

IF YOU'RE TRULY SERIOUS ABOUT
CREATION

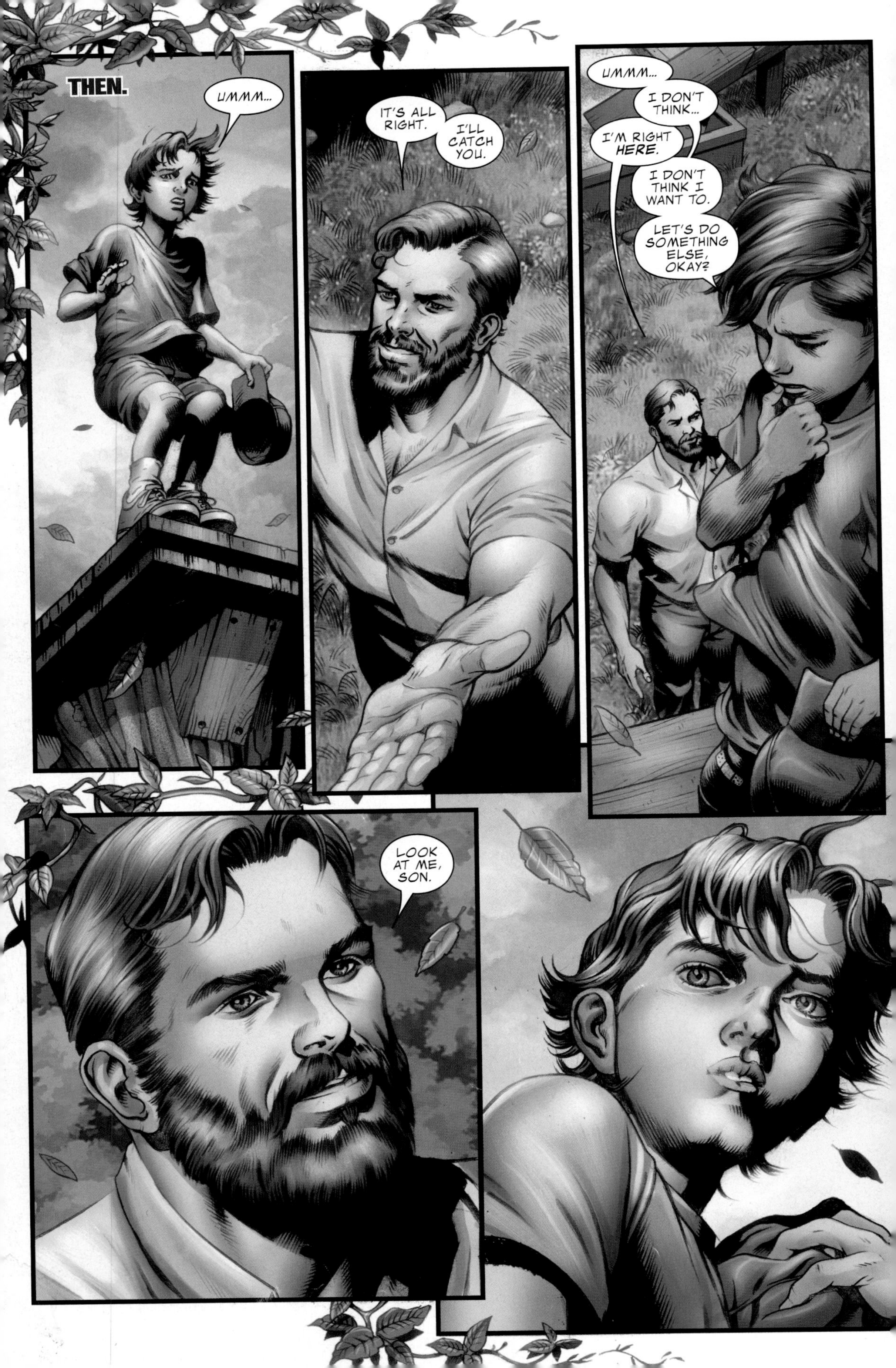
THEN.
UMMM...
IT'S ALL RIGHT.
I'LL CATCH YOU.
UMMM...
I DON'T THINK...
I'M RIGHT HERE.
I DON'T THINK I WANT TO.
LET'S DO SOMETHING ELSE, OKAY?
LOOK AT ME, SON.

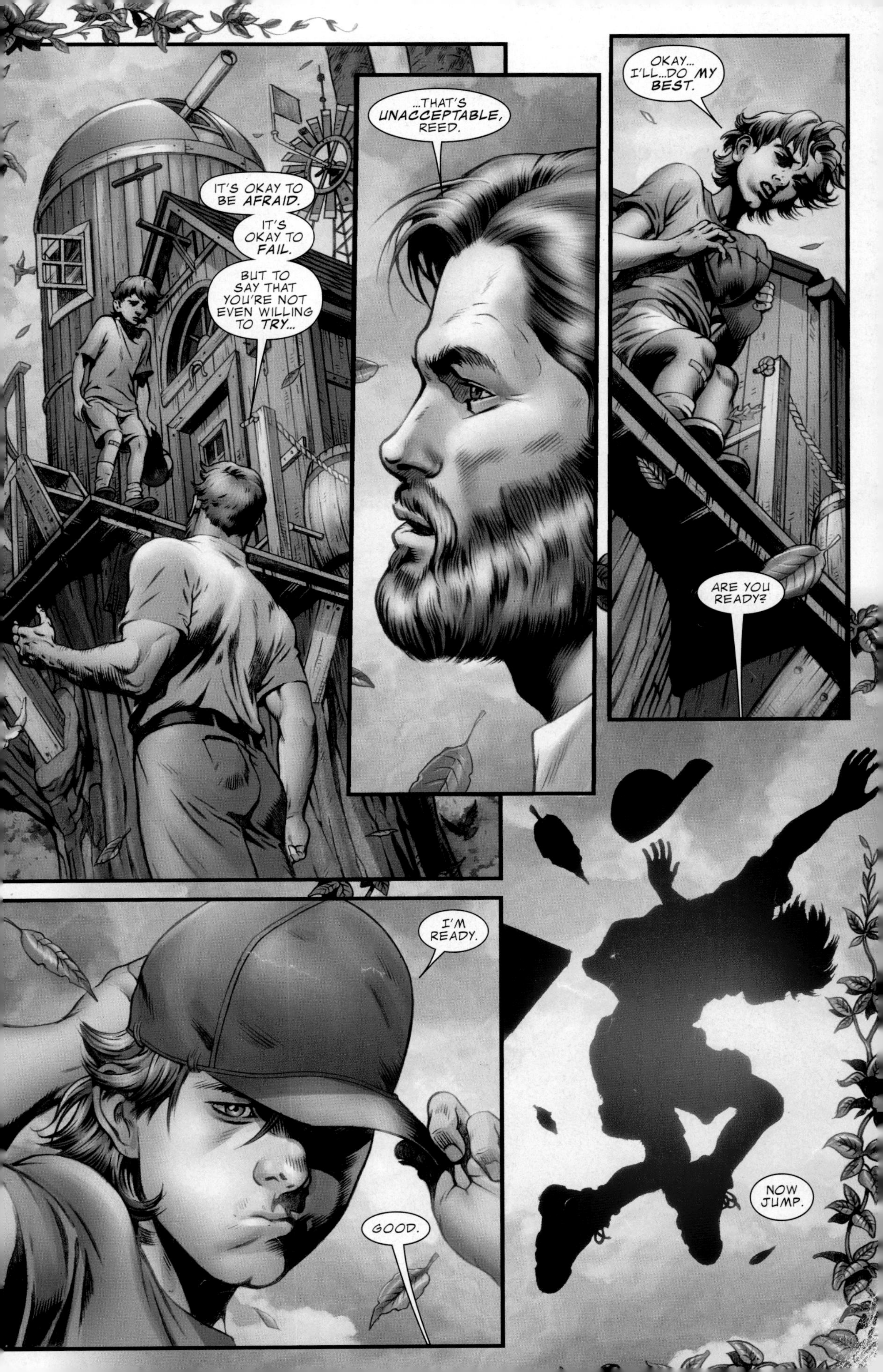
IT'S OKAY TO BE AFRAID.
IT'S OKAY TO FAIL.
BUT TO SAY THAT YOU'RE NOT EVEN WILLING TO TRY...
...THAT'S UNACCEPTABLE, REED.
OKAY... I'LL...DO MY BEST.
ARE YOU READY?
I'M READY.
GOOD.
NOW JUMP.

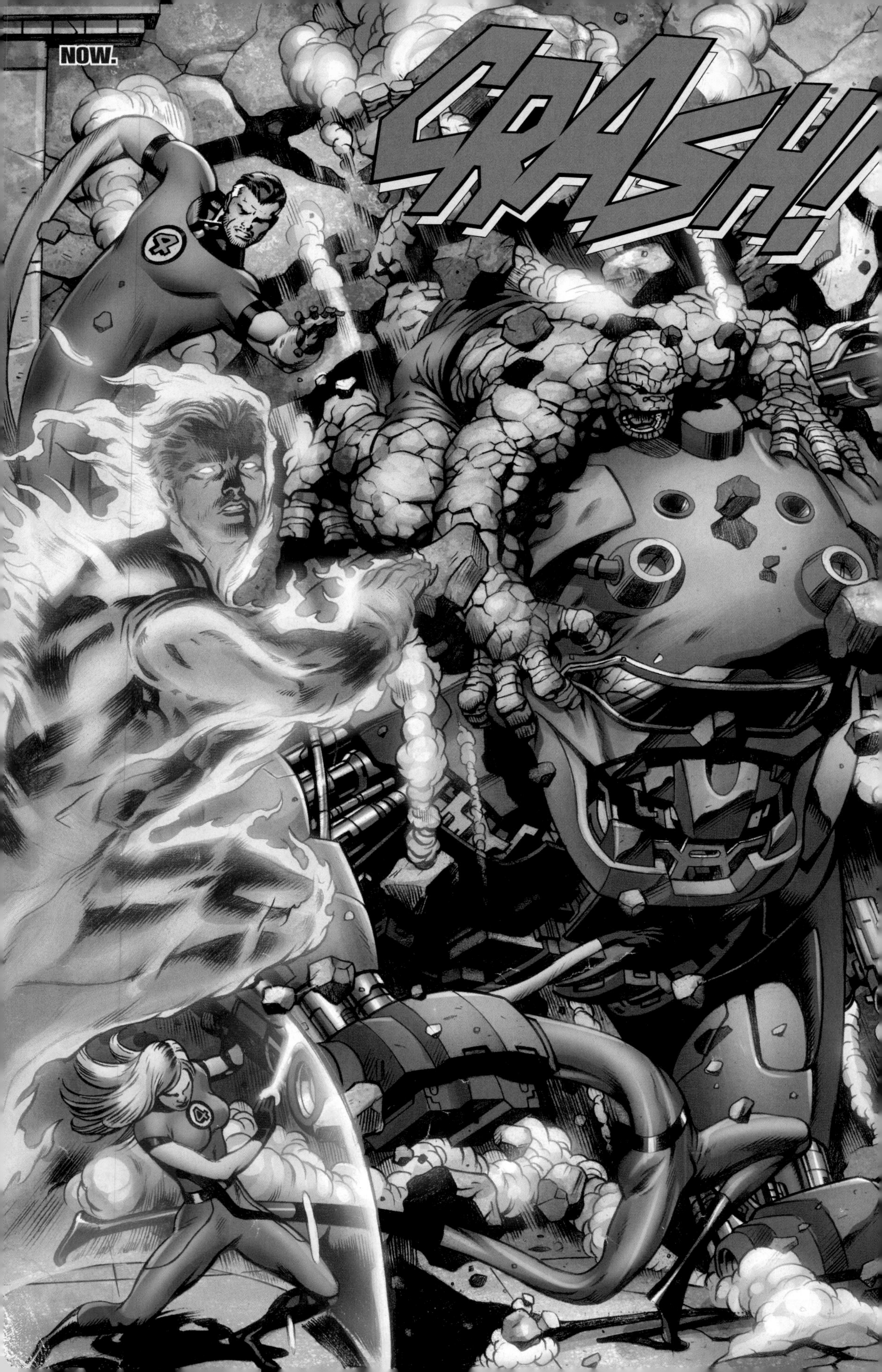
NOW.
CRASH!

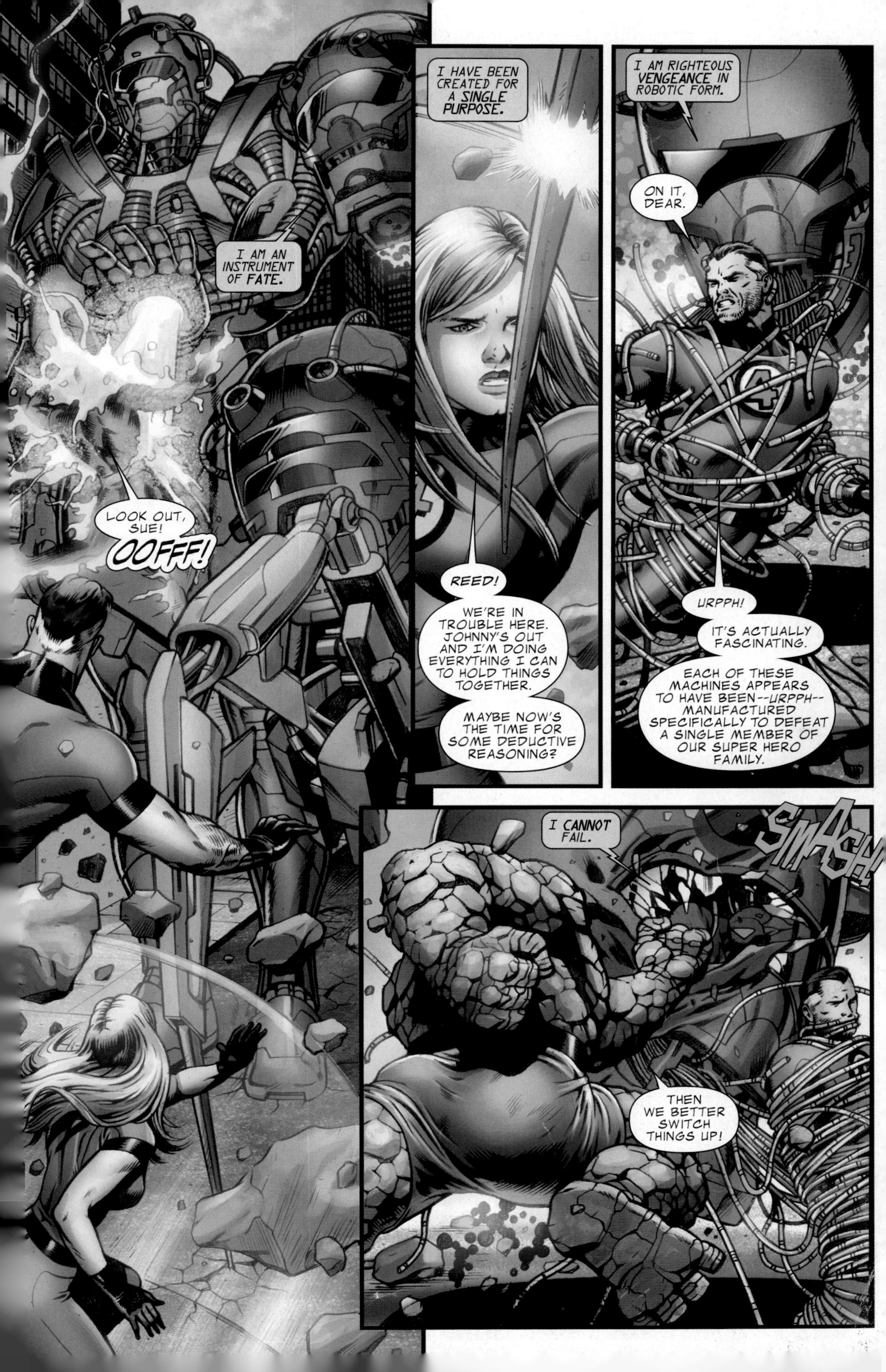
I AM AN INSTRUMENT OF FATE.
LOOK OUT, SUE!
OOFFF!
I HAVE BEEN CREATED FOR A SINGLE PURPOSE.
REED!
WE'RE IN TROUBLE HERE. JOHNNY'S OUT AND I'M DOING EVERYTHING I CAN TO HOLD THINGS TOGETHER.
MAYBE NOW'S THE TIME FOR SOME DEDUCTIVE REASONING?
I AM RIGHTEOUS VENGEANCE IN ROBOTIC FORM.
ON IT, DEAR.
URPPH!
IT'S ACTUALLY FASCINATING.
EACH OF THESE MACHINES APPEARS TO HAVE BEEN--URPPH--MANUFACTURED SPECIFICALLY TO DEFEAT A SINGLE MEMBER OF OUR SUPER HERO FAMILY.
I CANNOT FAIL.
SMASH!
THEN WE BETTER SWITCH THINGS UP!

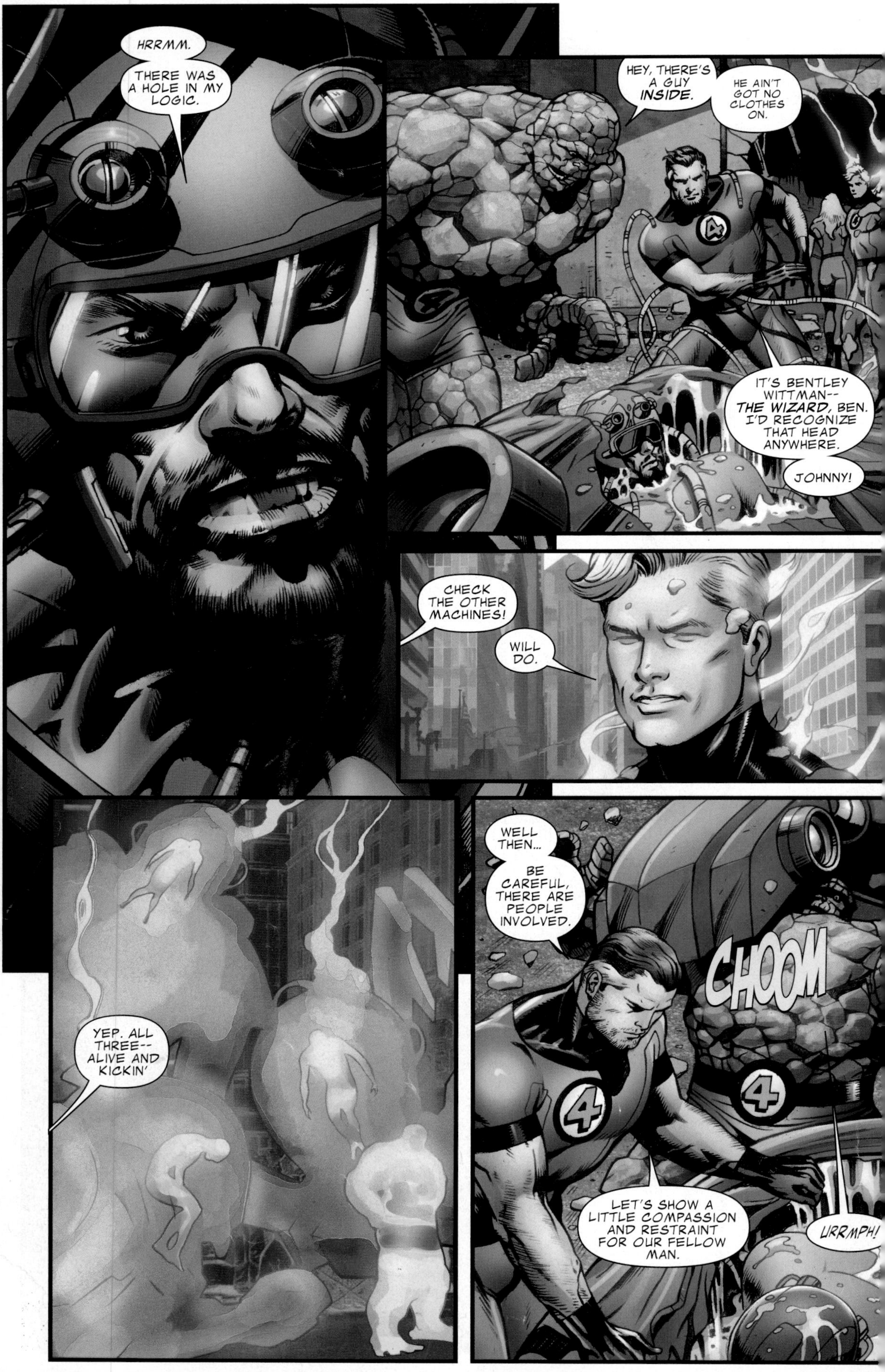
HRRMM.
THERE WAS A HOLE IN MY LOGIC.
HEY, THERE'S A GUY INSIDE.
HE AIN'T GOT NO CLOTHES ON.
IT'S BENTLEY WITTMAN-- THE WIZARD, BEN. I'D RECOGNIZE THAT HEAD ANYWHERE.
JOHNNY!
CHECK THE OTHER MACHINES!
WILL DO.
YEP. ALL THREE-- ALIVE AND KICKIN'
WELL THEN...
BE CAREFUL, THERE ARE PEOPLE INVOLVED.
CHOOM
LET'S SHOW A LITTLE COMPASSION AND RESTRAINT FOR OUR FELLOW MAN.
URRMPH!

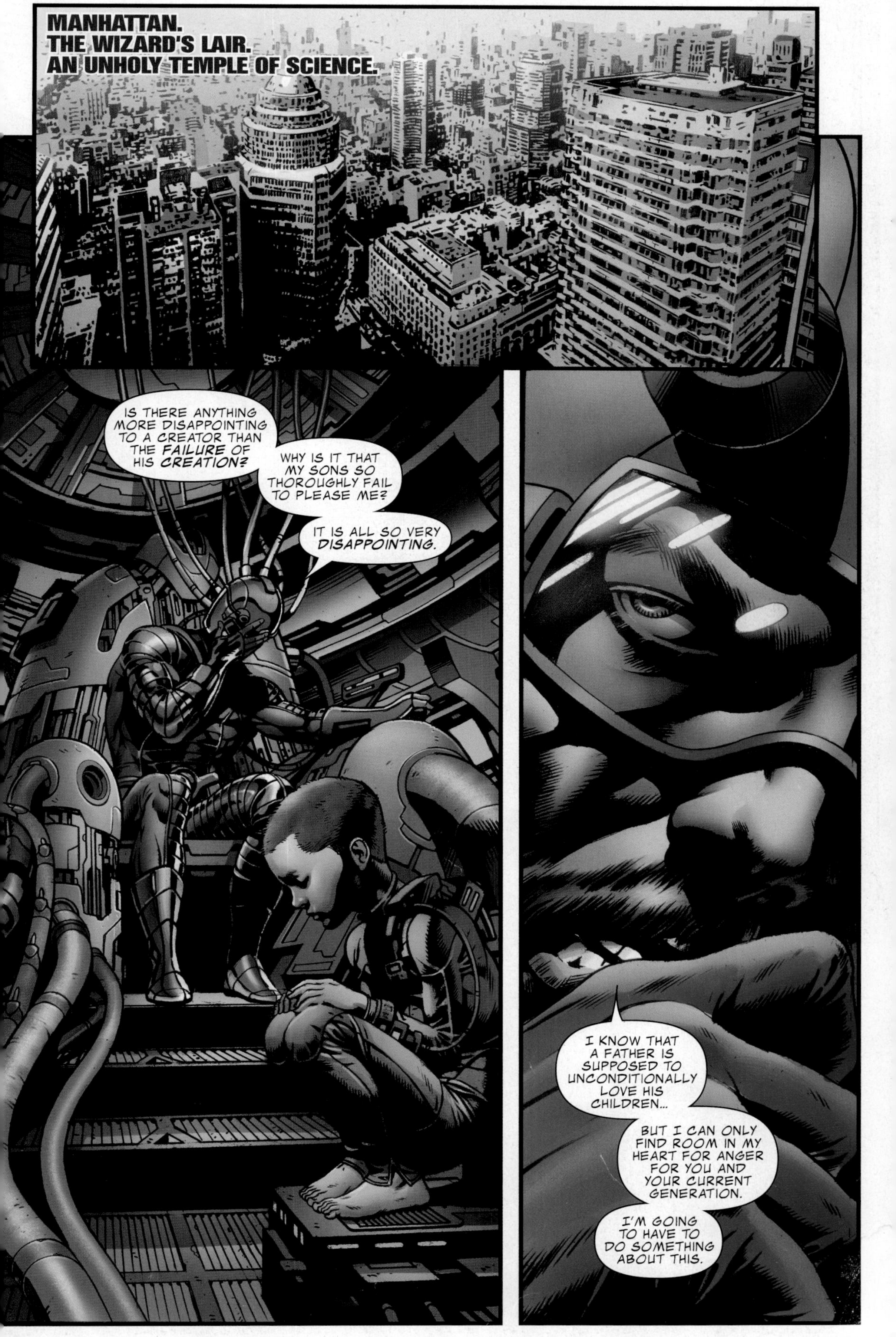
MANHATTAN.
THE WIZARD'S LAIR.
AN UNHOLY TEMPLE OF SCIENCE.
IS THERE ANYTHING MORE DISAPPOINTING TO A CREATOR THAN THE FAILURE OF HIS CREATION?
WHY IS IT THAT MY SONS SO THOROUGHLY FAIL TO PLEASE ME?
IT IS ALL SO VERY DISAPPOINTING.
I KNOW THAT A FATHER IS SUPPOSED TO UNCONDITIONALLY LOVE HIS CHILDREN...
BUT I CAN ONLY FIND ROOM IN MY HEART FOR ANGER FOR YOU AND YOUR CURRENT GENERATION.
I'M GOING TO HAVE TO DO SOMETHING ABOUT THIS.

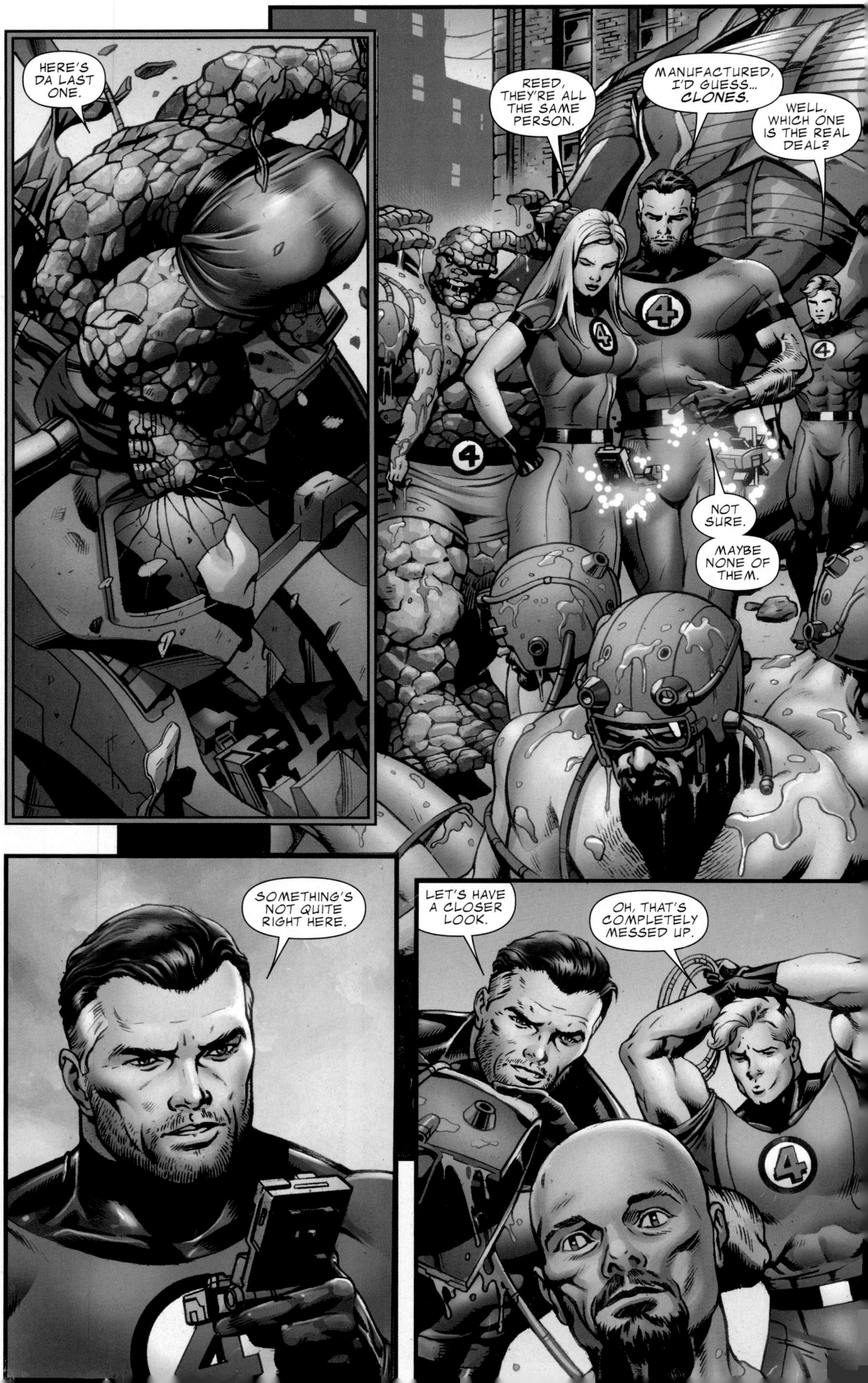
HERE'S DA LAST ONE.
REED, THEY'RE ALL THE SAME PERSON.
MANUFACTURED, I'D GUESS... CLONES.
WELL, WHICH ONE IS THE REAL DEAL?
NOT SURE.
MAYBE NONE OF THEM.
SOMETHING'S NOT QUITE RIGHT HERE.
LET'S HAVE A CLOSER LOOK.
OH, THAT'S COMPLETELY MESSED UP.

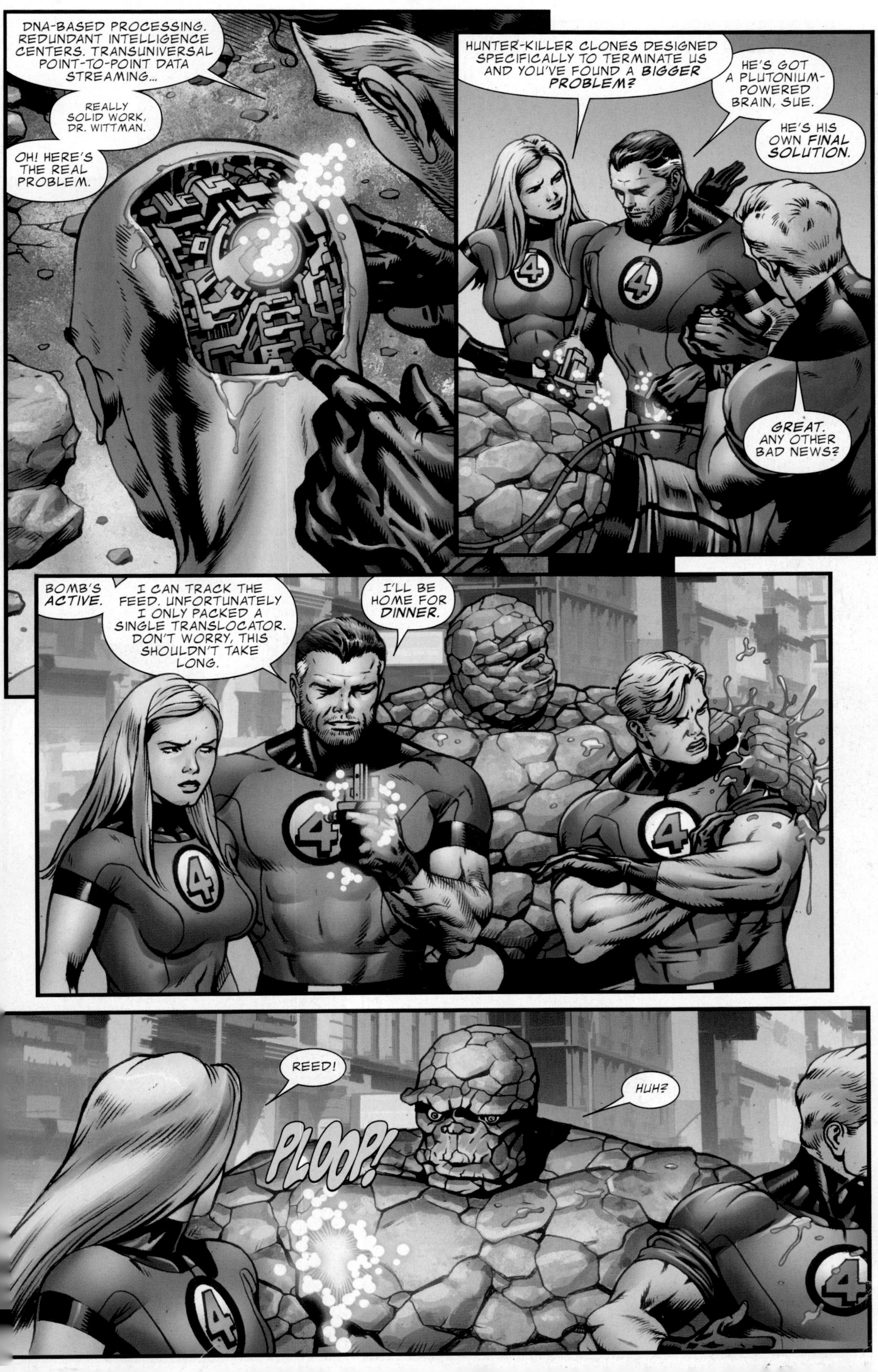
DNA-BASED PROCESSING. REDUNDANT INTELLIGENCE CENTERS. TRANSUNIVERSAL POINT-TO-POINT DATA STREAMING...
REALLY SOLID WORK, DR. WITTMAN.
OH! HERE'S THE REAL PROBLEM.
HUNTER-KILLER CLONES DESIGNED SPECIFICALLY TO TERMINATE US AND YOU'VE FOUND A BIGGER PROBLEM?
HE'S GOT A PLUTONIUM-POWERED BRAIN, SUE.
HE'S HIS OWN FINAL SOLUTION.
GREAT. ANY OTHER BAD NEWS?
BOMB'S ACTIVE.
I CAN TRACK THE FEED. UNFORTUNATELY I ONLY PACKED A SINGLE TRANSLOCATOR. DON'T WORRY, THIS SHOULDN'T TAKE LONG.
I'LL BE HOME FOR DINNER.
REED!
HUH?
PLOOP!

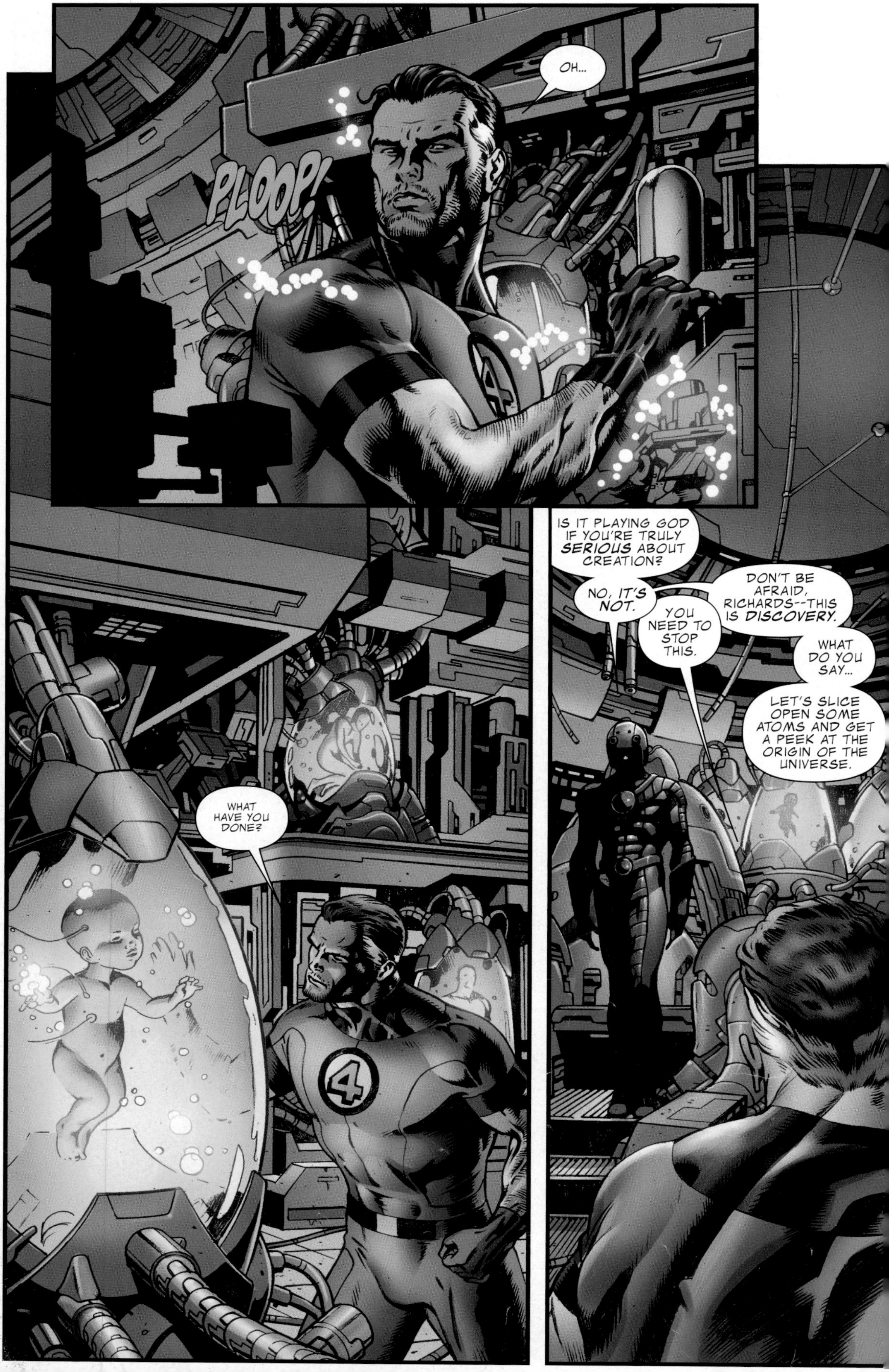
OH...
PLOOP!
WHAT HAVE YOU DONE?
IS IT PLAYING GOD IF YOU'RE TRULY SERIOUS ABOUT CREATION?
NO, IT'S NOT.
YOU NEED TO STOP THIS.
DON'T BE AFRAID, RICHARDS--THIS IS DISCOVERY.
WHAT DO YOU SAY...
LET'S SLICE OPEN SOME ATOMS AND GET A PEEK AT THE ORIGIN OF THE UNIVERSE.

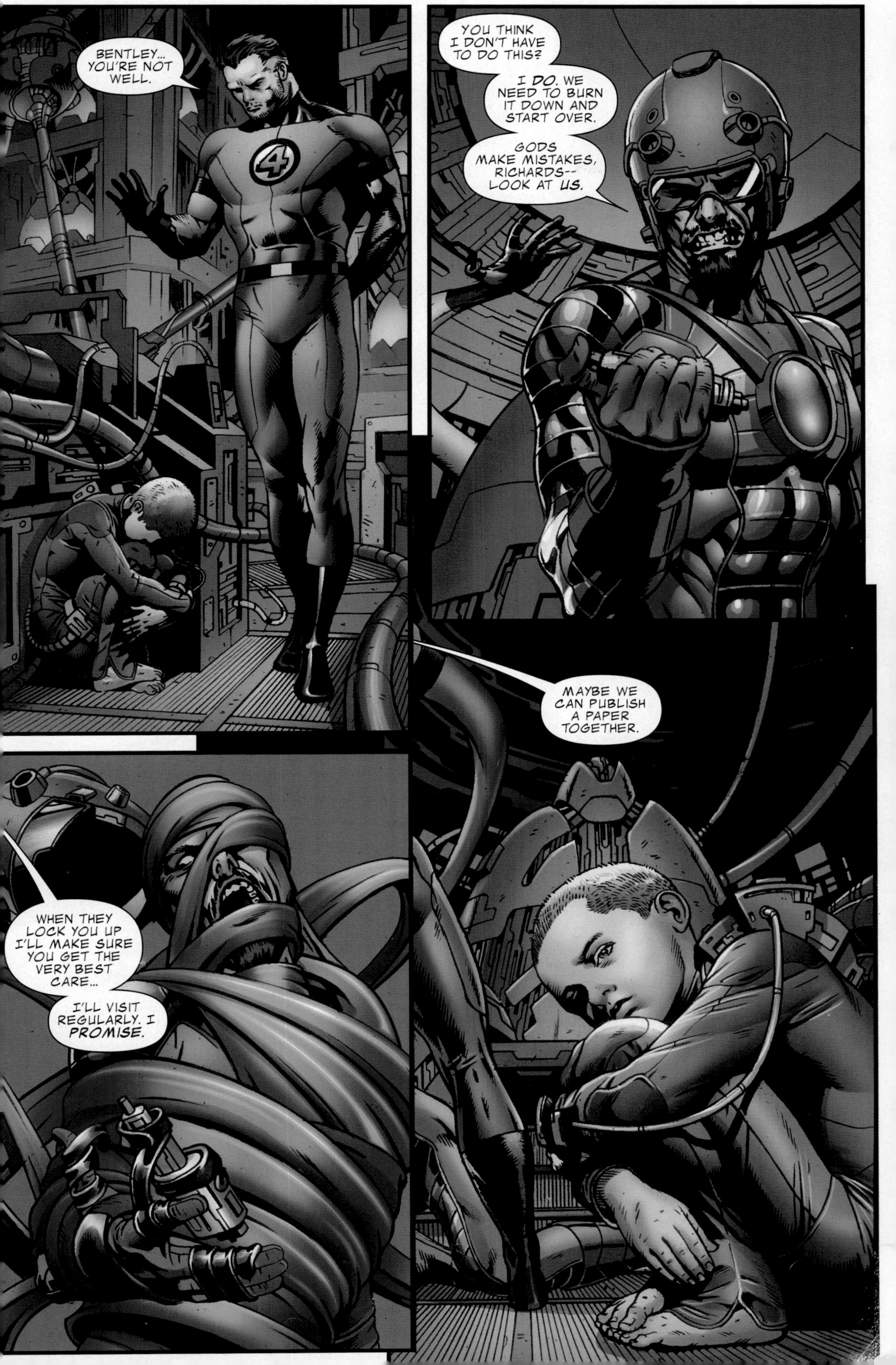
BENTLEY... YOU'RE NOT WELL.
YOU THINK I DON'T HAVE TO DO THIS?
I DO. WE NEED TO BURN IT DOWN AND START OVER.
GODS MAKE MISTAKES, RICHARDS-- LOOK AT US.
WHEN THEY LOCK YOU UP I'LL MAKE SURE YOU GET THE VERY BEST CARE...
I'LL VISIT REGULARLY. I PROMISE.
MAYBE WE CAN PUBLISH A PAPER TOGETHER.

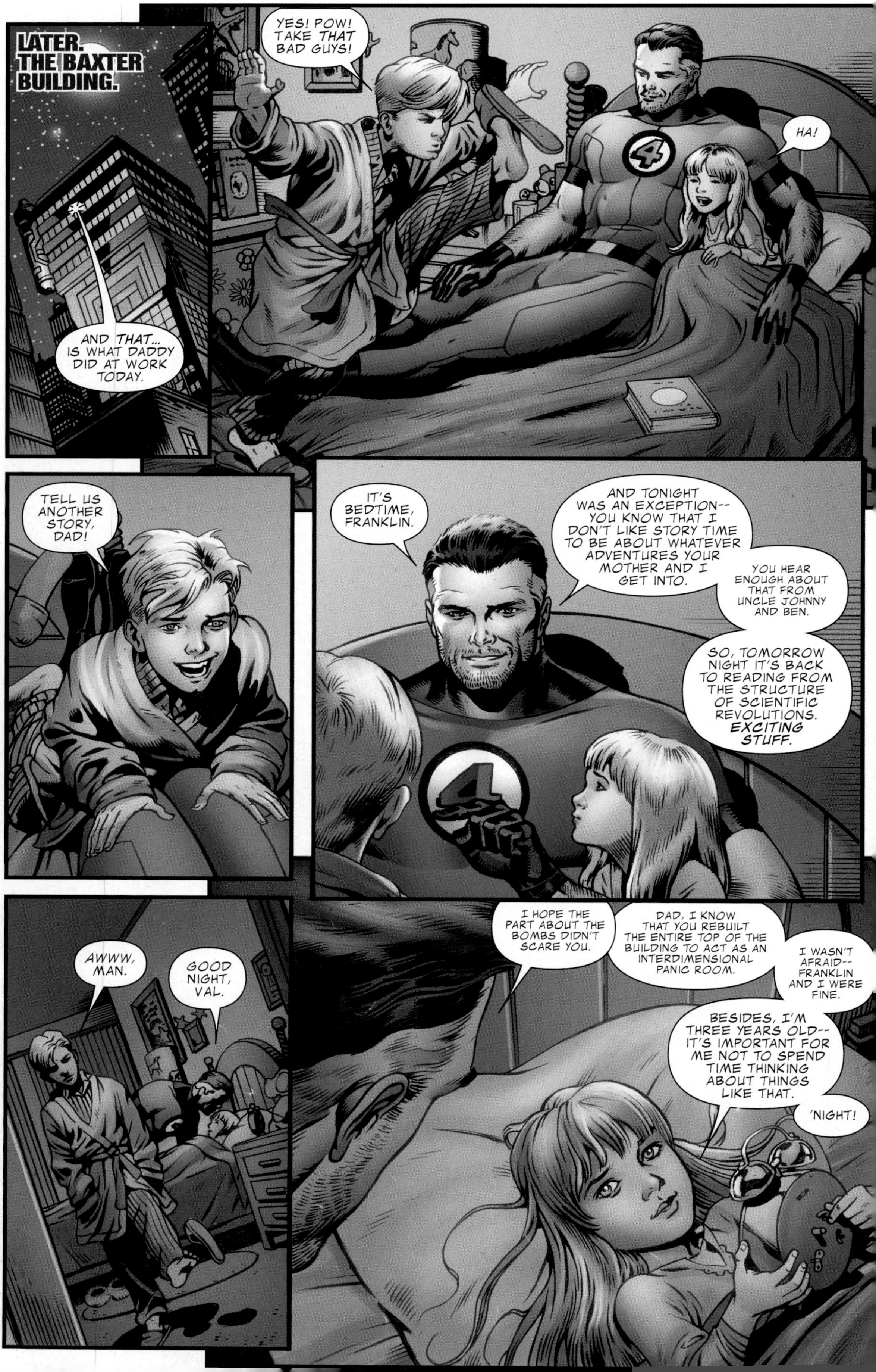
LATER. THE BAXTER BUILDING.
AND THAT... IS WHAT DADDY DID AT WORK TODAY.
YES! POW! TAKE THAT BAD GUYS!
HA!
TELL US ANOTHER STORY, DAD!
IT'S BEDTIME, FRANKLIN.
AND TONIGHT WAS AN EXCEPTION-- YOU KNOW THAT I DON'T LIKE STORY TIME TO BE ABOUT WHATEVER ADVENTURES YOUR MOTHER AND I GET INTO.
YOU HEAR ENOUGH ABOUT THAT FROM UNCLE JOHNNY AND BEN.
SO, TOMORROW NIGHT IT'S BACK TO READING FROM THE STRUCTURE OF SCIENTIFIC REVOLUTIONS. EXCITING STUFF.
AWWW, MAN.
GOOD NIGHT, VAL.
I HOPE THE PART ABOUT THE BOMBS DIDN'T SCARE YOU.
DAD, I KNOW THAT YOU REBUILT THE ENTIRE TOP OF THE BUILDING TO ACT AS AN INTERDIMENSIONAL PANIC ROOM.
I WASN'T AFRAID-- FRANKLIN AND I WERE FINE.
BESIDES, I'M THREE YEARS OLD-- IT'S IMPORTANT FOR ME NOT TO SPEND TIME THINKING ABOUT THINGS LIKE THAT.
'NIGHT!

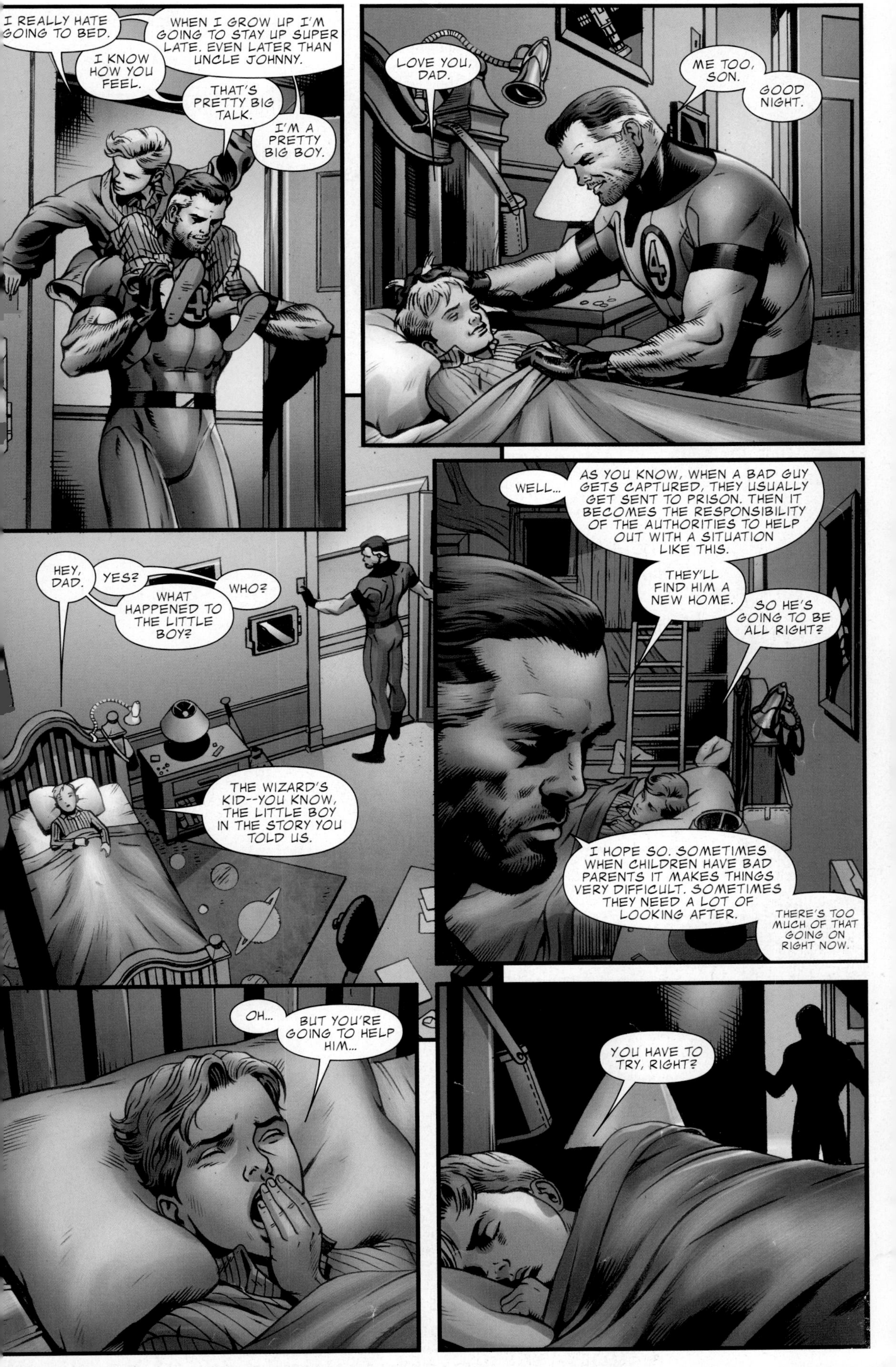
I REALLY HATE GOING TO BED.
WHEN I GROW UP I'M GOING TO STAY UP SUPER LATE. EVEN LATER THAN UNCLE JOHNNY.
I KNOW HOW YOU FEEL.
THAT'S PRETTY BIG TALK.
I'M A PRETTY BIG BOY.
LOVE YOU, DAD.
ME TOO, SON.
GOOD NIGHT.
HEY, DAD.
YES?
WHAT HAPPENED TO THE LITTLE BOY?
WHO?
THE WIZARD'S KID--YOU KNOW, THE LITTLE BOY IN THE STORY YOU TOLD US.
WELL...
AS YOU KNOW, WHEN A BAD GUY GETS CAPTURED, THEY USUALLY GET SENT TO PRISON. THEN IT BECOMES THE RESPONSIBILITY OF THE AUTHORITIES TO HELP OUT WITH A SITUATION LIKE THIS.
THEY'LL FIND HIM A NEW HOME.
SO HE'S GOING TO BE ALL RIGHT?
I HOPE SO. SOMETIMES WHEN CHILDREN HAVE BAD PARENTS IT MAKES THINGS VERY DIFFICULT. SOMETIMES THEY NEED A LOT OF LOOKING AFTER.
THERE'S TOO MUCH OF THAT GOING ON RIGHT NOW.
OH...
BUT YOU'RE GOING TO HELP HIM...
YOU HAVE TO TRY, RIGHT?

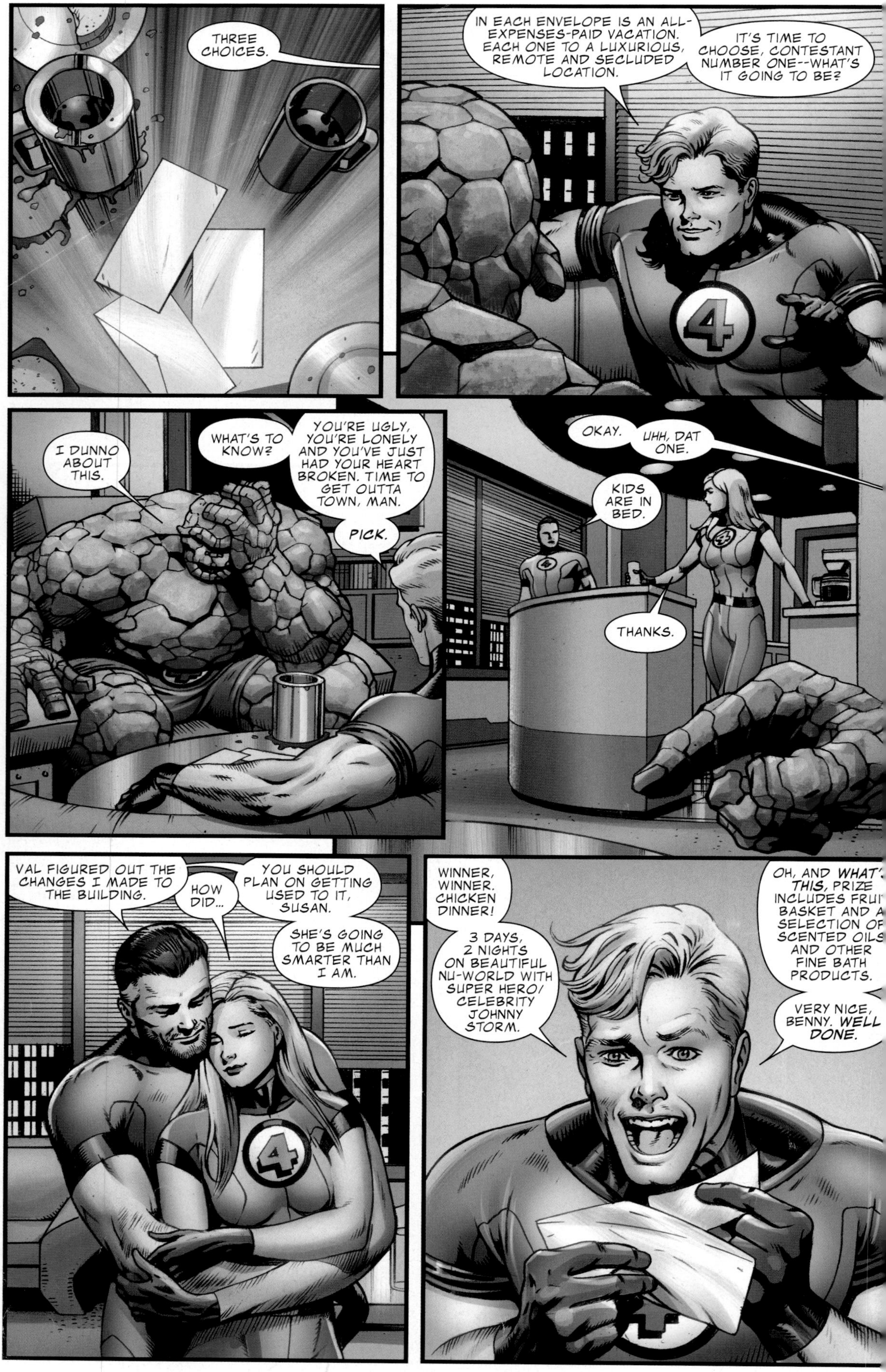

THREE CHOICES.
IN EACH ENVELOPE IS AN ALL-EXPENSES-PAID VACATION. EACH ONE TO A LUXURIOUS, REMOTE AND SECLUDED LOCATION.
IT'S TIME TO CHOOSE, CONTESTANT NUMBER ONE--WHAT'S IT GOING TO BE?
I DUNNO ABOUT THIS.
WHAT'S TO KNOW?
YOU'RE UGLY, YOU'RE LONELY AND YOU'VE JUST HAD YOUR HEART BROKEN. TIME TO GET OUTTA TOWN, MAN.
PICK.
OKAY.
UHH, DAT ONE.
KIDS ARE IN BED.
THANKS.
VAL FIGURED OUT THE CHANGES I MADE TO THE BUILDING.
HOW DID...
YOU SHOULD PLAN ON GETTING USED TO IT, SUSAN.
SHE'S GOING TO BE MUCH SMARTER THAN I AM.
WINNER, WINNER. CHICKEN DINNER!
3 DAYS, 2 NIGHTS ON BEAUTIFUL NU-WORLD WITH SUPER HERO/ CELEBRITY JOHNNY STORM.
VERY NICE, BENNY. WELL DONE.

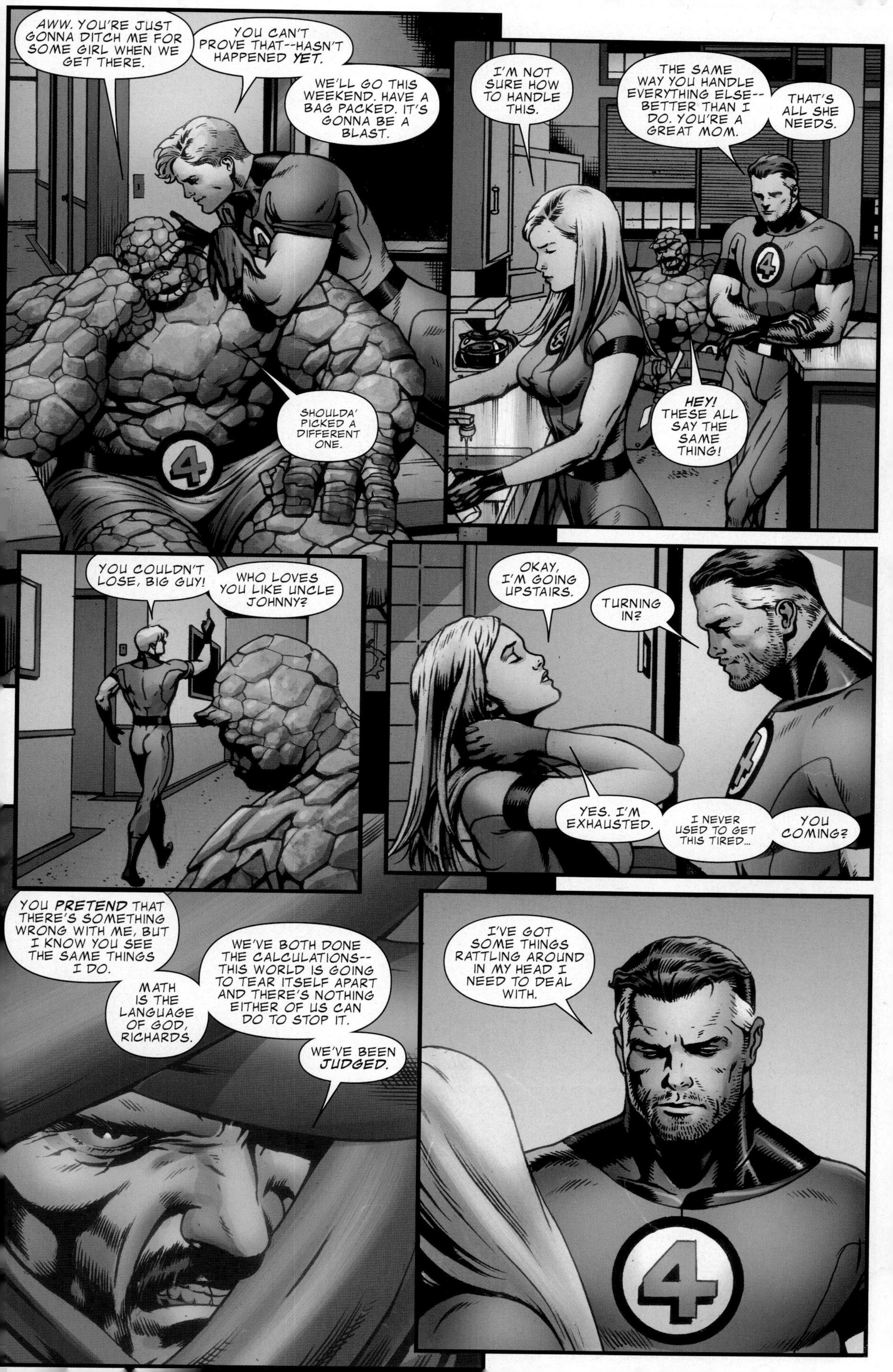
AWW. YOU'RE JUST GONNA DITCH ME FOR SOME GIRL WHEN WE GET THERE.
YOU CAN'T PROVE THAT--HASN'T HAPPENED YET.
WE'LL GO THIS WEEKEND. HAVE A BAG PACKED. IT'S GONNA BE A BLAST.
SHOULDA' PICKED A DIFFERENT ONE.
I'M NOT SURE HOW TO HANDLE THIS.
THE SAME WAY YOU HANDLE EVERYTHING ELSE--BETTER THAN I DO. YOU'RE A GREAT MOM.
THAT'S ALL SHE NEEDS.
HEY! THESE ALL SAY THE SAME THING!
YOU COULDN'T LOSE, BIG GUY!
WHO LOVES YOU LIKE UNCLE JOHNNY?
OKAY, I'M GOING UPSTAIRS.
TURNING IN?
YES. I'M EXHAUSTED.
I NEVER USED TO GET THIS TIRED...
YOU COMING?
YOU PRETEND THAT THERE'S SOMETHING WRONG WITH ME, BUT I KNOW YOU SEE THE SAME THINGS I DO.
MATH IS THE LANGUAGE OF GOD, RICHARDS.
WE'VE BOTH DONE THE CALCULATIONS--THIS WORLD IS GOING TO TEAR ITSELF APART AND THERE'S NOTHING EITHER OF US CAN DO TO STOP IT.
WE'VE BEEN JUDGED.
I'VE GOT SOME THINGS RATTLING AROUND IN MY HEAD I NEED TO DEAL WITH.

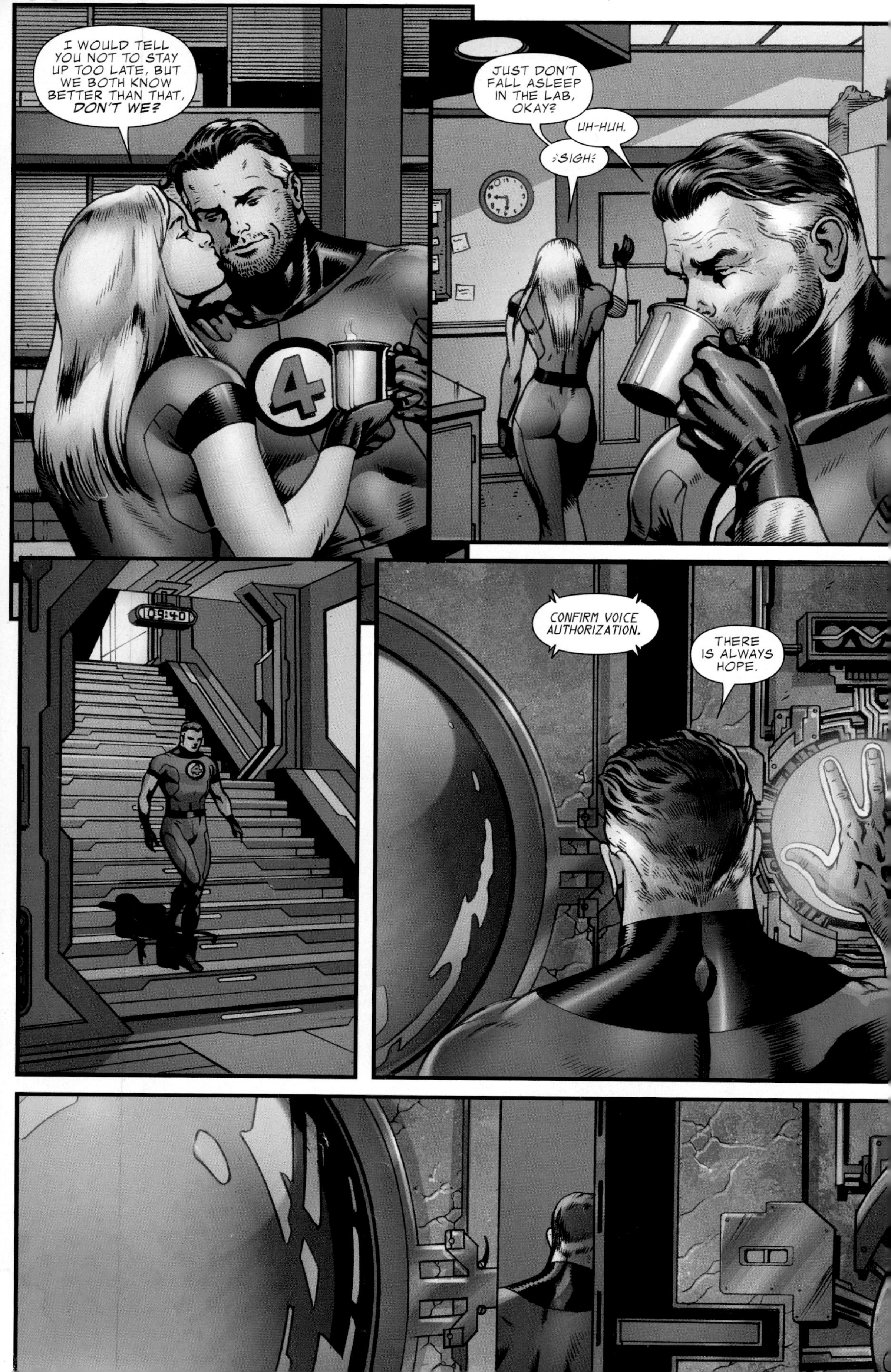
I WOULD TELL YOU NOT TO STAY UP TOO LATE, BUT WE BOTH KNOW BETTER THAN THAT, DON'T WE?
JUST DON'T FALL ASLEEP IN THE LAB, OKAY?
UH-HUH.
SIGH
CONFIRM VOICE AUTHORIZATION.
THERE IS ALWAYS HOPE.

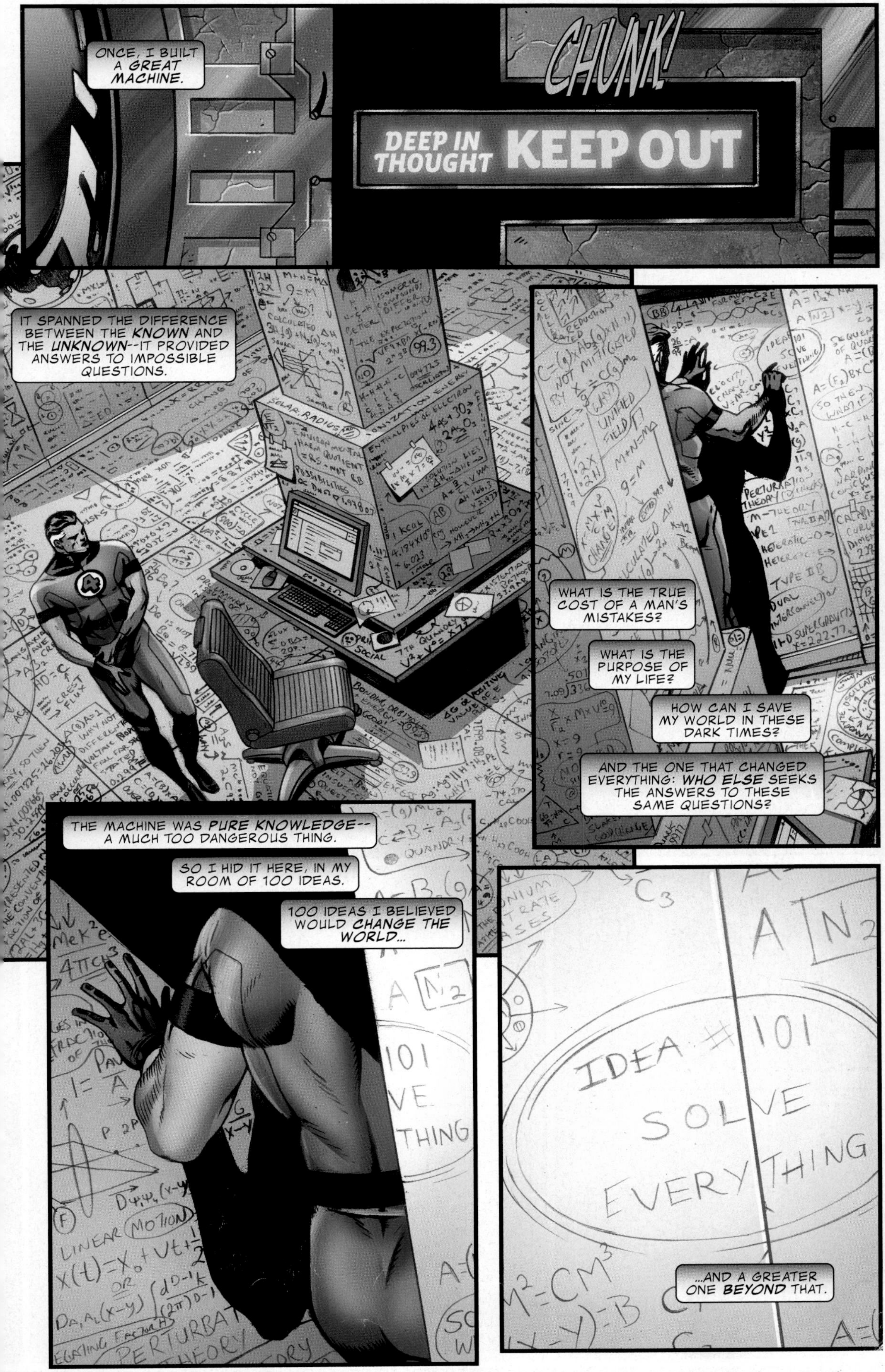
ONCE, I BUILT A GREAT MACHINE.
CHUNK!
DEEP IN THOUGHT
KEEP OUT
IT SPANNED THE DIFFERENCE BETWEEN THE KNOWN AND THE UNKNOWN--IT PROVIDED ANSWERS TO IMPOSSIBLE QUESTIONS.
WHAT IS THE TRUE COST OF A MAN'S MISTAKES?
WHAT IS THE PURPOSE OF MY LIFE?
HOW CAN I SAVE MY WORLD IN THESE DARK TIMES?
AND THE ONE THAT CHANGED EVERYTHING: WHO ELSE SEEKS THE ANSWERS TO THESE SAME QUESTIONS?
THE MACHINE WAS PURE KNOWLEDGE-- A MUCH TOO DANGEROUS THING.
SO I HID IT HERE, IN MY ROOM OF 100 IDEAS.
100 IDEAS I BELIEVED WOULD CHANGE THE WORLD...
IDEA #101
SOLVE EVERYTHING
...AND A GREATER ONE BEYOND THAT.

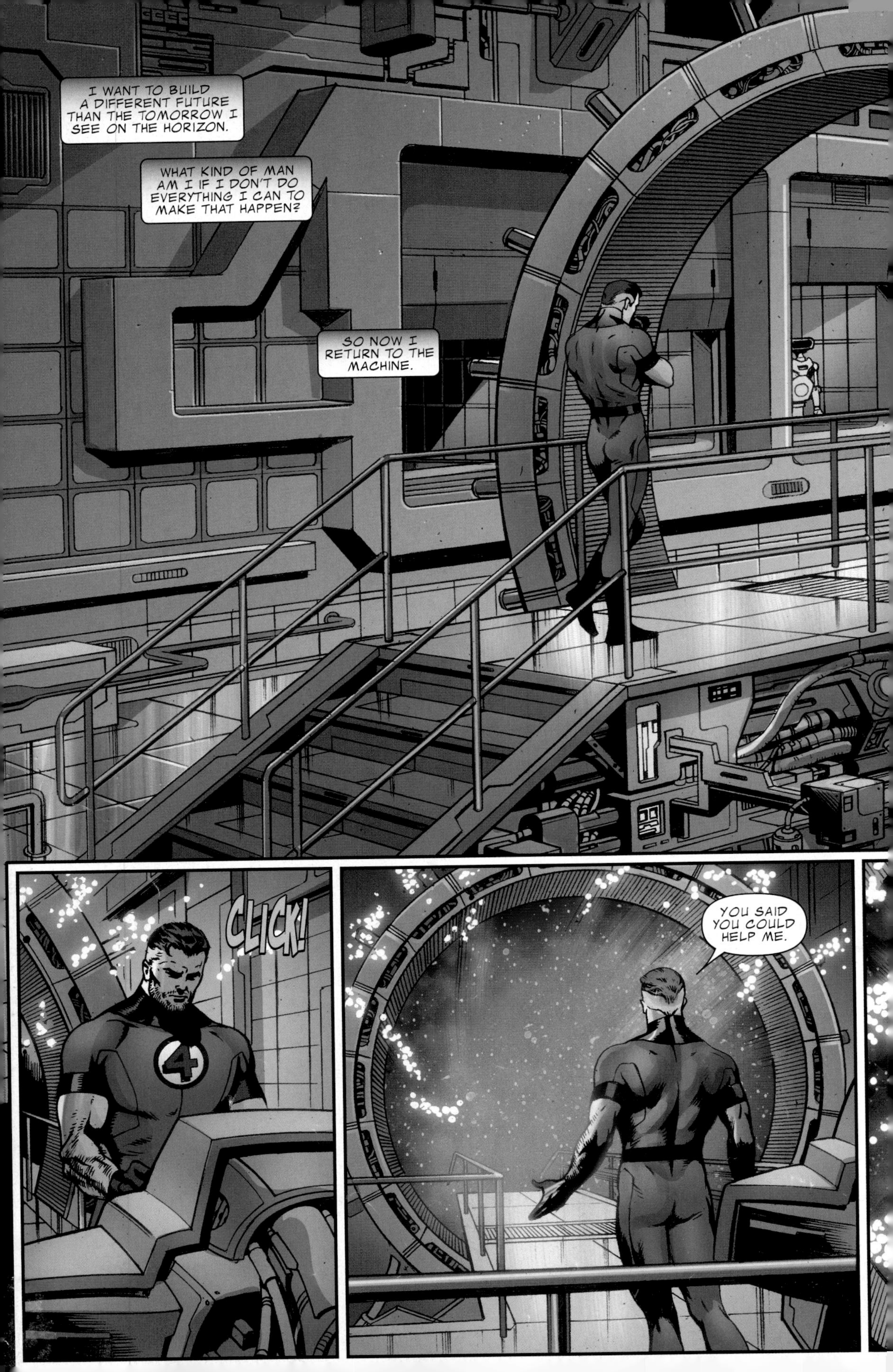
I WANT TO BUILD A DIFFERENT FUTURE THAN THE TOMORROW I SEE ON THE HORIZON.
WHAT KIND OF MAN AM I IF I DON'T DO EVERYTHING I CAN TO MAKE THAT HAPPEN?
SO NOW I RETURN TO THE MACHINE.
CLICK!
YOU SAID YOU COULD HELP ME.

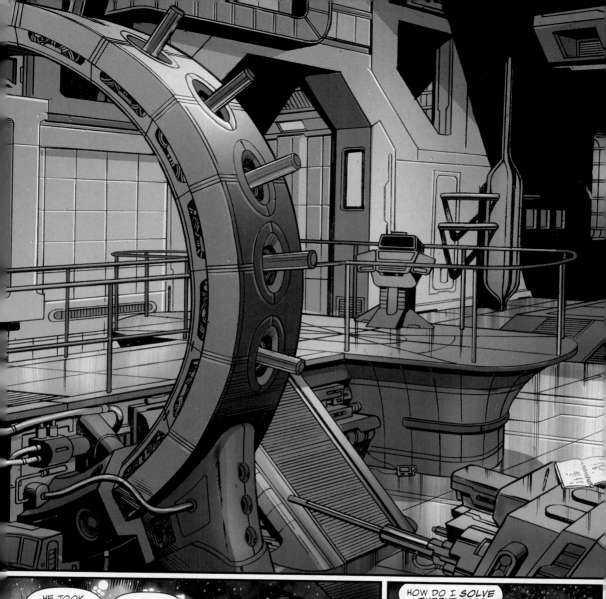

HE TOOK THREE DAYS LONGER THAN NORMAL.

IT'S TO BE EXPECTED.

HE'S A TROUBLED AND CONFLICTED MAN.

HOW CAN WE HELP YOU, REED RICHARDS?

HOW DO I SOLVE EVERYTHING?

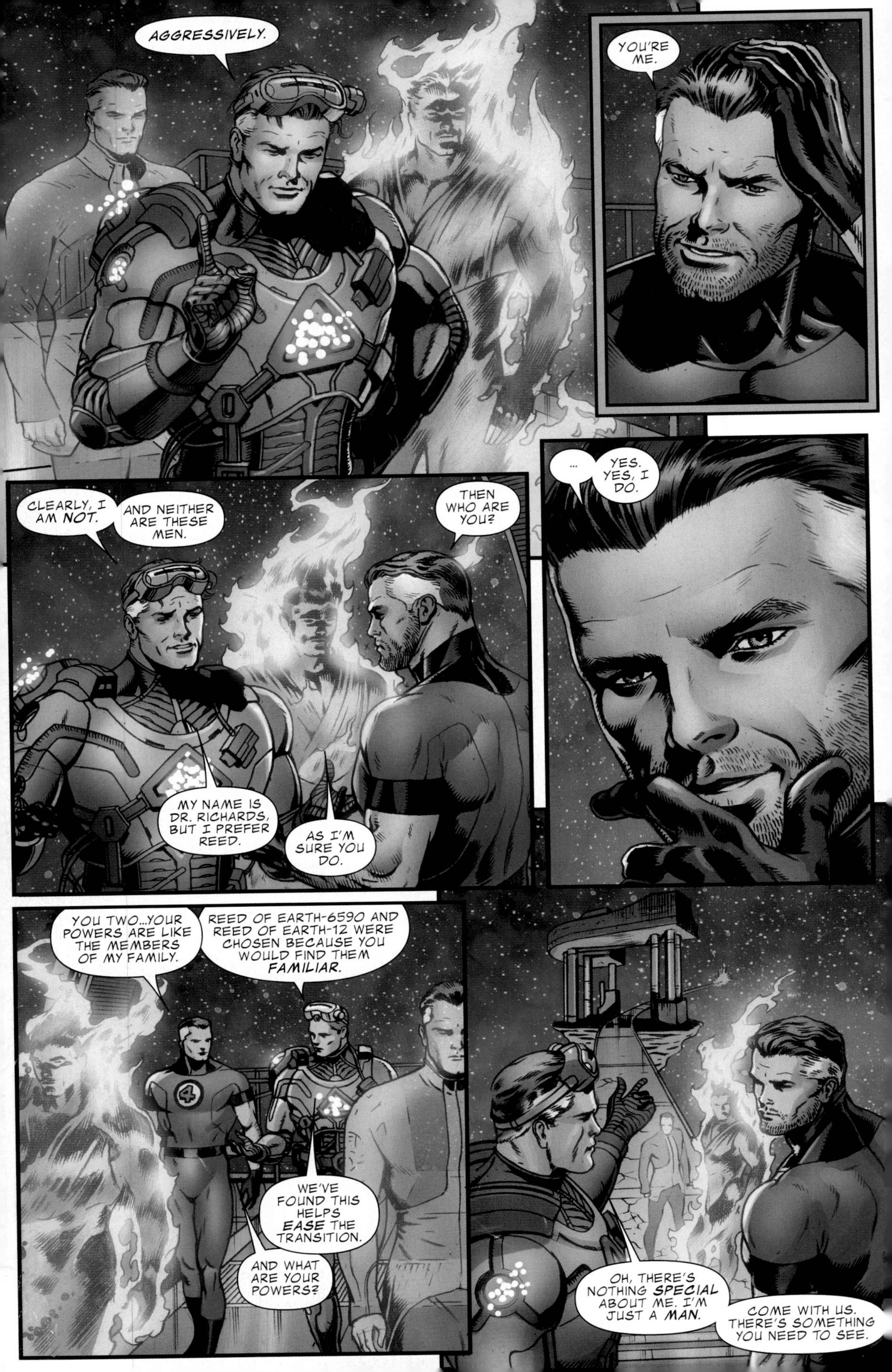
AGGRESSIVELY.
YOU'RE ME.
CLEARLY, I AM NOT.
AND NEITHER ARE THESE MEN.
THEN WHO ARE YOU?
MY NAME IS DR. RICHARDS, BUT I PREFER REED.
AS I'M SURE YOU DO.
...
YES. YES, I DO.
YOU TWO...YOUR POWERS ARE LIKE THE MEMBERS OF MY FAMILY.
REED OF EARTH-6590 AND REED OF EARTH-12 WERE CHOSEN BECAUSE YOU WOULD FIND THEM FAMILIAR.
WE'VE FOUND THIS HELPS EASE THE TRANSITION.
AND WHAT ARE YOUR POWERS?
OH, THERE'S NOTHING SPECIAL ABOUT ME. I'M JUST A MAN.
COME WITH US. THERE'S SOMETHING YOU NEED TO SEE.

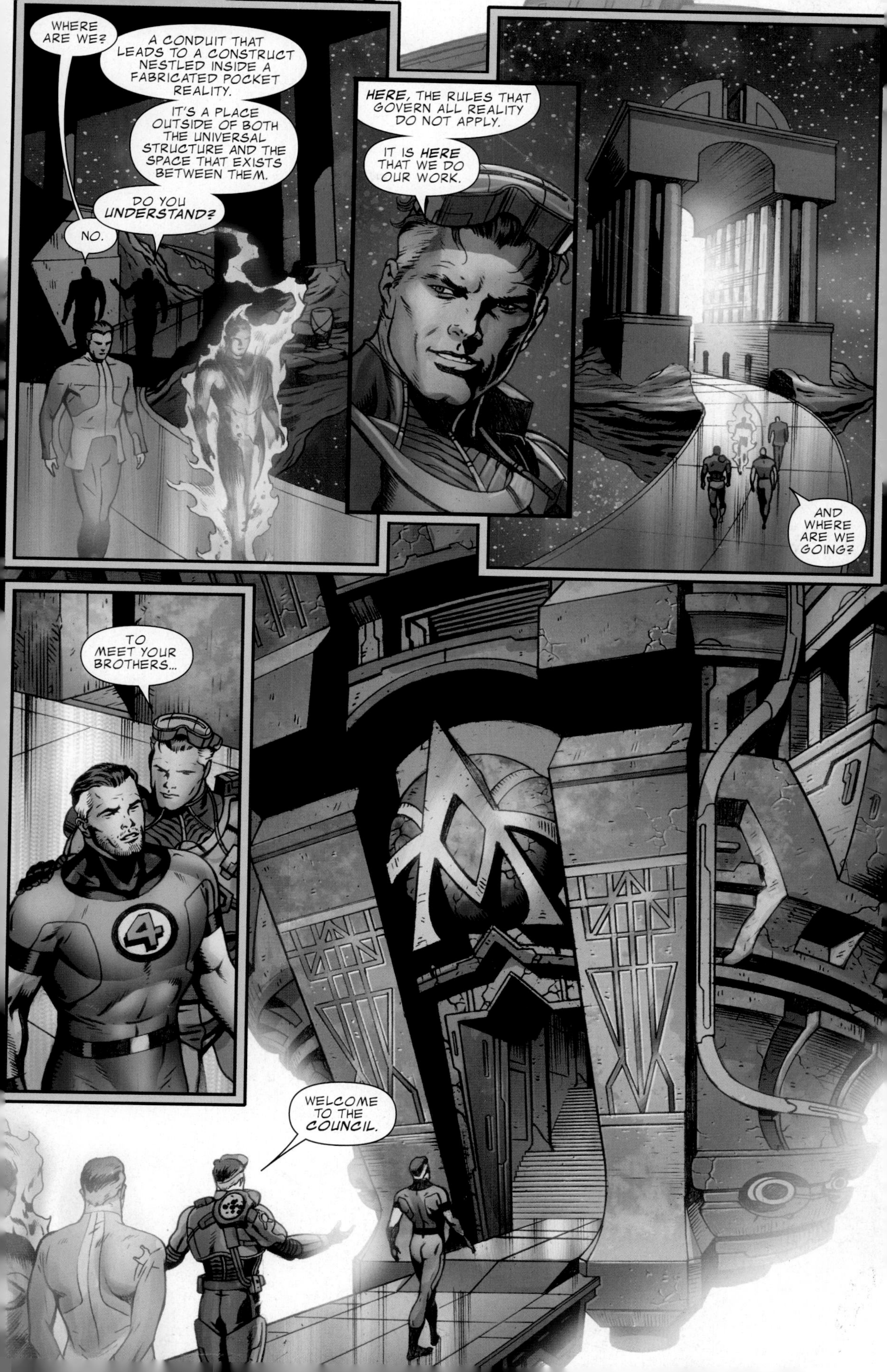
WHERE ARE WE?
A CONDUIT THAT LEADS TO A CONSTRUCT NESTLED INSIDE A FABRICATED POCKET REALITY.
IT'S A PLACE OUTSIDE OF BOTH THE UNIVERSAL STRUCTURE AND THE SPACE THAT EXISTS BETWEEN THEM.
DO YOU UNDERSTAND?
NO.
HERE, THE RULES THAT GOVERN ALL REALITY DO NOT APPLY.
IT IS HERE THAT WE DO OUR WORK.
AND WHERE ARE WE GOING?
TO MEET YOUR BROTHERS...
WELCOME TO THE COUNCIL.

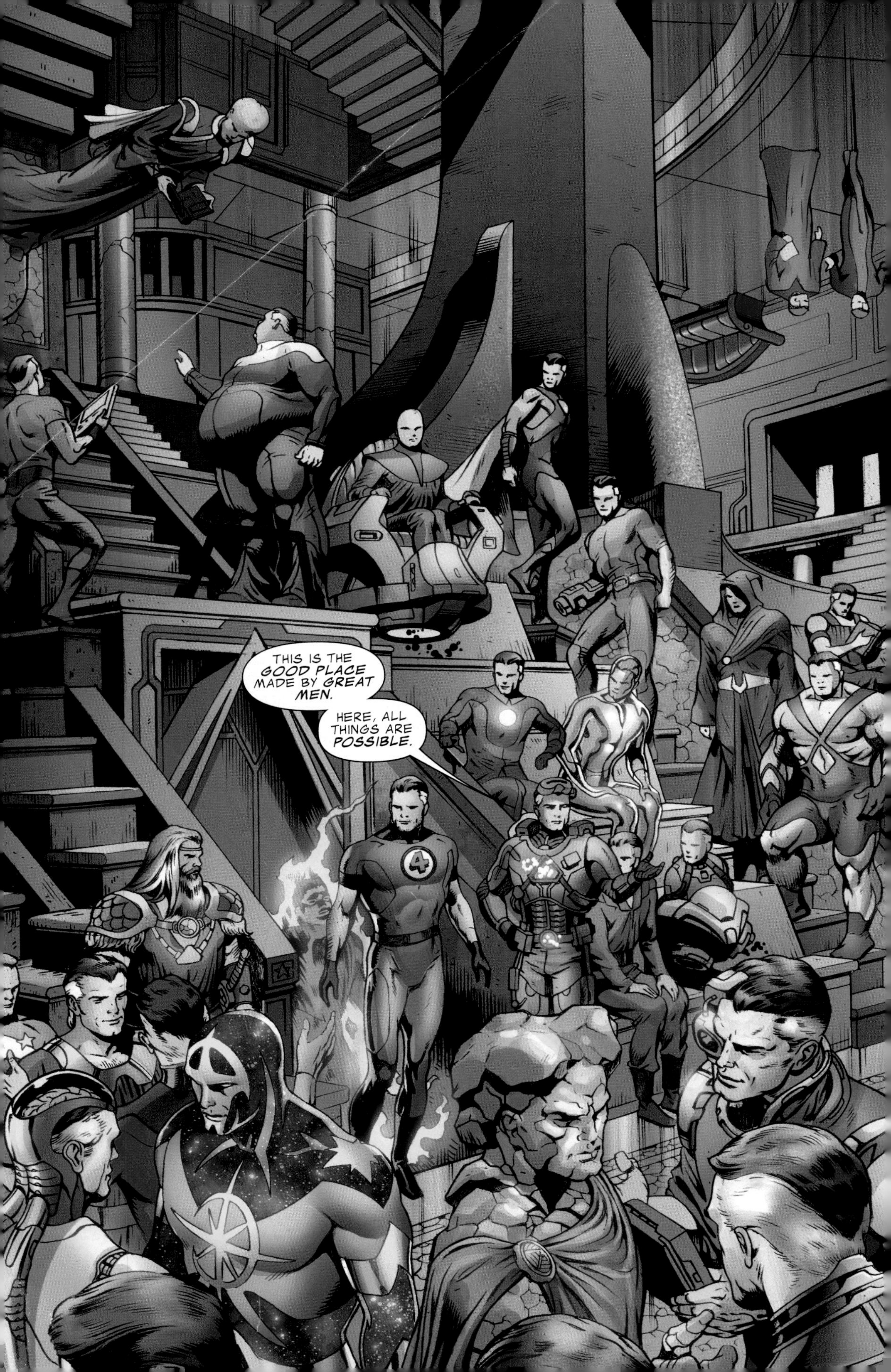
THIS IS THE GOOD PLACE MADE BY GREAT MEN.
HERE, ALL THINGS ARE POSSIBLE.

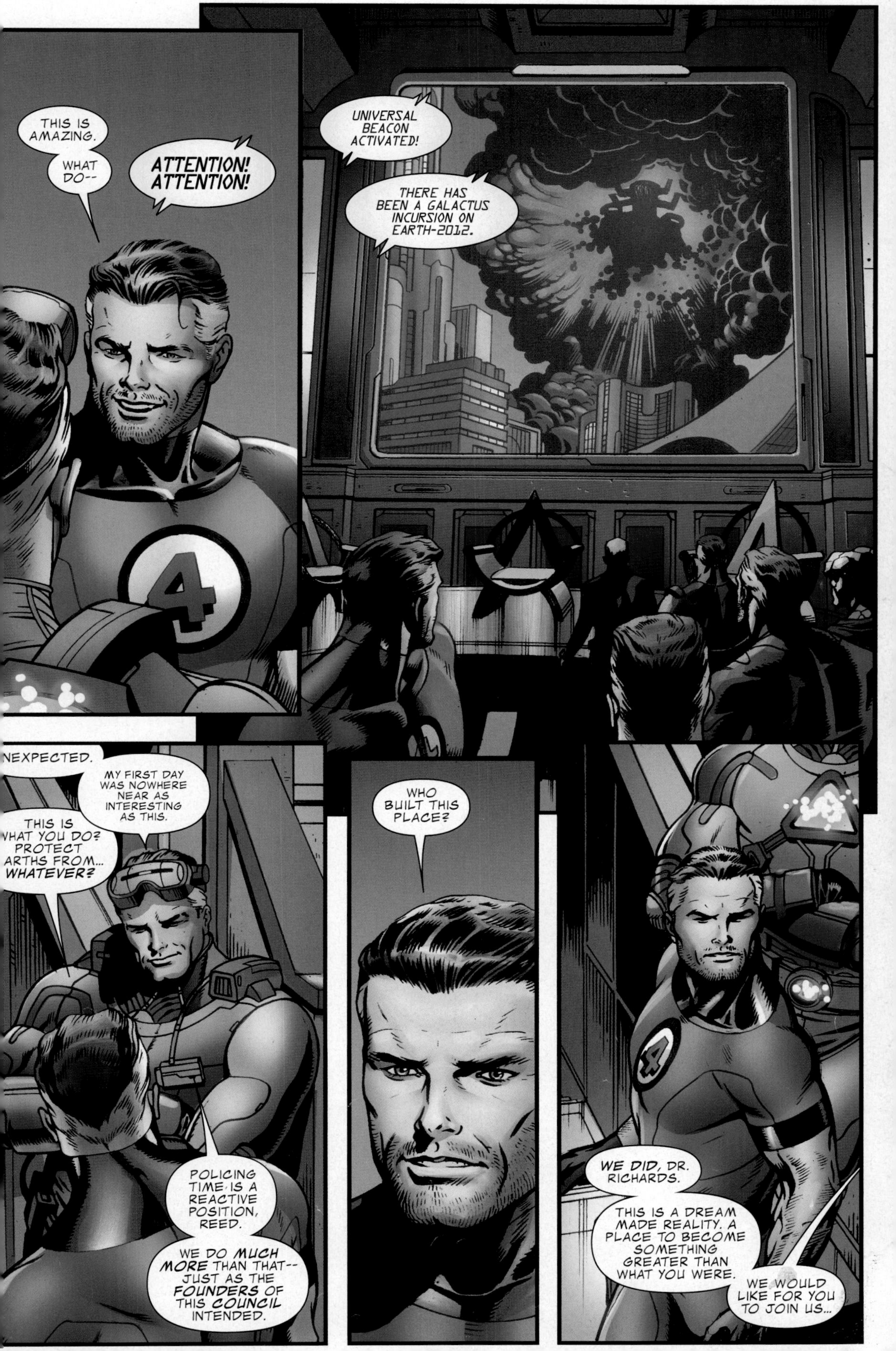

THIS IS AMAZING.
WHAT DO--
ATTENTION! ATTENTION!
UNIVERSAL BEACON ACTIVATED!
THERE HAS BEEN A GALACTUS INCURSION ON EARTH-2012.
NEXPECTED.
MY FIRST DAY WAS NOWHERE NEAR AS INTERESTING AS THIS.
THIS IS WHAT YOU DO? PROTECT ARTHS FROM... WHATEVER?
POLICING TIME IS A REACTIVE POSITION, REED.
WE DO MUCH MORE THAN THAT-- JUST AS THE FOUNDERS OF THIS COUNCIL INTENDED.
WHO BUILT THIS PLACE?
WE DID, DR. RICHARDS.
THIS IS A DREAM MADE REALITY. A PLACE TO BECOME SOMETHING GREATER THAN WHAT YOU WERE.
WE WOULD LIKE FOR YOU TO JOIN US...

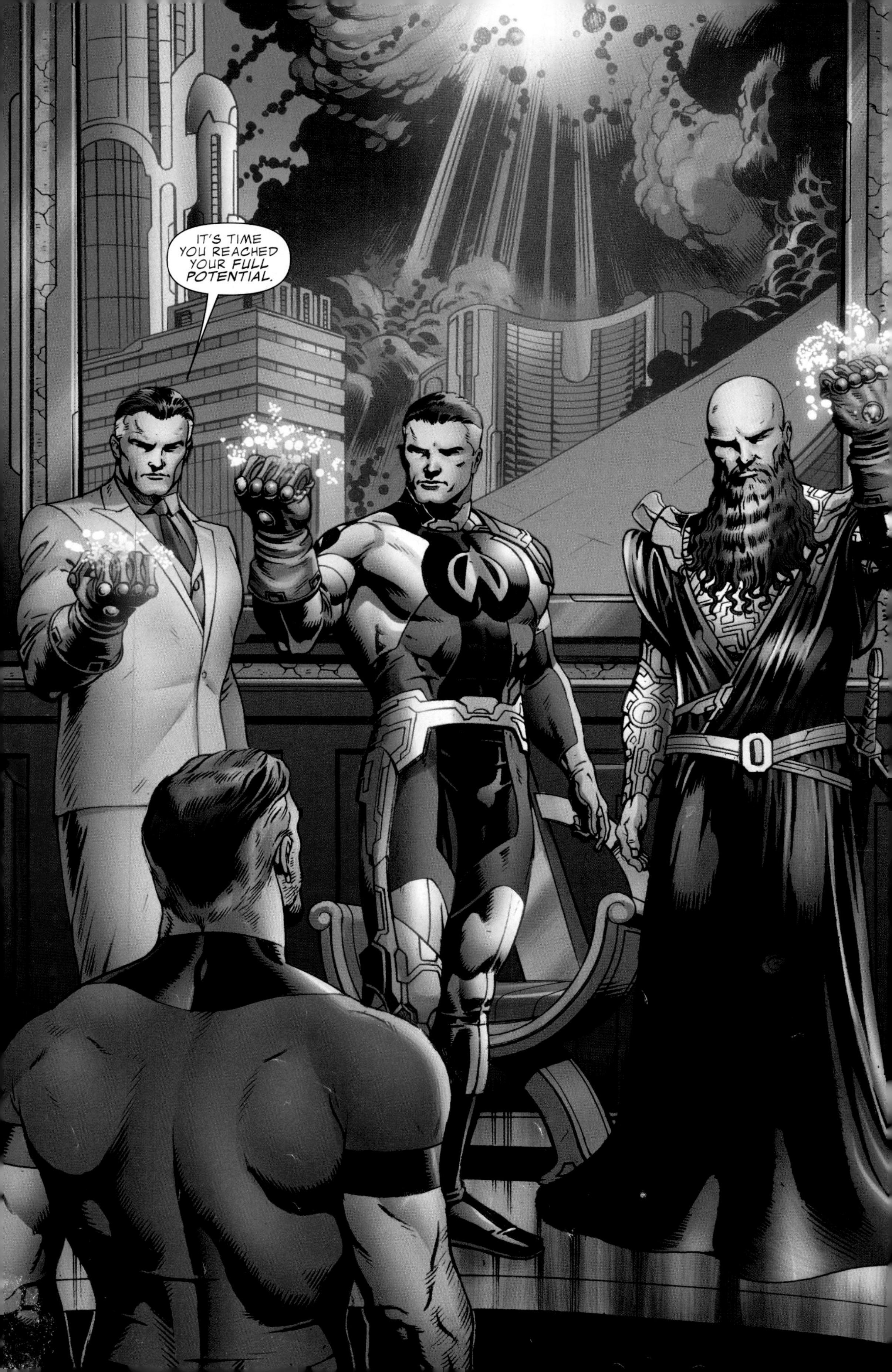
IT'S TIME YOU REACHED YOUR FULL POTENTIAL.

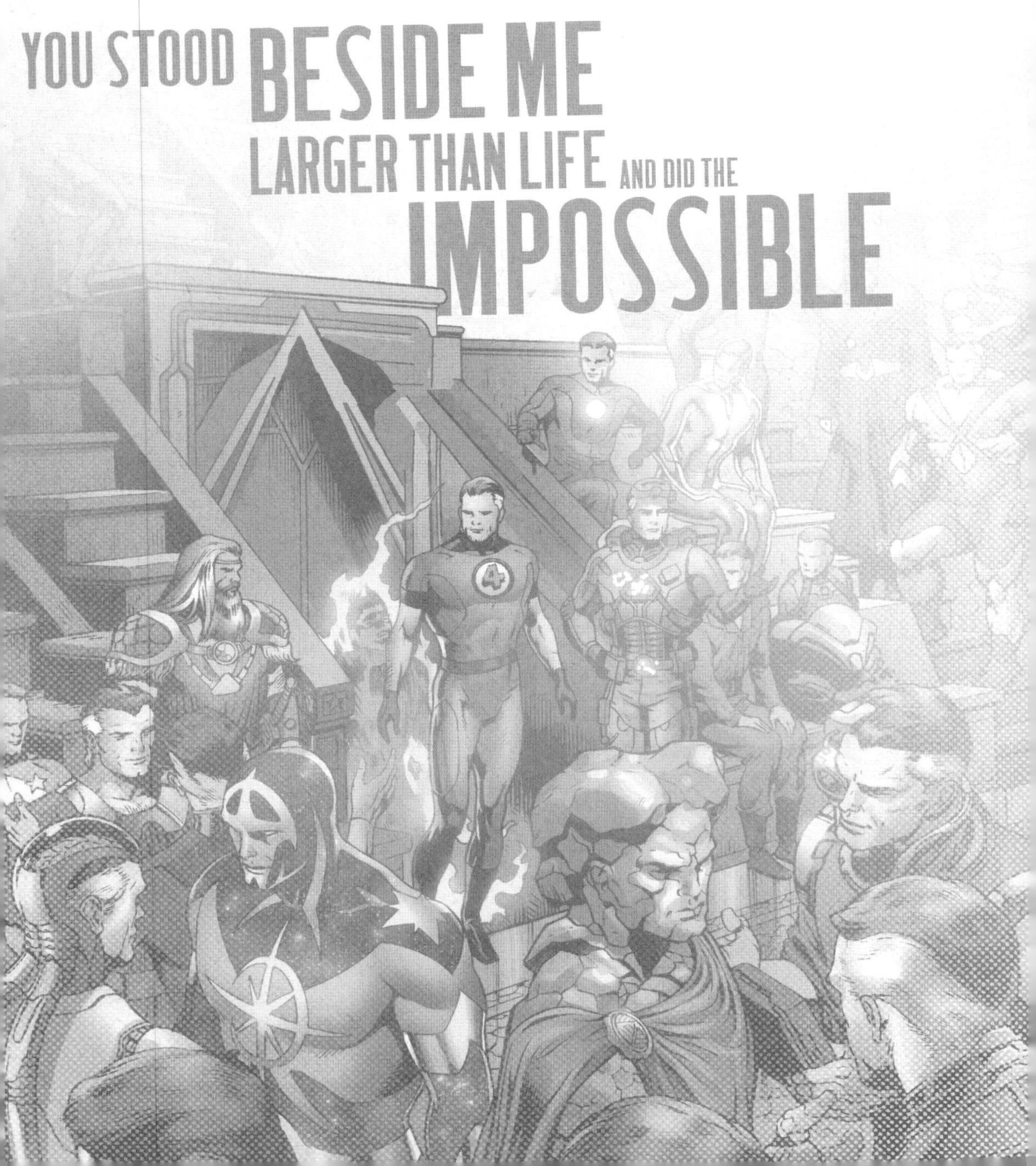
YOU STOOD BESIDE ME
LARGER THAN LIFE AND DID THE
IMPOSSIBLE

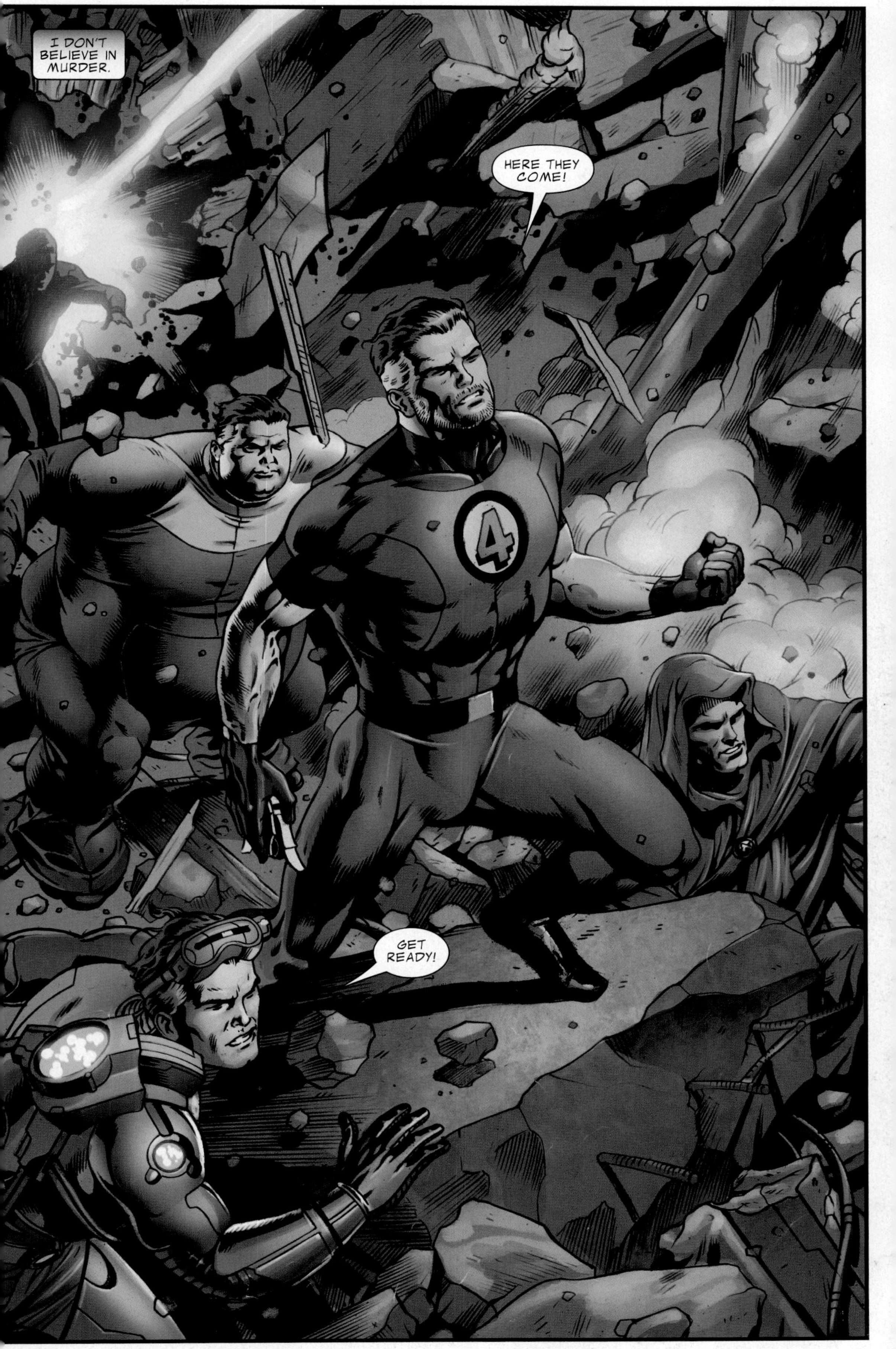
I DON'T BELIEVE IN MURDER.
HERE THEY COME!
GET READY!

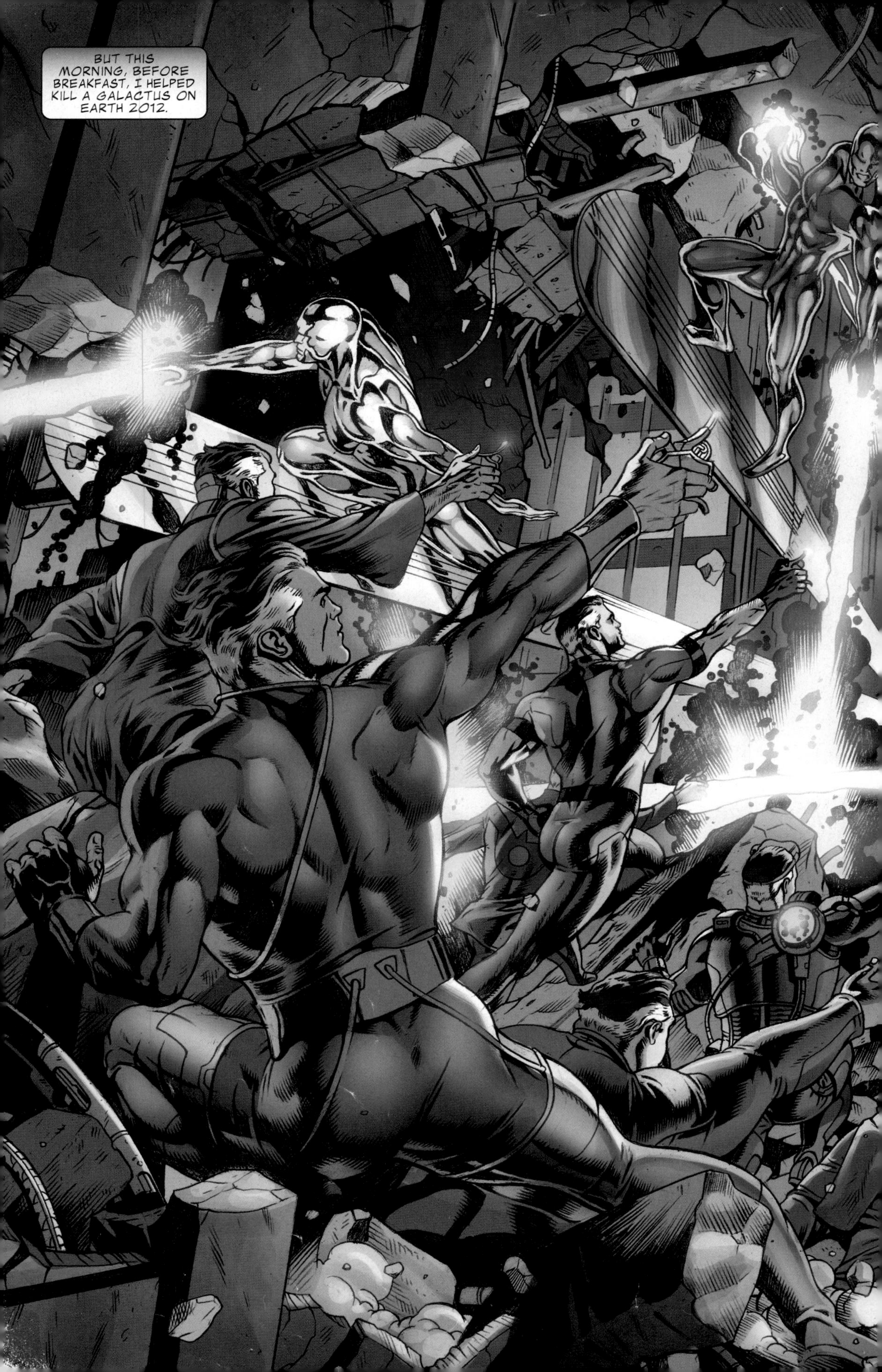
BUT THIS MORNING, BEFORE BREAKFAST, I HELPED KILL A GALACTUS ON EARTH 2012.

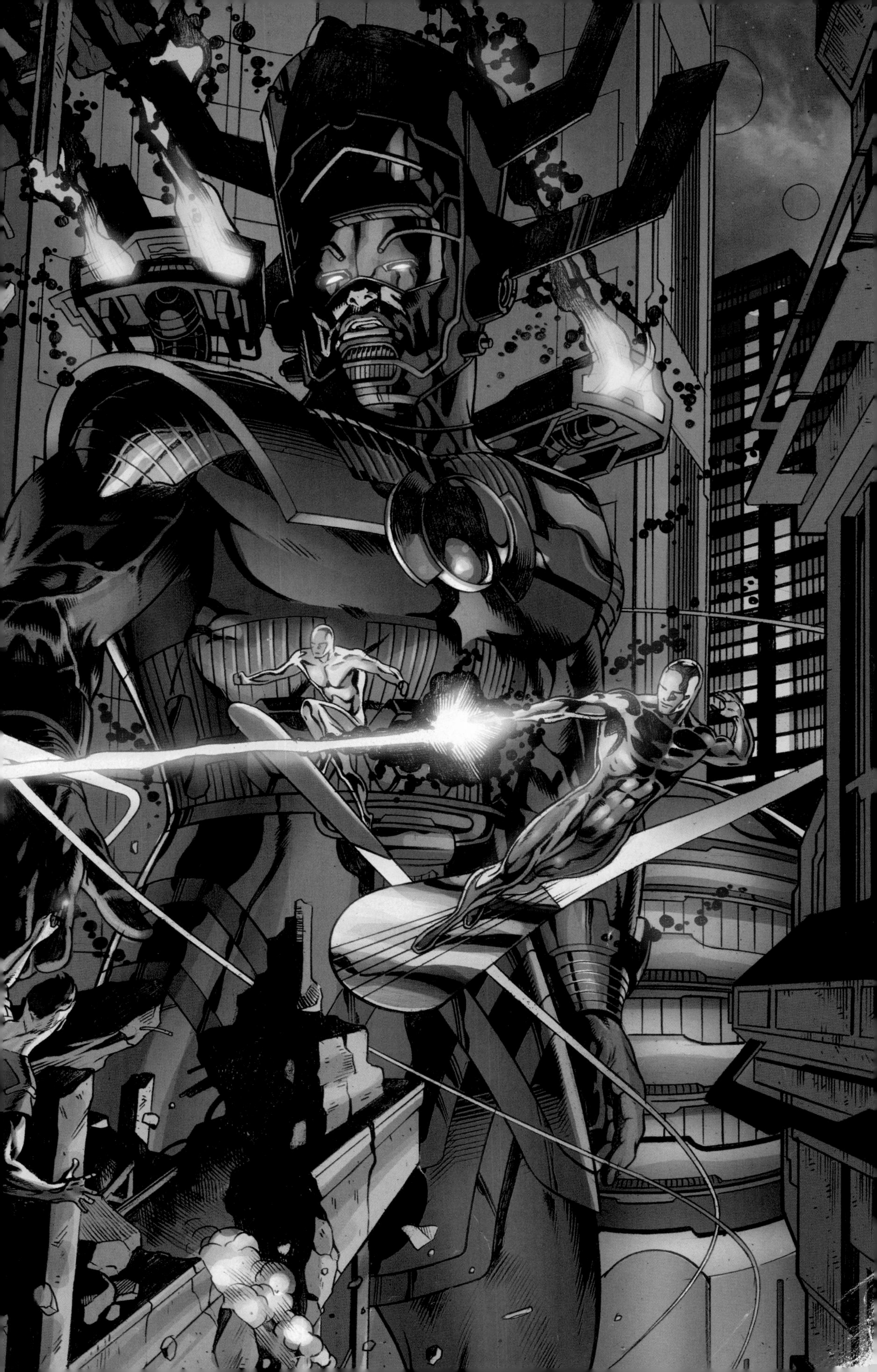

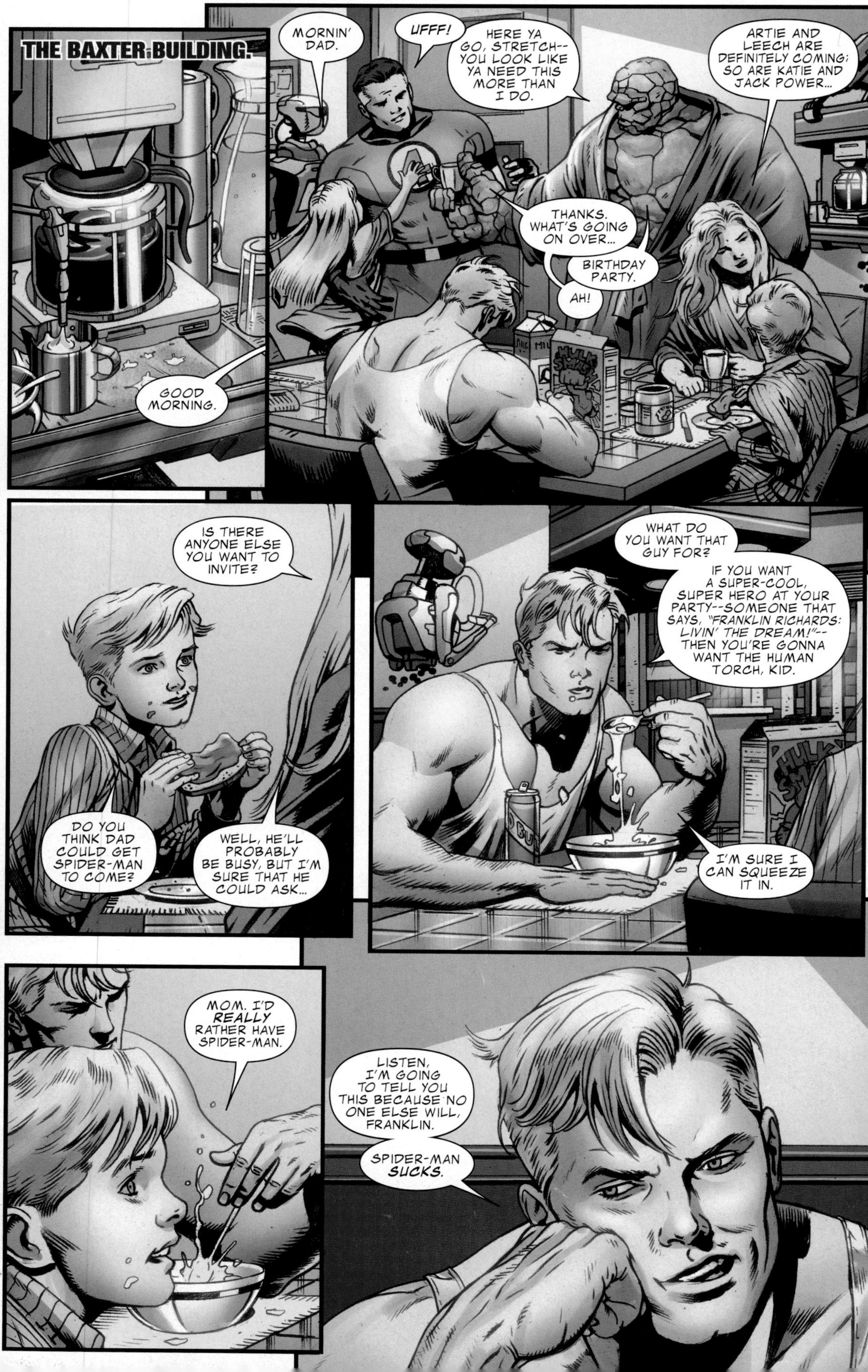
THE BAXTER BUILDING.
GOOD MORNING.
MORNIN' DAD.
UFFF!
HERE YA GO, STRETCH-- YOU LOOK LIKE YA NEED THIS MORE THAN I DO.
ARTIE AND LEECH ARE DEFINITELY COMING; SO ARE KATIE AND JACK POWER...
THANKS. WHAT'S GOING ON OVER...
BIRTHDAY PARTY.
AH!
IS THERE ANYONE ELSE YOU WANT TO INVITE?
DO YOU THINK DAD COULD GET SPIDER-MAN TO COME?
WELL, HE'LL PROBABLY BE BUSY, BUT I'M SURE THAT HE COULD ASK...
WHAT DO YOU WANT THAT GUY FOR?
IF YOU WANT A SUPER-COOL, SUPER HERO AT YOUR PARTY--SOMEONE THAT SAYS, "FRANKLIN RICHARDS: LIVIN' THE DREAM!"-- THEN YOU'RE GONNA WANT THE HUMAN TORCH, KID.
I'M SURE I CAN SQUEEZE IT IN.
MOM. I'D REALLY RATHER HAVE SPIDER-MAN.
LISTEN, I'M GOING TO TELL YOU THIS BECAUSE NO ONE ELSE WILL, FRANKLIN.
SPIDER-MAN SUCKS.

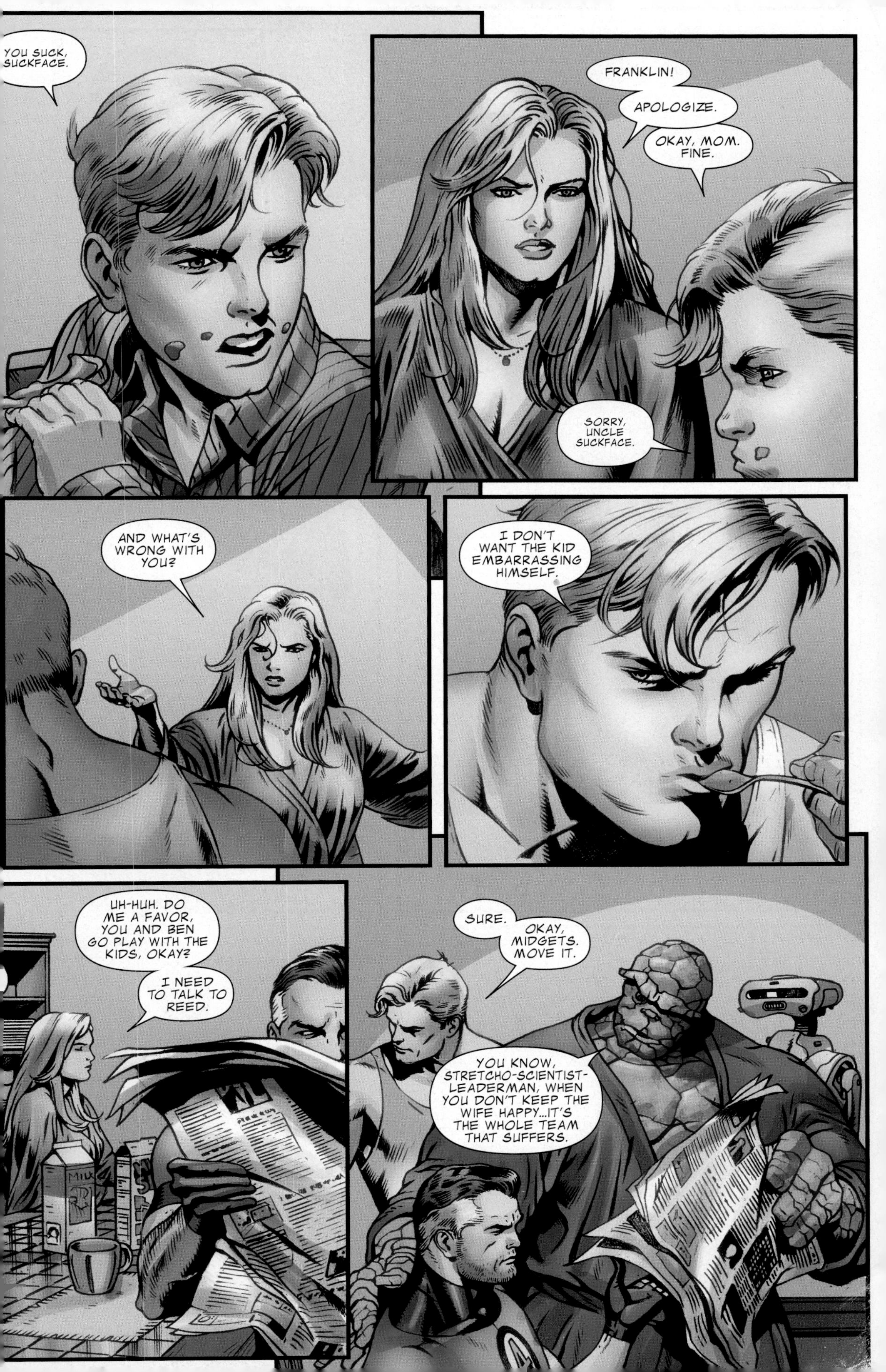
YOU SUCK, SUCKFACE.
FRANKLIN!
APOLOGIZE.
OKAY, MOM. FINE.
SORRY, UNCLE SUCKFACE.
AND WHAT'S WRONG WITH YOU?
I DON'T WANT THE KID EMBARRASSING HIMSELF.
UH-HUH. DO ME A FAVOR, YOU AND BEN GO PLAY WITH THE KIDS, OKAY?
I NEED TO TALK TO REED.
SURE.
OKAY, MIDGETS. MOVE IT.
YOU KNOW, STRETCHO-SCIENTIST-LEADERMAN, WHEN YOU DON'T KEEP THE WIFE HAPPY...IT'S THE WHOLE TEAM THAT SUFFERS.

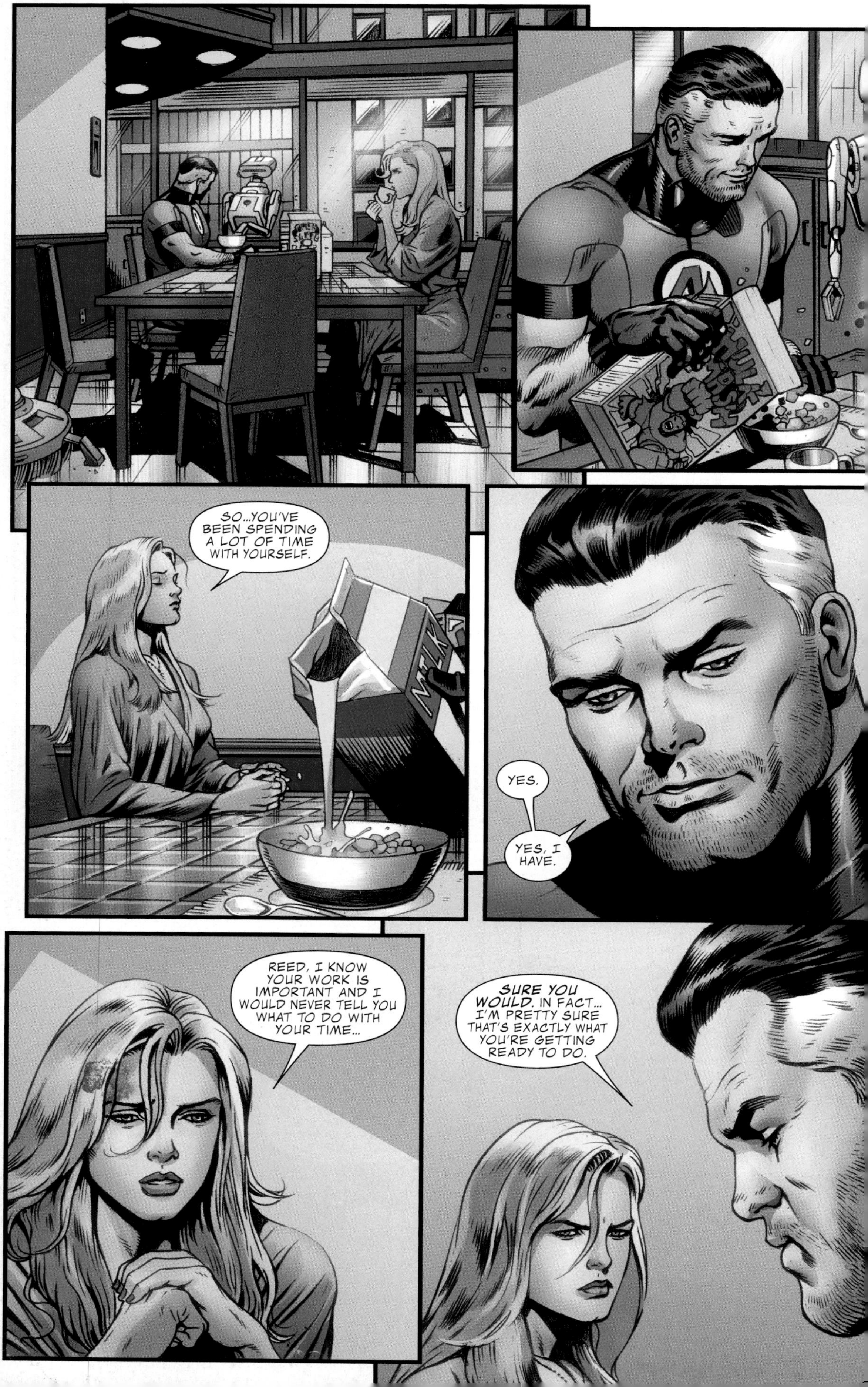

SO...YOU'VE BEEN SPENDING A LOT OF TIME WITH YOURSELF.
YES.
YES, I HAVE.
REED, I KNOW YOUR WORK IS IMPORTANT AND I WOULD NEVER TELL YOU WHAT TO DO WITH YOUR TIME...
SURE YOU WOULD. IN FACT... I'M PRETTY SURE THAT'S EXACTLY WHAT YOU'RE GETTING READY TO DO.

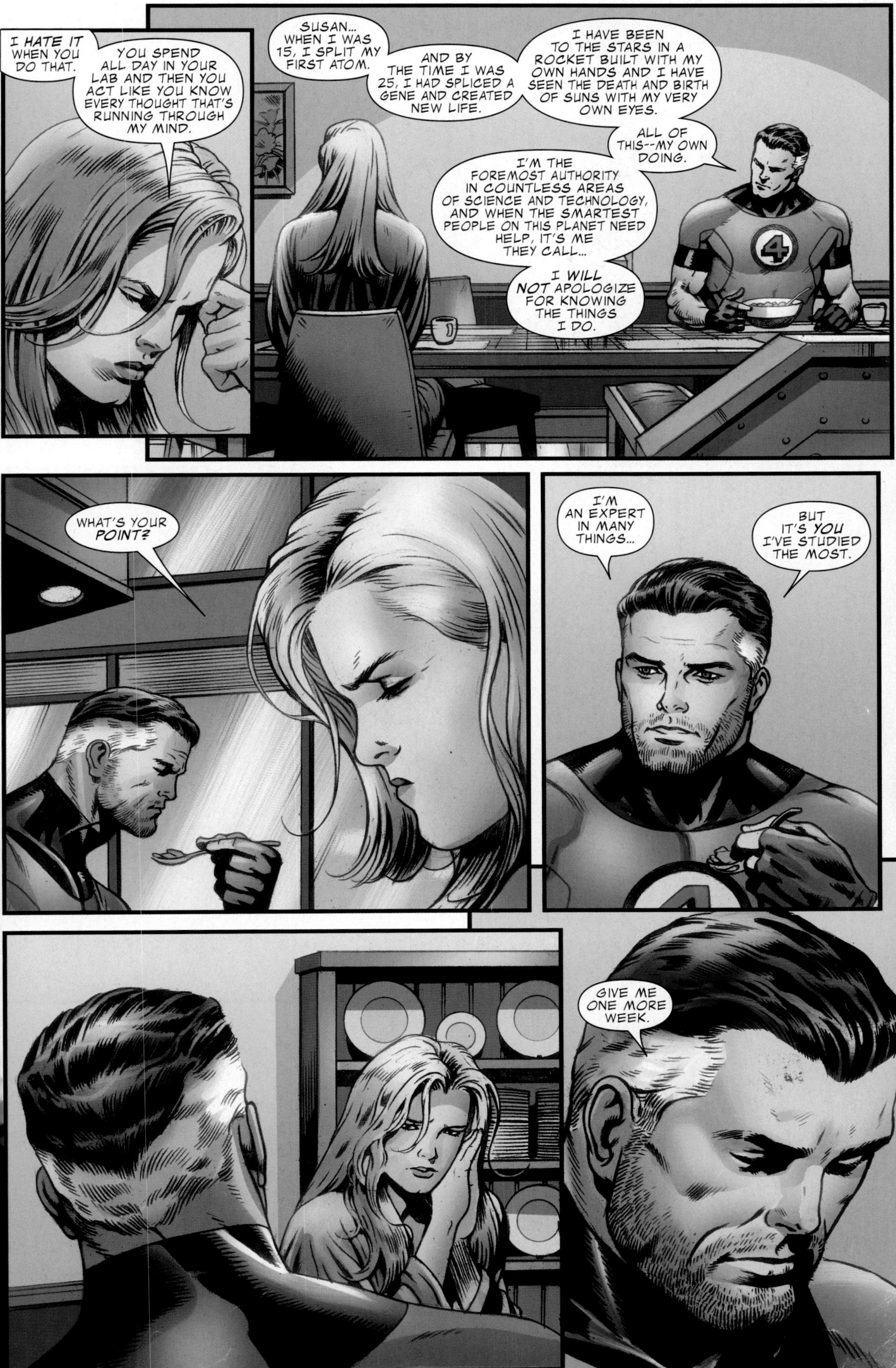
I HATE IT WHEN YOU DO THAT.
YOU SPEND ALL DAY IN YOUR LAB AND THEN YOU ACT LIKE YOU KNOW EVERY THOUGHT THAT'S RUNNING THROUGH MY MIND.
SUSAN... WHEN I WAS 15, I SPLIT MY FIRST ATOM.
AND BY THE TIME I WAS 25, I HAD SPLICED A GENE AND CREATED NEW LIFE.
I HAVE BEEN TO THE STARS IN A ROCKET BUILT WITH MY OWN HANDS AND I HAVE SEEN THE DEATH AND BIRTH OF SUNS WITH MY VERY OWN EYES.
ALL OF THIS--MY OWN DOING.
I'M THE FOREMOST AUTHORITY IN COUNTLESS AREAS OF SCIENCE AND TECHNOLOGY, AND WHEN THE SMARTEST PEOPLE ON THIS PLANET NEED HELP, IT'S ME THEY CALL...
I WILL NOT APOLOGIZE FOR KNOWING THE THINGS I DO.
WHAT'S YOUR POINT?
I'M AN EXPERT IN MANY THINGS...
BUT IT'S YOU I'VE STUDIED THE MOST.
GIVE ME ONE MORE WEEK.

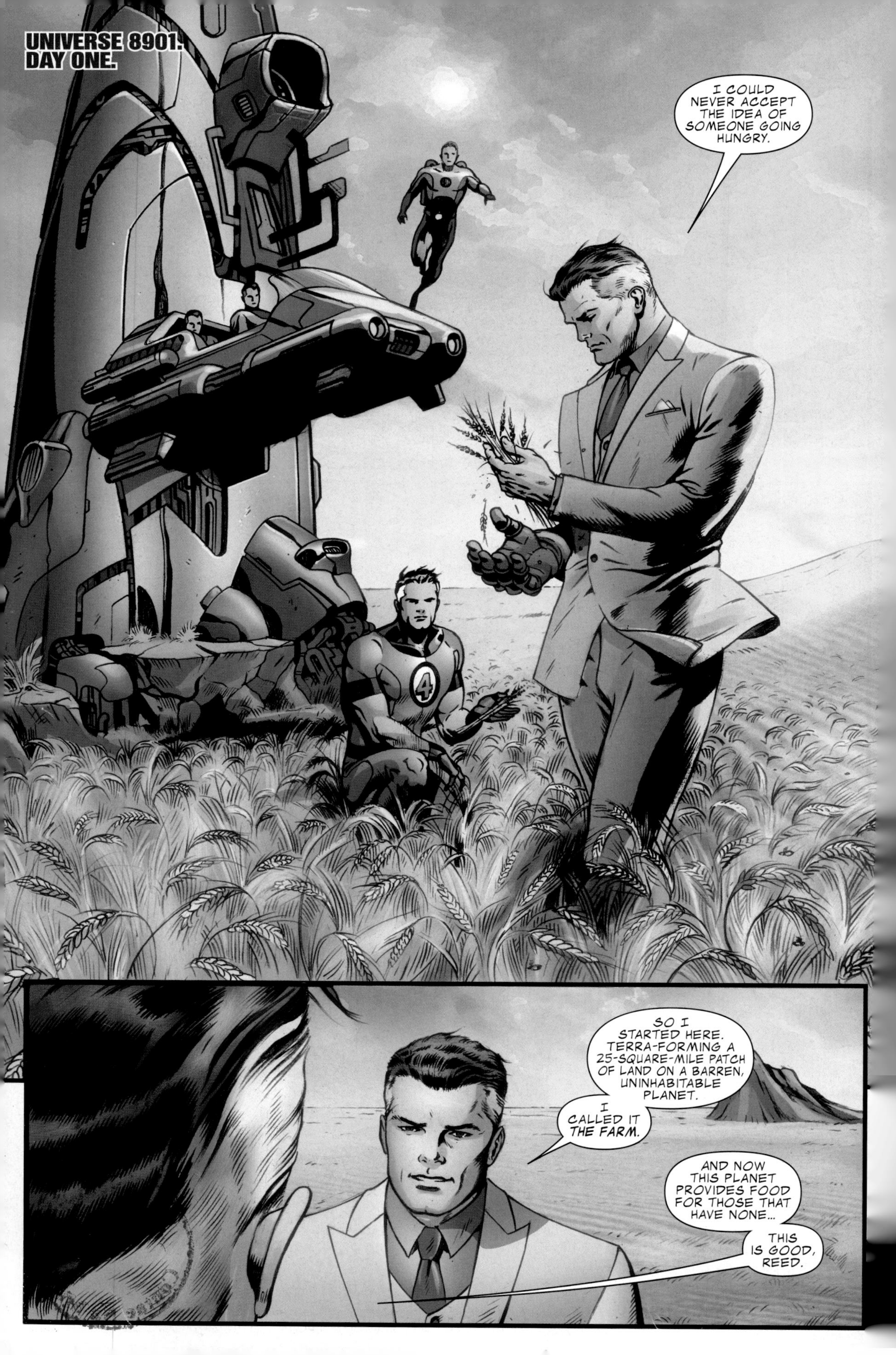
UNIVERSE 8901. DAY ONE.
I COULD NEVER ACCEPT THE IDEA OF SOMEONE GOING HUNGRY.
SO I STARTED HERE. TERRA-FORMING A 25-SQUARE-MILE PATCH OF LAND ON A BARREN, UNINHABITABLE PLANET.
I CALLED IT THE FARM.
AND NOW THIS PLANET PROVIDES FOOD FOR THOSE THAT HAVE NONE...
THIS IS GOOD, REED.

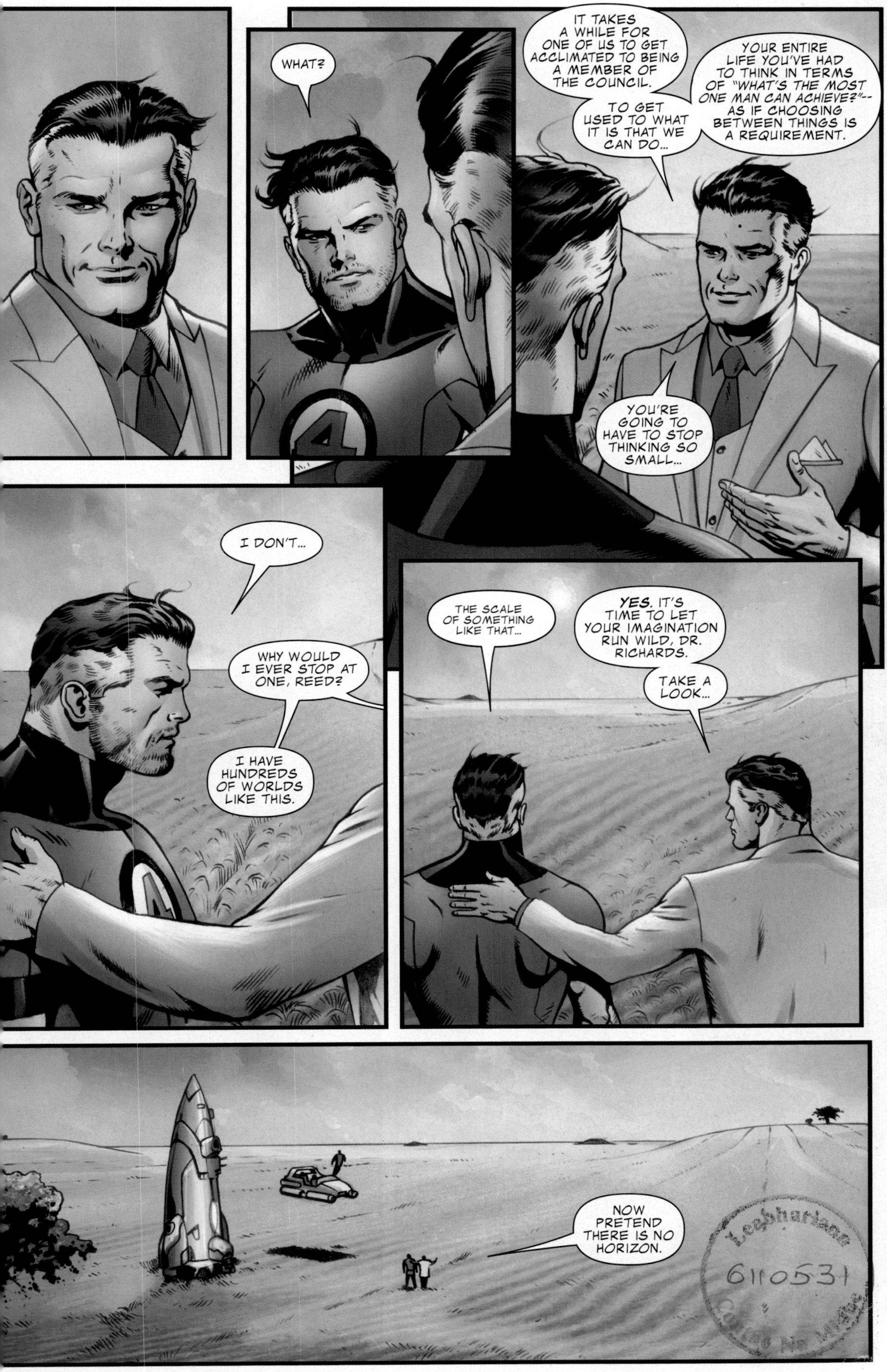
WHAT?
IT TAKES A WHILE FOR ONE OF US TO GET ACCLIMATED TO BEING A MEMBER OF THE COUNCIL.
TO GET USED TO WHAT IT IS THAT WE CAN DO...
YOUR ENTIRE LIFE YOU'VE HAD TO THINK IN TERMS OF "WHAT'S THE MOST ONE MAN CAN ACHIEVE?"-- AS IF CHOOSING BETWEEN THINGS IS A REQUIREMENT.
YOU'RE GOING TO HAVE TO STOP THINKING SO SMALL...
I DON'T...
WHY WOULD I EVER STOP AT ONE, REED?
I HAVE HUNDREDS OF WORLDS LIKE THIS.
THE SCALE OF SOMETHING LIKE THAT...
YES. IT'S TIME TO LET YOUR IMAGINATION RUN WILD, DR. RICHARDS.
TAKE A LOOK...
NOW PRETEND THERE IS NO HORIZON.

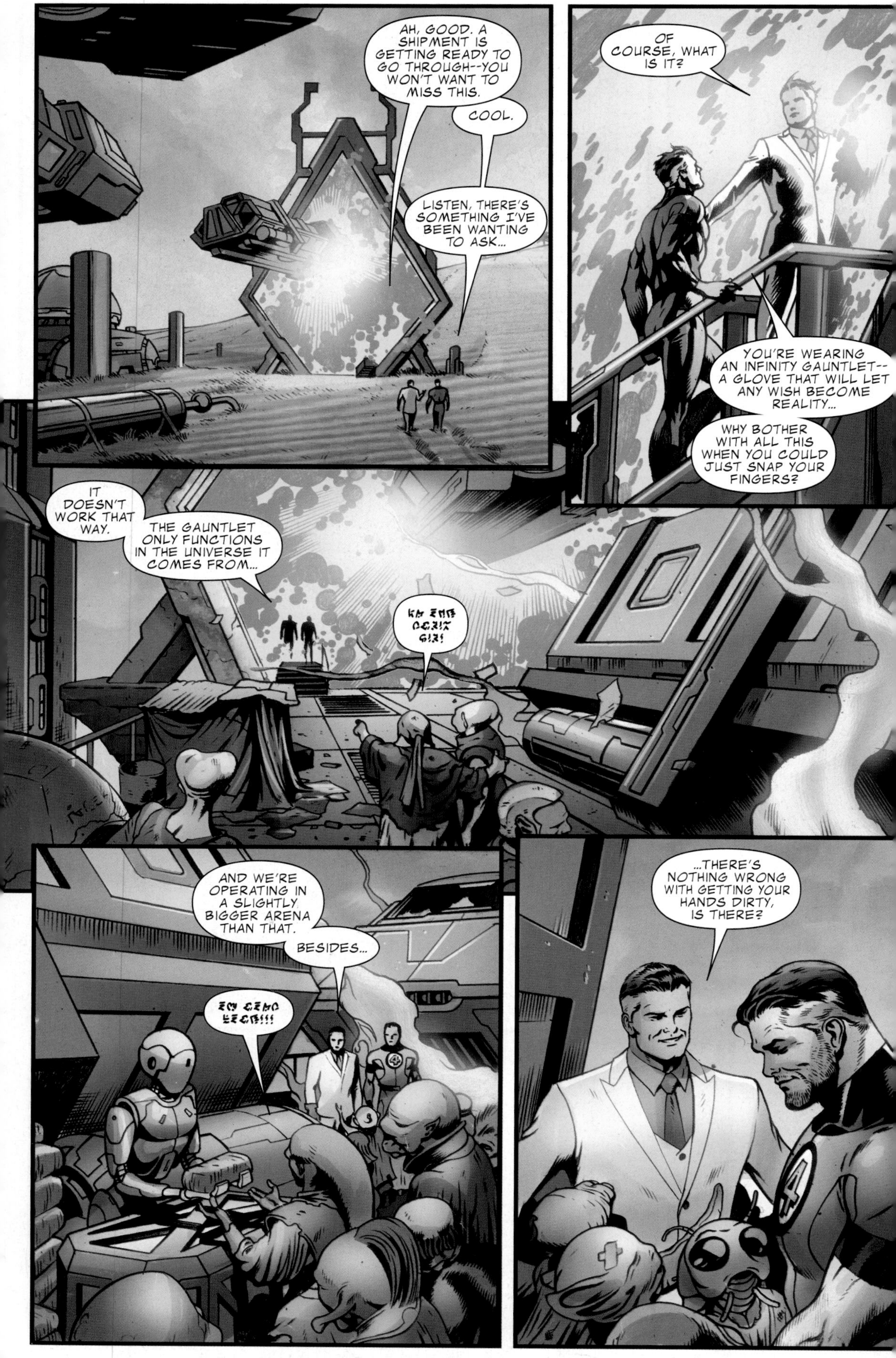
AH, GOOD. A SHIPMENT IS GETTING READY TO GO THROUGH--YOU WON'T WANT TO MISS THIS.
COOL.
LISTEN, THERE'S SOMETHING I'VE BEEN WANTING TO ASK...
OF COURSE, WHAT IS IT?
YOU'RE WEARING AN INFINITY GAUNTLET-- A GLOVE THAT WILL LET ANY WISH BECOME REALITY...
WHY BOTHER WITH ALL THIS WHEN YOU COULD JUST SNAP YOUR FINGERS?
IT DOESN'T WORK THAT WAY.
THE GAUNTLET ONLY FUNCTIONS IN THE UNIVERSE IT COMES FROM...
AND WE'RE OPERATING IN A SLIGHTLY BIGGER ARENA THAN THAT.
BESIDES...
...THERE'S NOTHING WRONG WITH GETTING YOUR HANDS DIRTY, IS THERE?

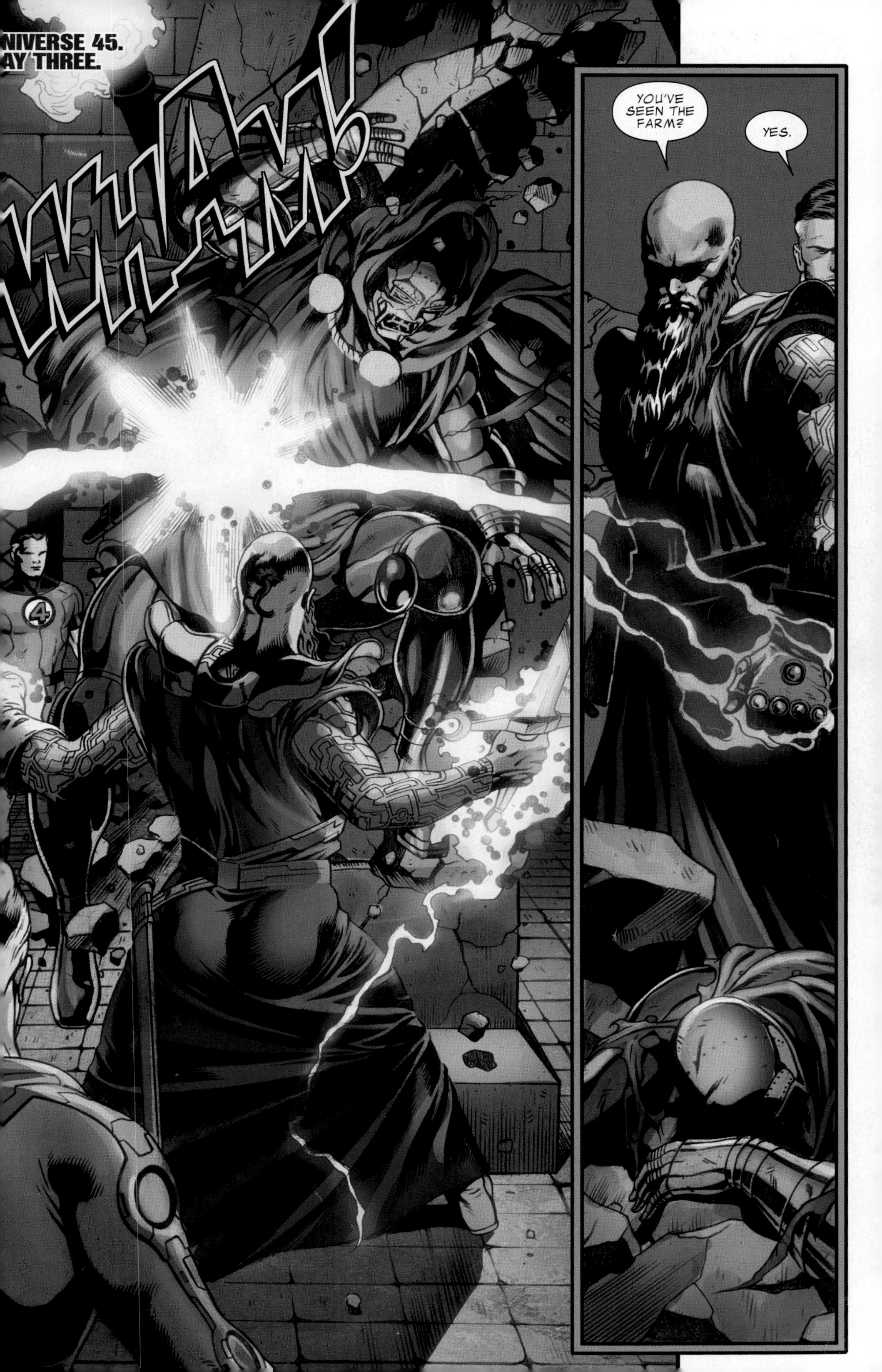
NIVERSE 45.
AY THREE.
WHAM!
YOU'VE SEEN THE FARM?
YES.

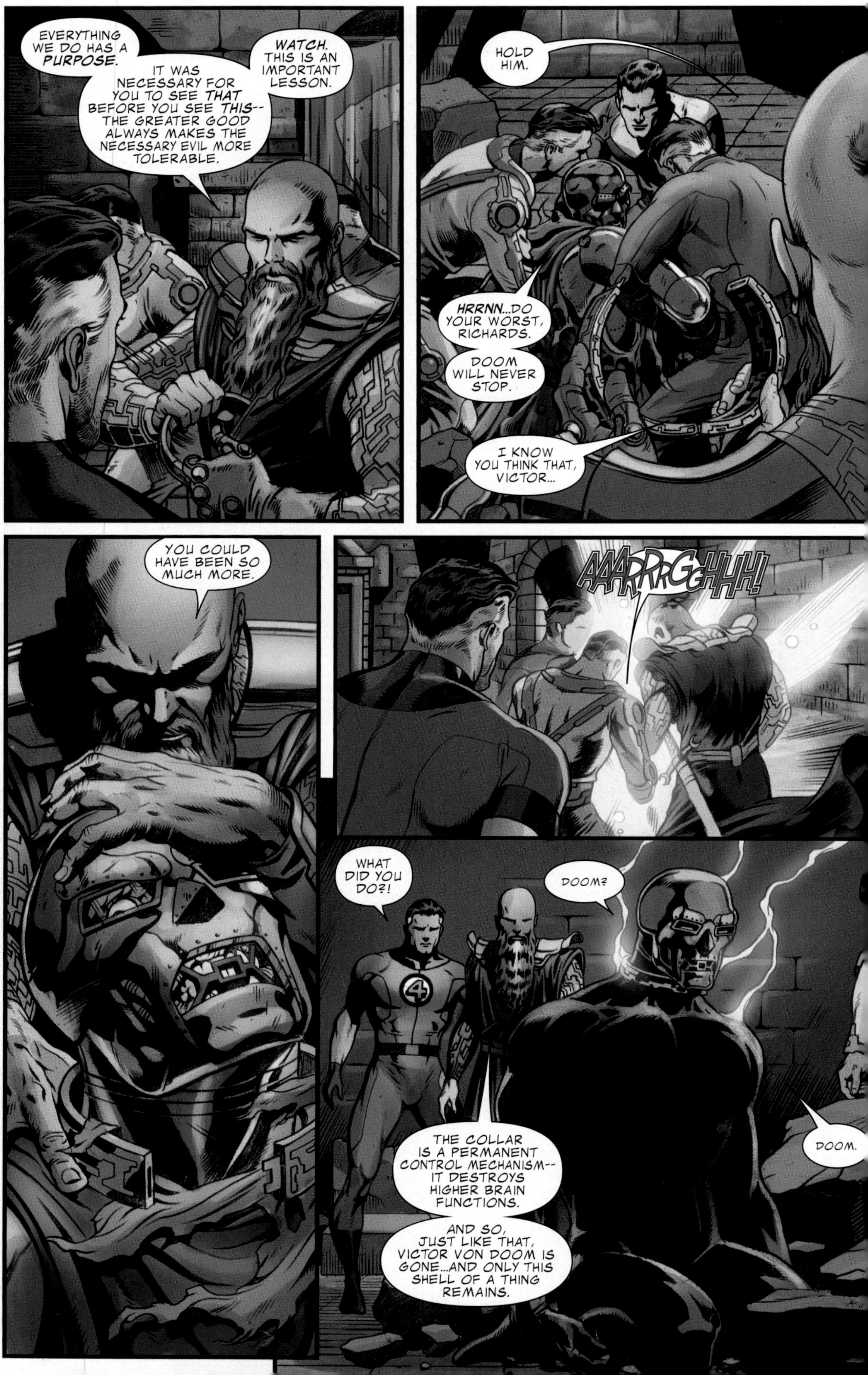
EVERYTHING WE DO HAS A PURPOSE.
IT WAS NECESSARY FOR YOU TO SEE THAT BEFORE YOU SEE THIS-- THE GREATER GOOD ALWAYS MAKES THE NECESSARY EVIL MORE TOLERABLE.
WATCH. THIS IS AN IMPORTANT LESSON.
HOLD HIM.
HRRNN...DO YOUR WORST, RICHARDS.
DOOM WILL NEVER STOP.
I KNOW YOU THINK THAT, VICTOR...
YOU COULD HAVE BEEN SO MUCH MORE.
AAARRRGGHHH!
WHAT DID YOU DO?!
DOOM?
THE COLLAR IS A PERMANENT CONTROL MECHANISM-- IT DESTROYS HIGHER BRAIN FUNCTIONS.
AND SO, JUST LIKE THAT, VICTOR VON DOOM IS GONE...AND ONLY THIS SHELL OF A THING REMAINS.
DOOM.

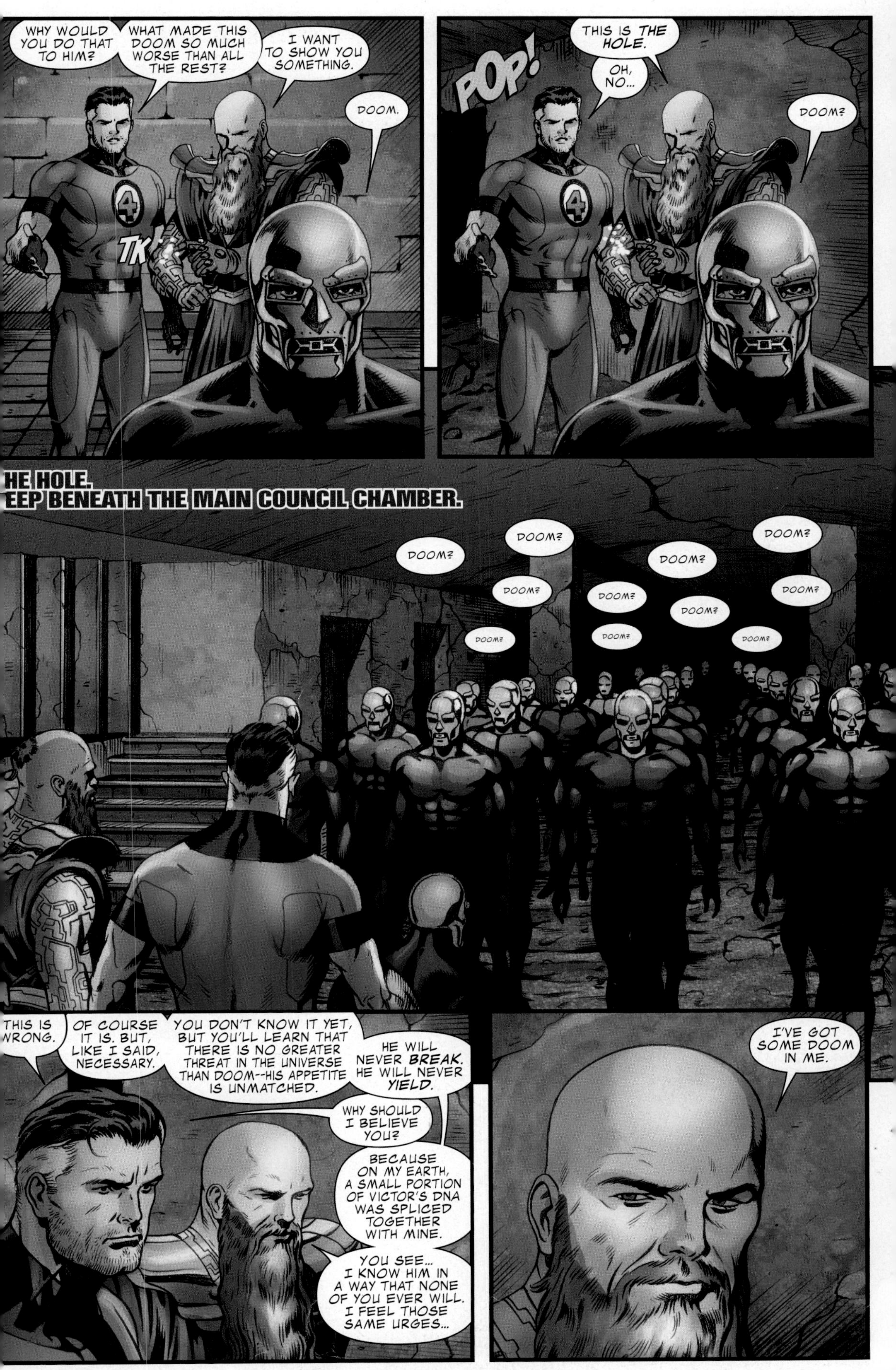
WHY WOULD YOU DO THAT TO HIM?
WHAT MADE THIS DOOM SO MUCH WORSE THAN ALL THE REST?
I WANT TO SHOW YOU SOMETHING.
DOOM.
TK
POP!
THIS IS THE HOLE.
OH, NO...
DOOM?
HE HOLE.
EEP BENEATH THE MAIN COUNCIL CHAMBER.
DOOM?
DOOM?
DOOM?
DOOM?
DOOM?
DOOM?
DOOM?
DOOM?
DOOM?
DOOM?
DOOM?
THIS IS WRONG.
OF COURSE IT IS. BUT, LIKE I SAID, NECESSARY.
YOU DON'T KNOW IT YET, BUT YOU'LL LEARN THAT THERE IS NO GREATER THREAT IN THE UNIVERSE THAN DOOM--HIS APPETITE IS UNMATCHED.
HE WILL NEVER BREAK. HE WILL NEVER YIELD.
WHY SHOULD I BELIEVE YOU?
BECAUSE ON MY EARTH, A SMALL PORTION OF VICTOR'S DNA WAS SPLICED TOGETHER WITH MINE.
YOU SEE... I KNOW HIM IN A WAY THAT NONE OF YOU EVER WILL. I FEEL THOSE SAME URGES...
I'VE GOT SOME DOOM IN ME.

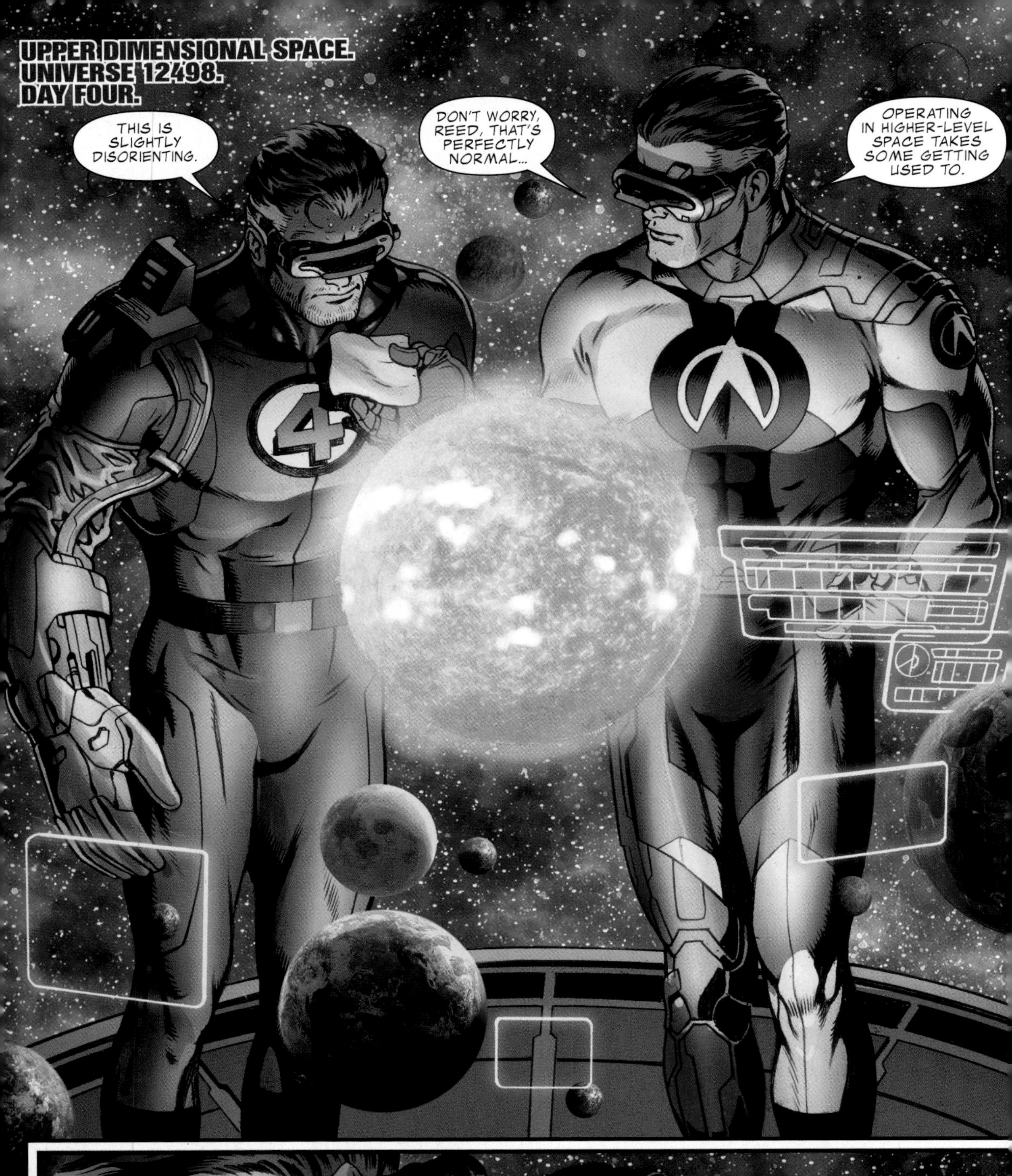
UPPER DIMENSIONAL SPACE. UNIVERSE 12498. DAY FOUR.
THIS IS SLIGHTLY DISORIENTING.
DON'T WORRY, REED, THAT'S PERFECTLY NORMAL...
OPERATING IN HIGHER-LEVEL SPACE TAKES SOME GETTING USED TO.

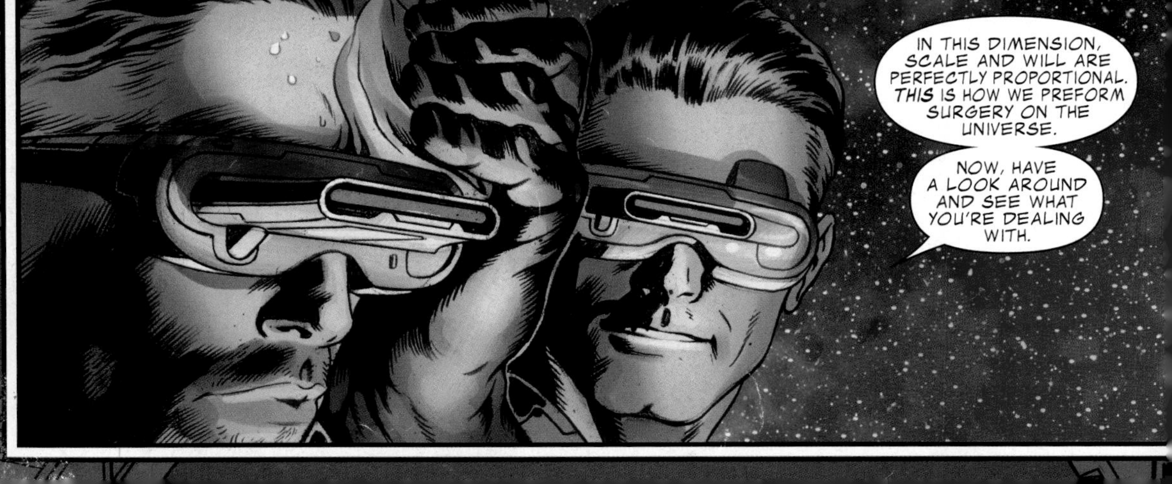
IN THIS DIMENSION, SCALE AND WILL ARE PERFECTLY PROPORTIONAL. THIS IS HOW WE PREFORM SURGERY ON THE UNIVERSE.
NOW, HAVE A LOOK AROUND AND SEE WHAT YOU'RE DEALING WITH.

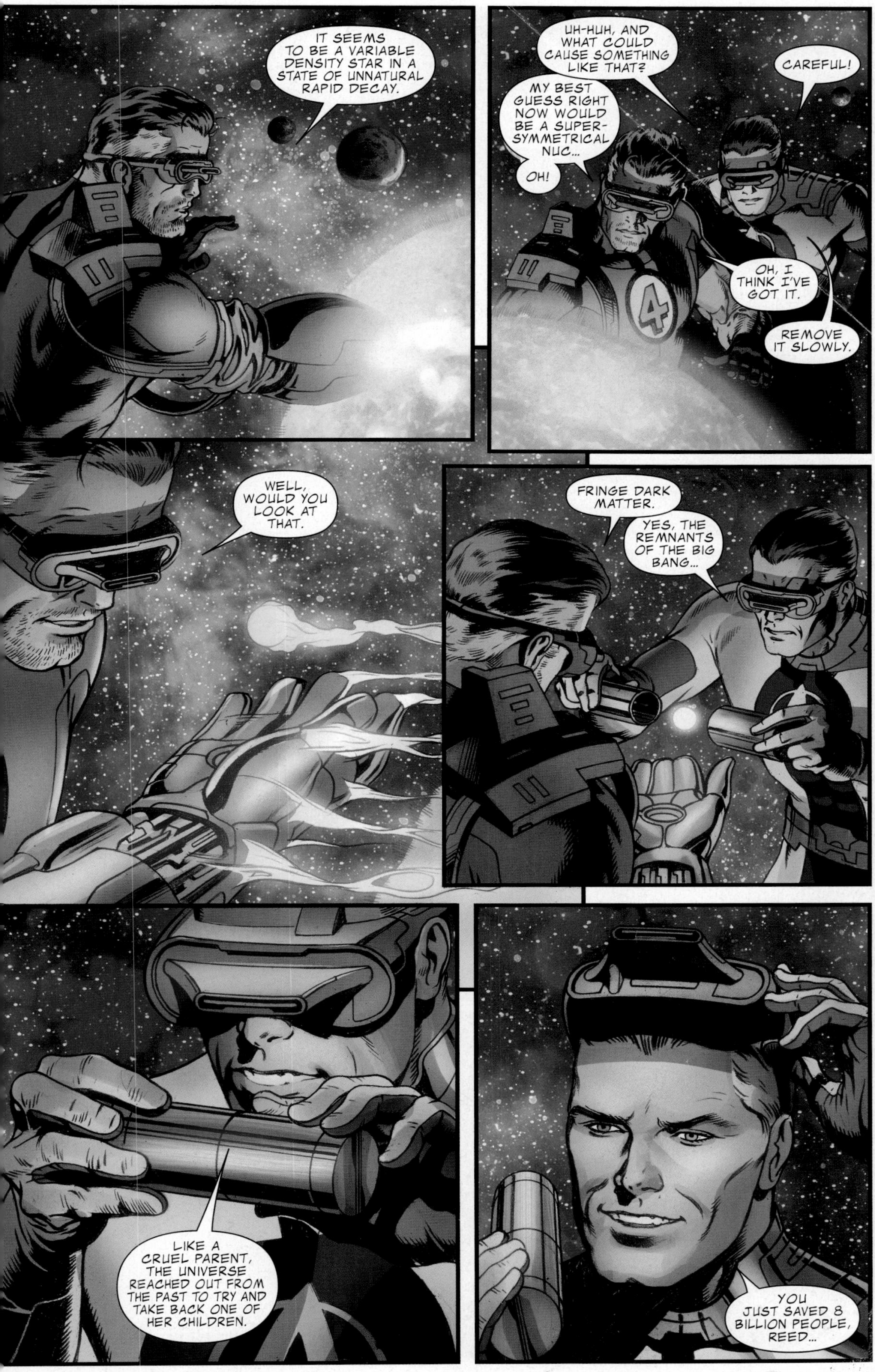
IT SEEMS TO BE A VARIABLE DENSITY STAR IN A STATE OF UNNATURAL RAPID DECAY.
UH-HUH, AND WHAT COULD CAUSE SOMETHING LIKE THAT?
MY BEST GUESS RIGHT NOW WOULD BE A SUPER-SYMMETRICAL NUC...
OH!
CAREFUL!
OH, I THINK I'VE GOT IT.
REMOVE IT SLOWLY.
WELL, WOULD YOU LOOK AT THAT.
FRINGE DARK MATTER.
YES, THE REMNANTS OF THE BIG BANG...
LIKE A CRUEL PARENT, THE UNIVERSE REACHED OUT FROM THE PAST TO TRY AND TAKE BACK ONE OF HER CHILDREN.
YOU JUST SAVED 8 BILLION PEOPLE, REED...

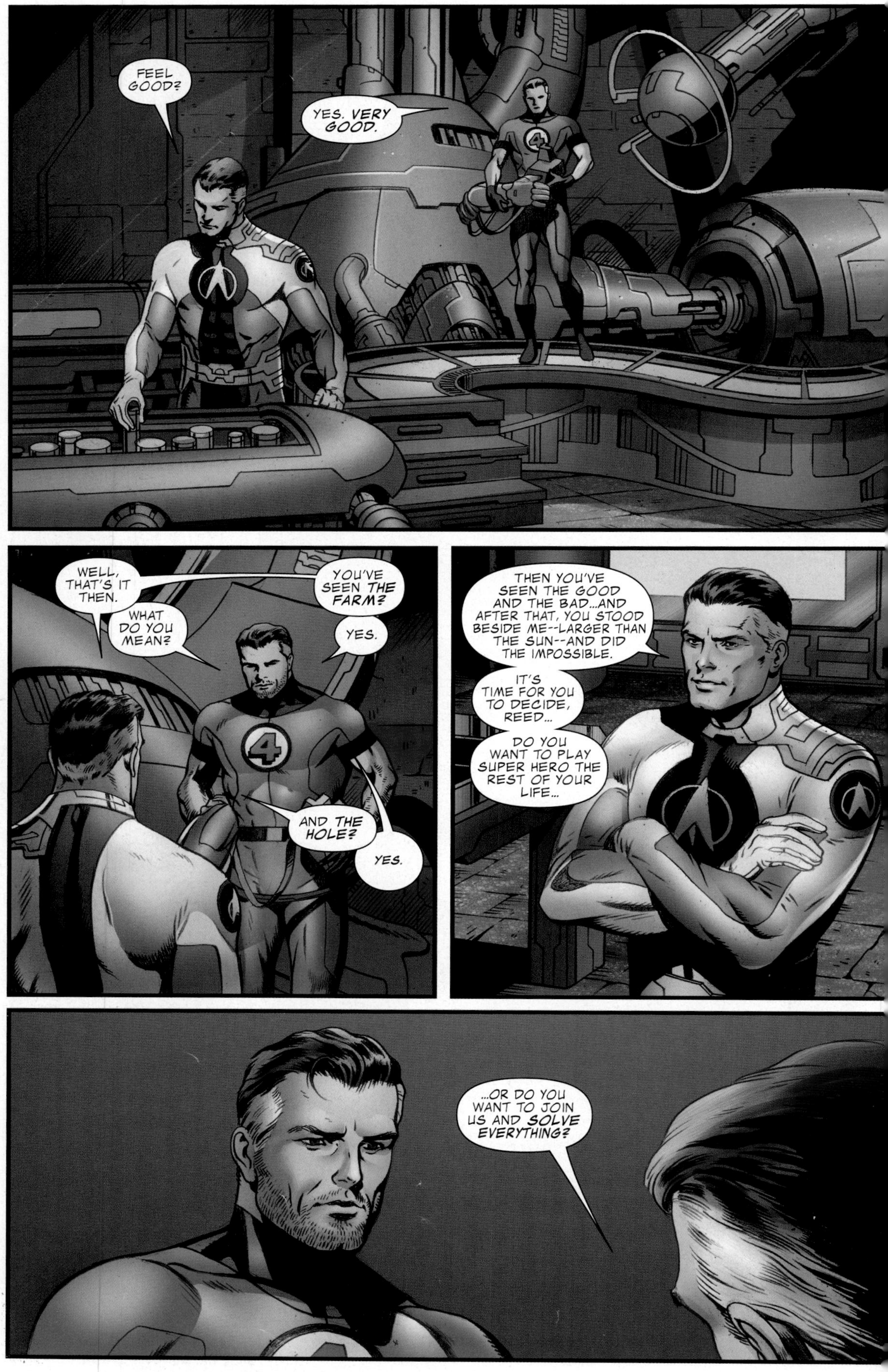
FEEL GOOD?
YES. VERY GOOD.
WELL, THAT'S IT THEN.
WHAT DO YOU MEAN?
YOU'VE SEEN THE FARM?
YES.
AND THE HOLE?
YES.
THEN YOU'VE SEEN THE GOOD AND THE BAD...AND AFTER THAT, YOU STOOD BESIDE ME--LARGER THAN THE SUN--AND DID THE IMPOSSIBLE.
IT'S TIME FOR YOU TO DECIDE, REED...
DO YOU WANT TO PLAY SUPER HERO THE REST OF YOUR LIFE...
...OR DO YOU WANT TO JOIN US AND SOLVE EVERYTHING?

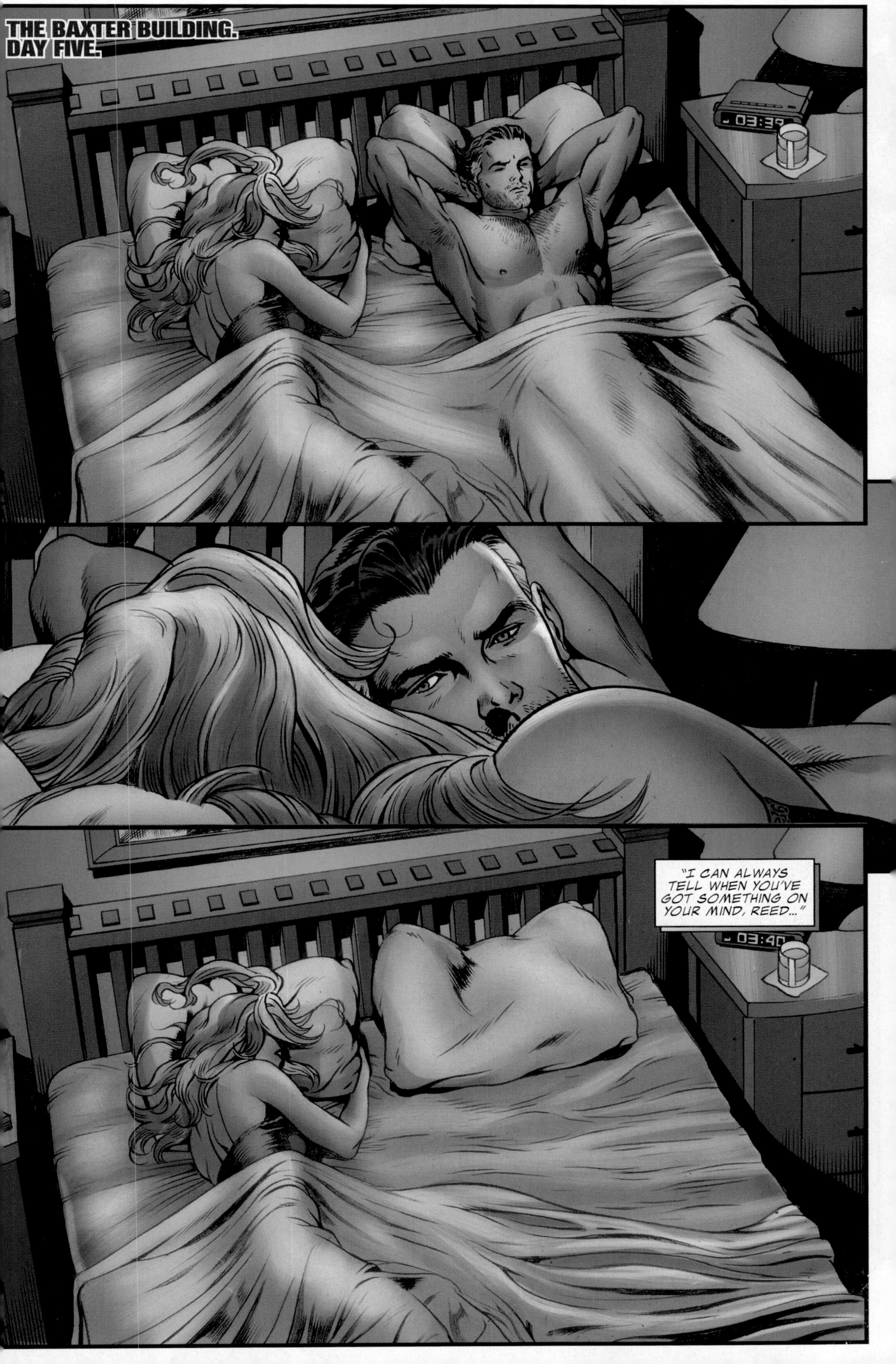
THE BAXTER BUILDING. DAY FIVE.
03:39
03:40
"I CAN ALWAYS TELL WHEN YOU'VE GOT SOMETHING ON YOUR MIND, REED..."

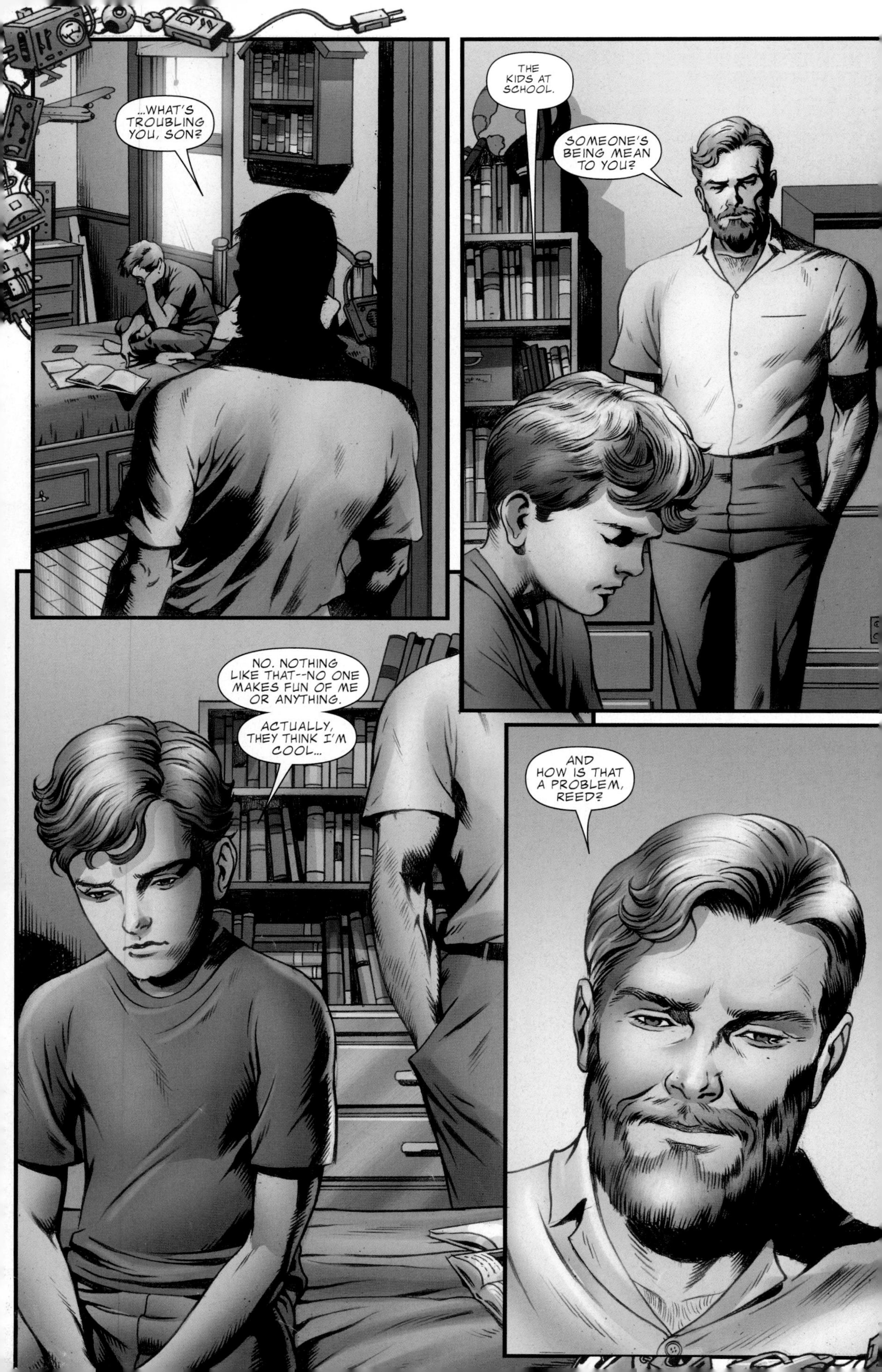
...WHAT'S TROUBLING YOU, SON?
THE KIDS AT SCHOOL.
SOMEONE'S BEING MEAN TO YOU?
NO. NOTHING LIKE THAT--NO ONE MAKES FUN OF ME OR ANYTHING.
ACTUALLY, THEY THINK I'M COOL...
AND HOW IS THAT A PROBLEM, REED?

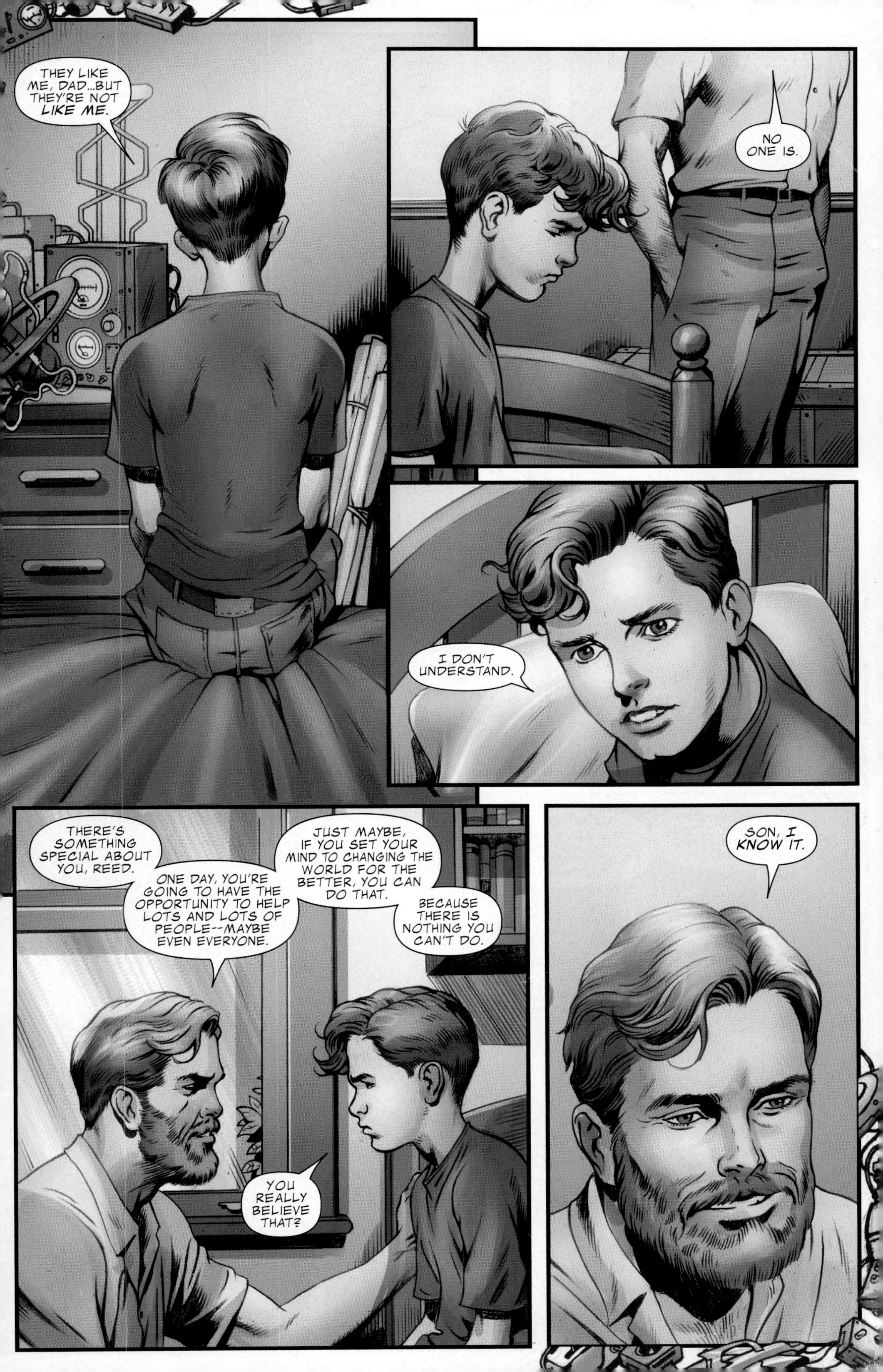
THEY LIKE ME, DAD...BUT THEY'RE NOT *LIKE ME.*
NO ONE IS.
I DON'T UNDERSTAND.
THERE'S SOMETHING SPECIAL ABOUT YOU, REED.
ONE DAY, YOU'RE GOING TO HAVE THE OPPORTUNITY TO HELP LOTS AND LOTS OF PEOPLE--MAYBE EVEN EVERYONE.
JUST MAYBE, IF YOU SET YOUR MIND TO CHANGING THE WORLD FOR THE BETTER, YOU CAN DO THAT.
BECAUSE THERE IS NOTHING YOU CAN'T DO.
YOU REALLY BELIEVE THAT?
SON, I *KNOW IT.*

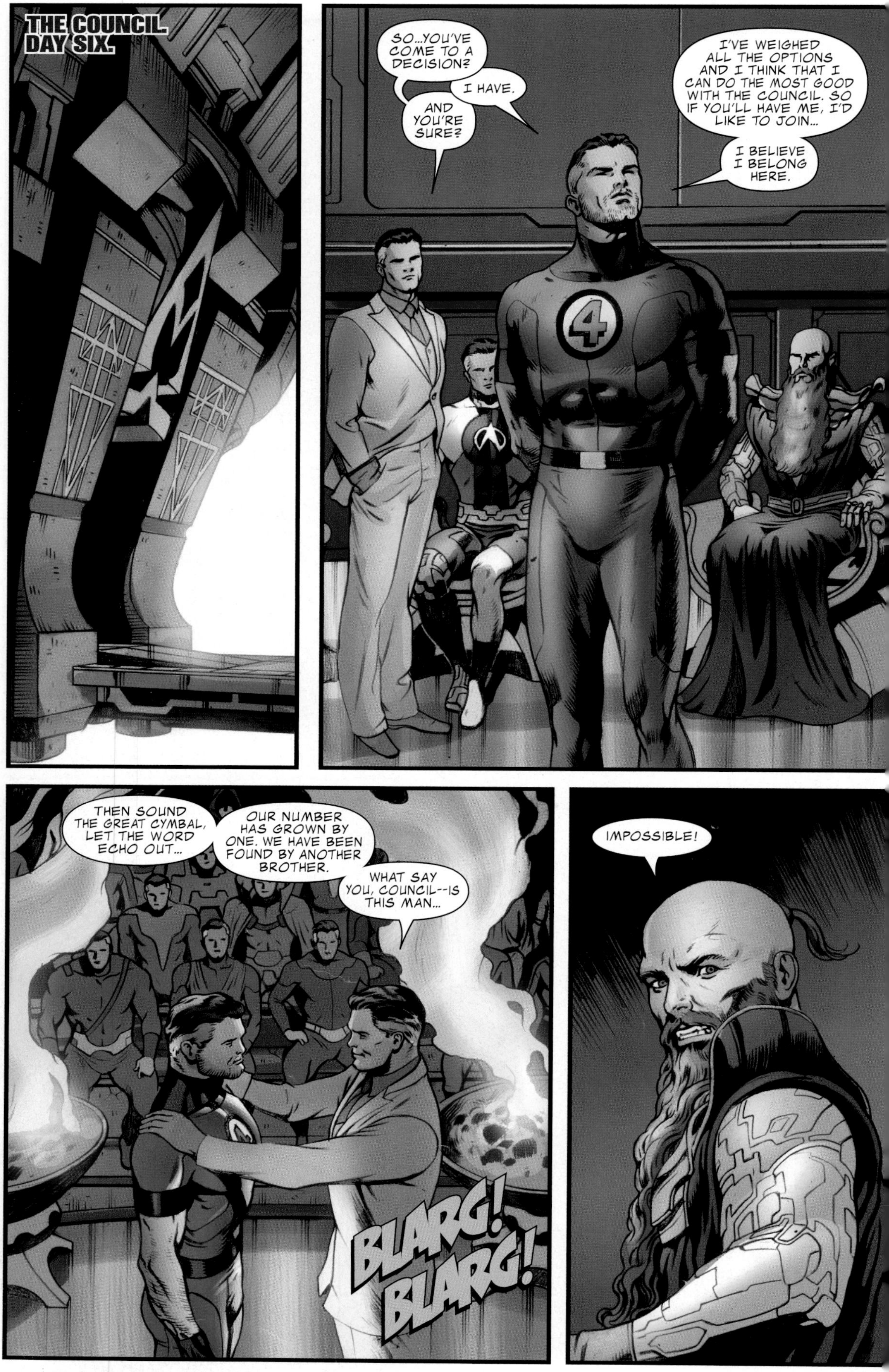
THE COUNCIL. DAY SIX.
SO...YOU'VE COME TO A DECISION?
I HAVE.
AND YOU'RE SURE?
I'VE WEIGHED ALL THE OPTIONS AND I THINK THAT I CAN DO THE MOST GOOD WITH THE COUNCIL. SO IF YOU'LL HAVE ME, I'D LIKE TO JOIN...
I BELIEVE I BELONG HERE.
THEN SOUND THE GREAT CYMBAL, LET THE WORD ECHO OUT...
OUR NUMBER HAS GROWN BY ONE. WE HAVE BEEN FOUND BY ANOTHER BROTHER.
WHAT SAY YOU, COUNCIL--IS THIS MAN...
BLARG! BLARG!
IMPOSSIBLE!

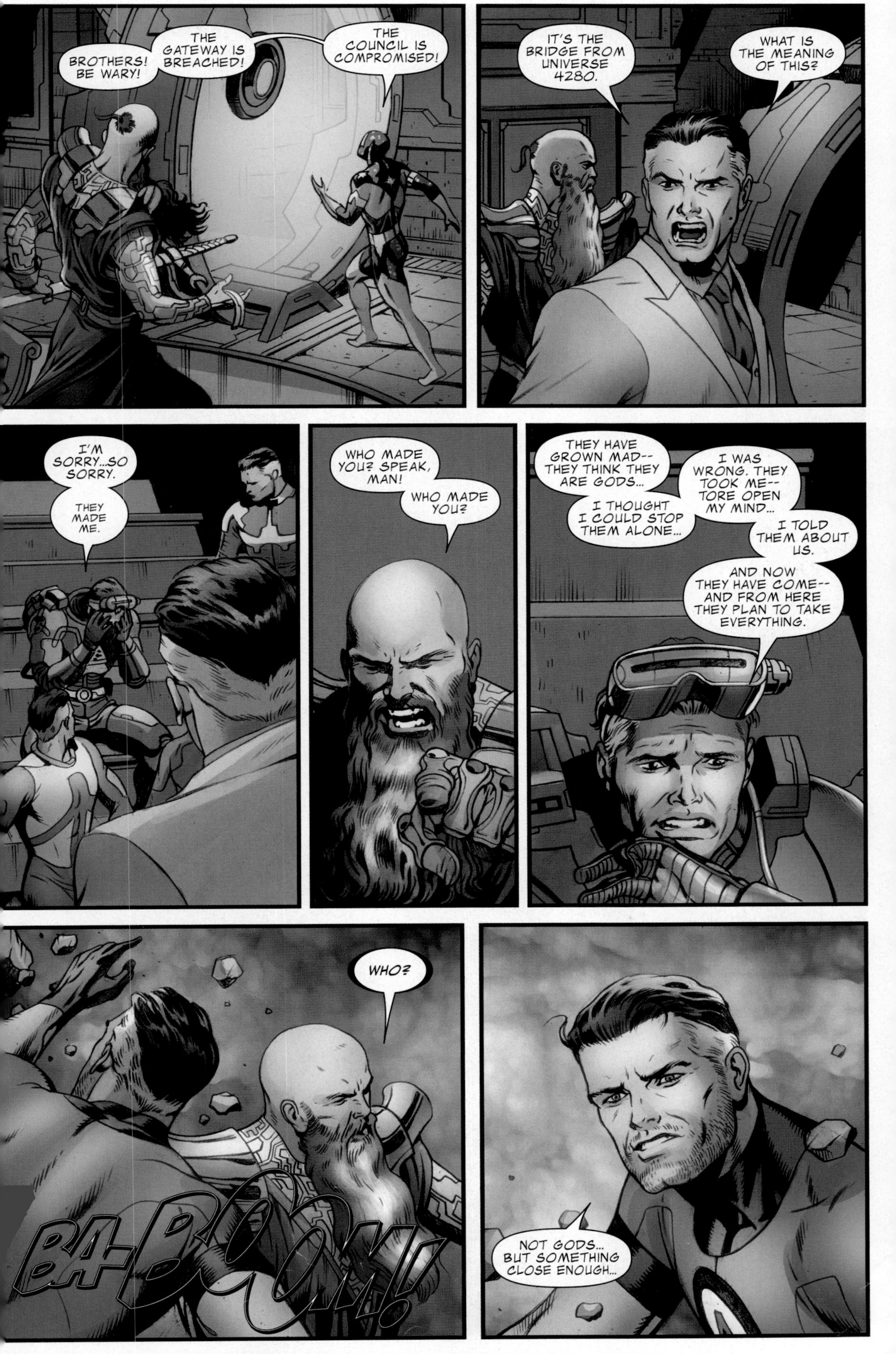
BROTHERS! BE WARY!
THE GATEWAY IS BREACHED!
THE COUNCIL IS COMPROMISED!
IT'S THE BRIDGE FROM UNIVERSE 4280.
WHAT IS THE MEANING OF THIS?
I'M SORRY...SO SORRY.
THEY MADE ME.
WHO MADE YOU? SPEAK, MAN!
WHO MADE YOU?
THEY HAVE GROWN MAD-- THEY THINK THEY ARE GODS...
I THOUGHT I COULD STOP THEM ALONE...
I WAS WRONG. THEY TOOK ME-- TORE OPEN MY MIND...
I TOLD THEM ABOUT US.
AND NOW THEY HAVE COME-- AND FROM HERE THEY PLAN TO TAKE EVERYTHING.
WHO?
BA-BOOM!
NOT GODS... BUT SOMETHING CLOSE ENOUGH...

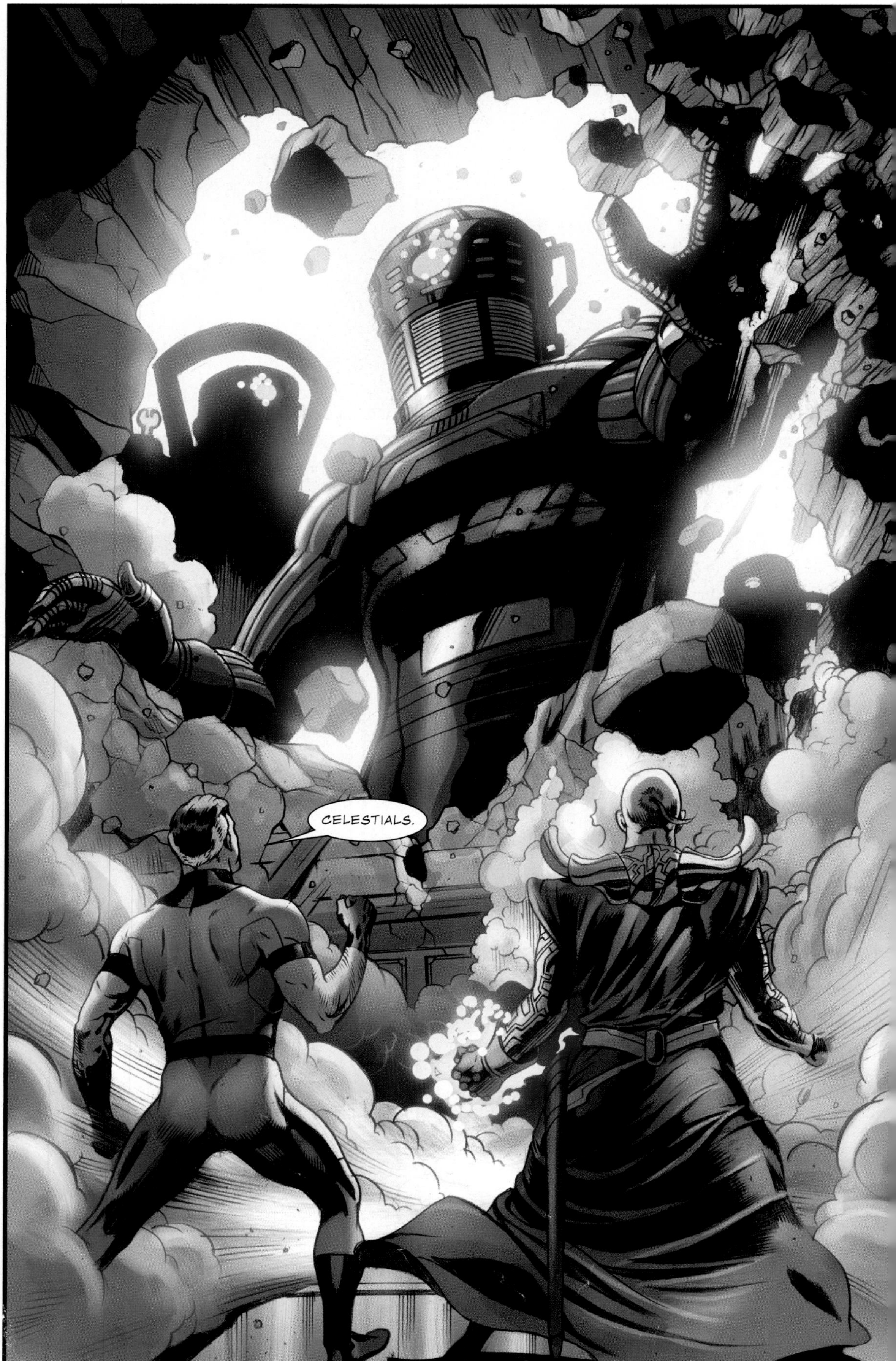
CELESTIALS.

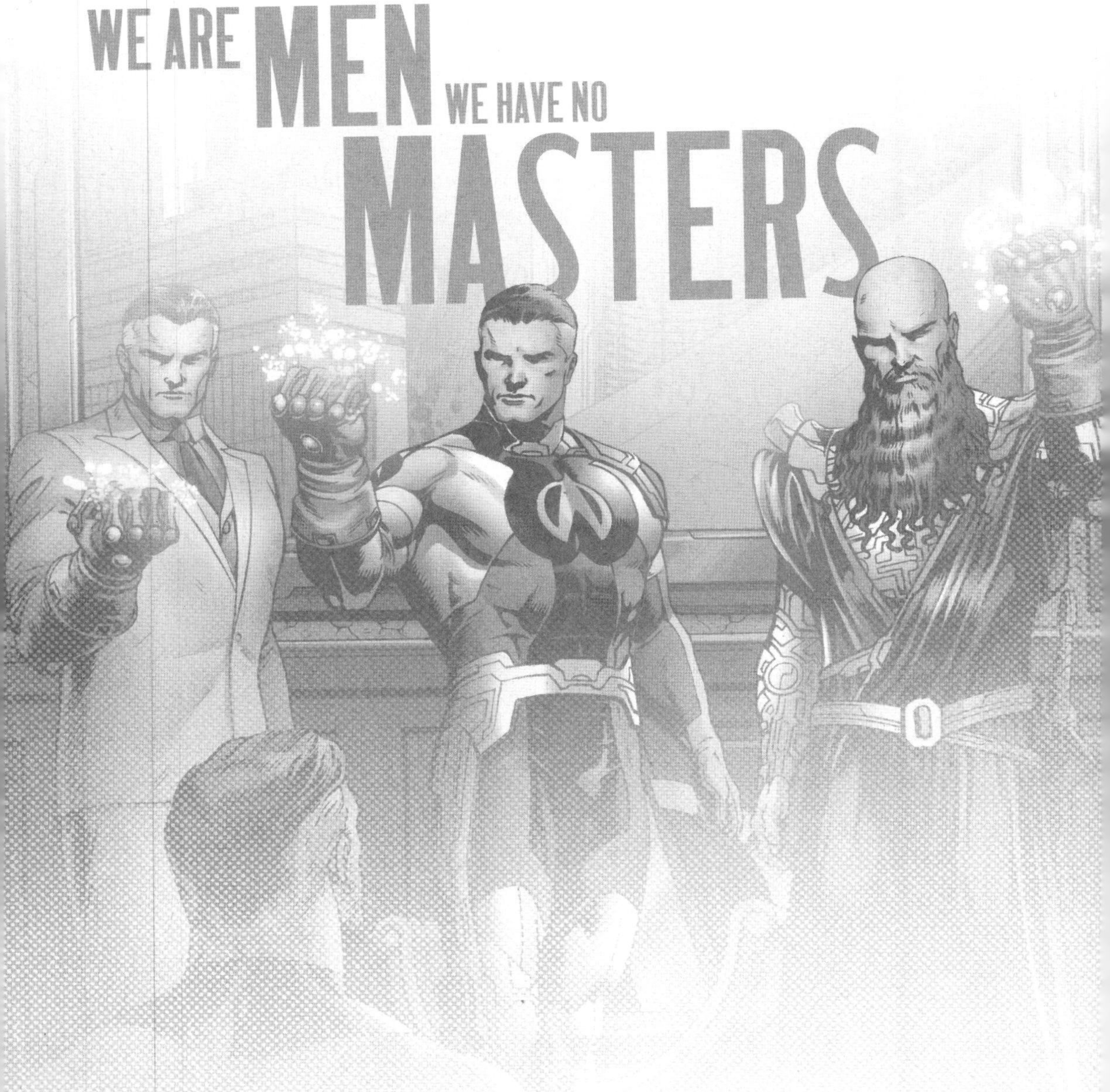
WE ARE MEN WE HAVE NO
MASTERS

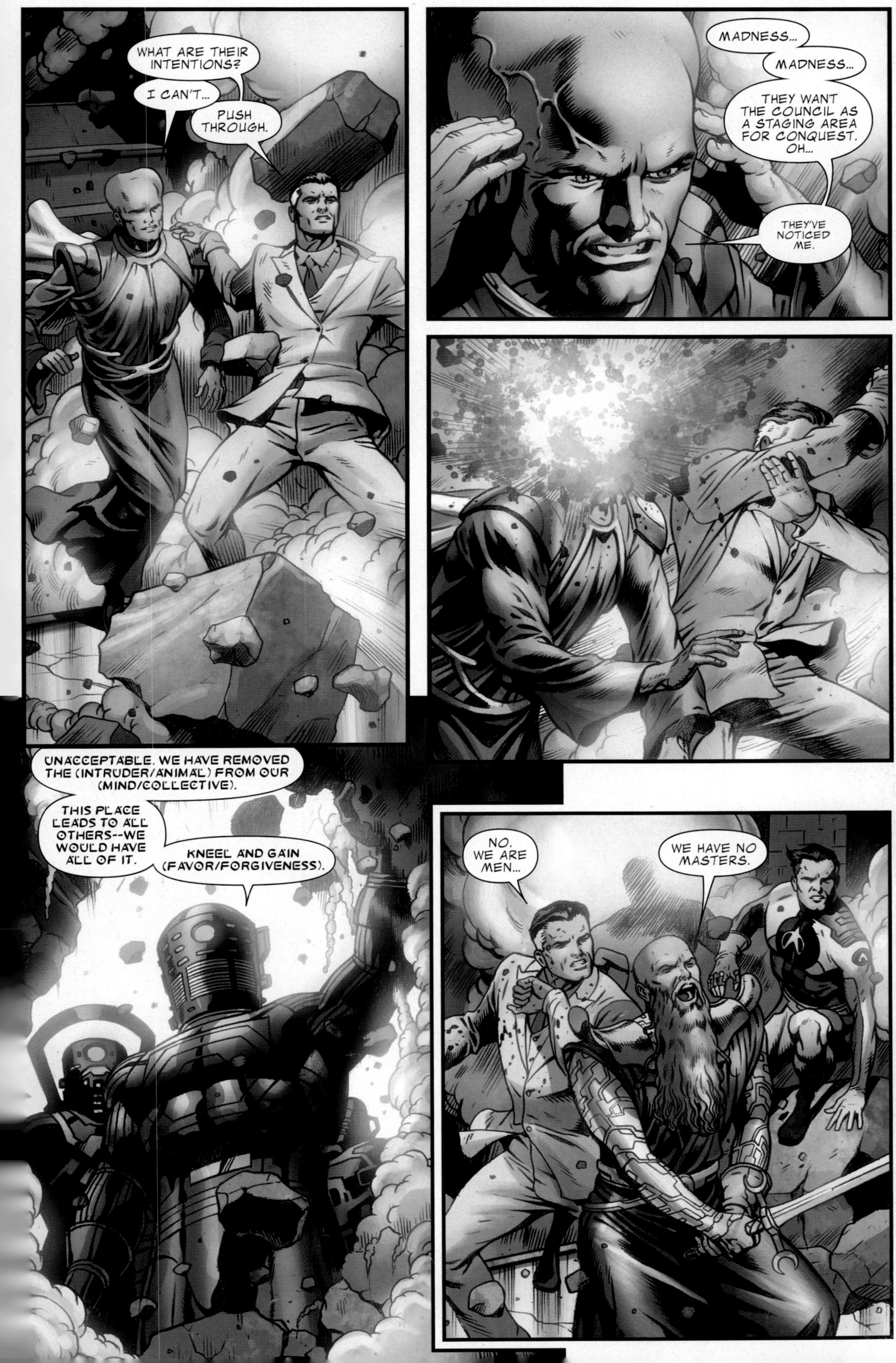
WHAT ARE THEIR INTENTIONS?
I CAN'T...
PUSH THROUGH.
MADNESS...
MADNESS...
THEY WANT THE COUNCIL AS A STAGING AREA FOR CONQUEST. OH...
THEY'VE NOTICED ME.
UNACCEPTABLE. WE HAVE REMOVED THE (INTRUDER/ANIMAL) FROM OUR (MIND/COLLECTIVE).
THIS PLACE LEADS TO ALL OTHERS--WE WOULD HAVE ALL OF IT.
KNEEL AND GAIN (FAVOR/FORGIVENESS).
NO. WE ARE MEN...
WE HAVE NO MASTERS.

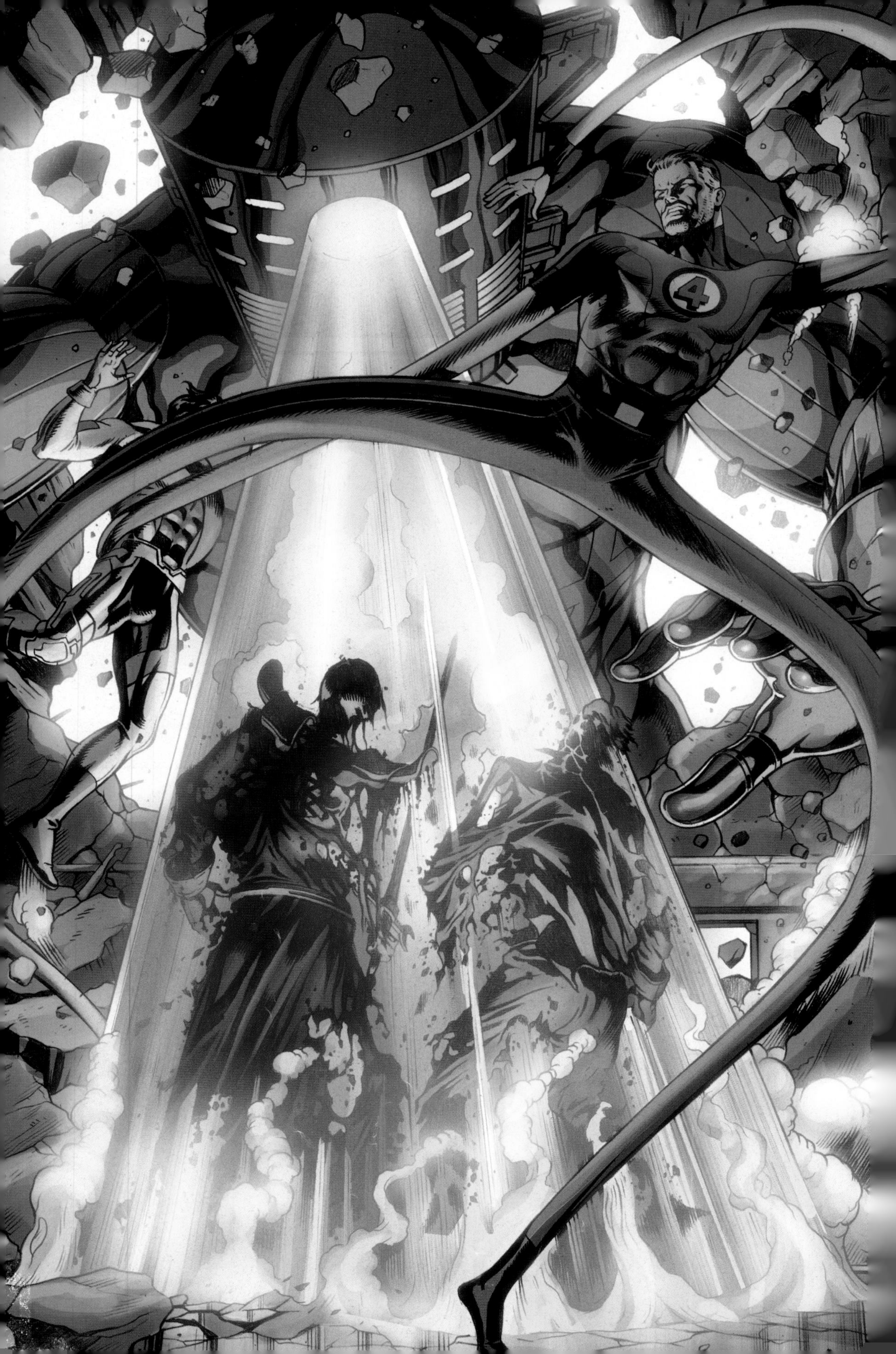

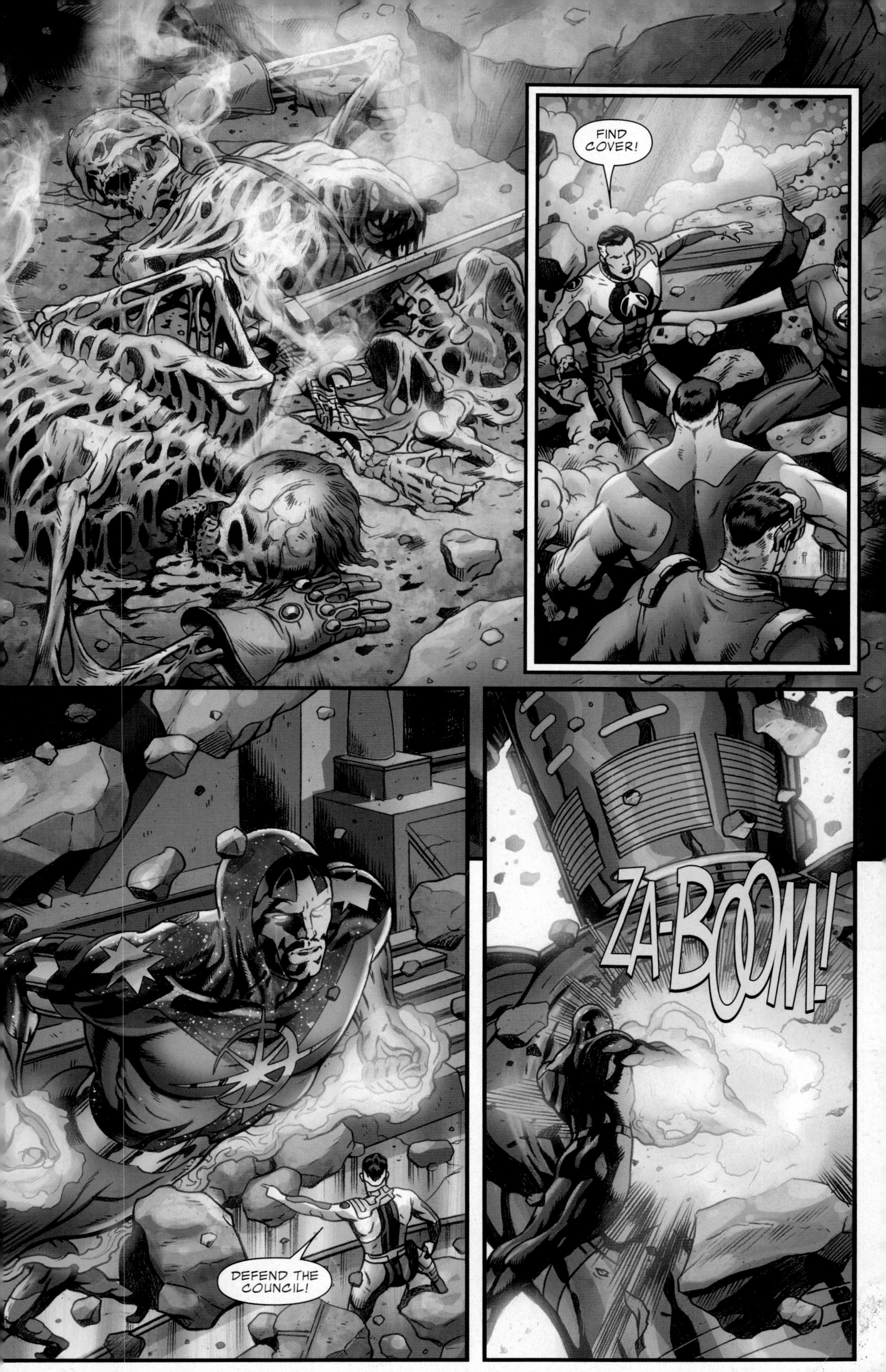
FIND COVER!
DEFEND THE COUNCIL!
ZA-BOOM!

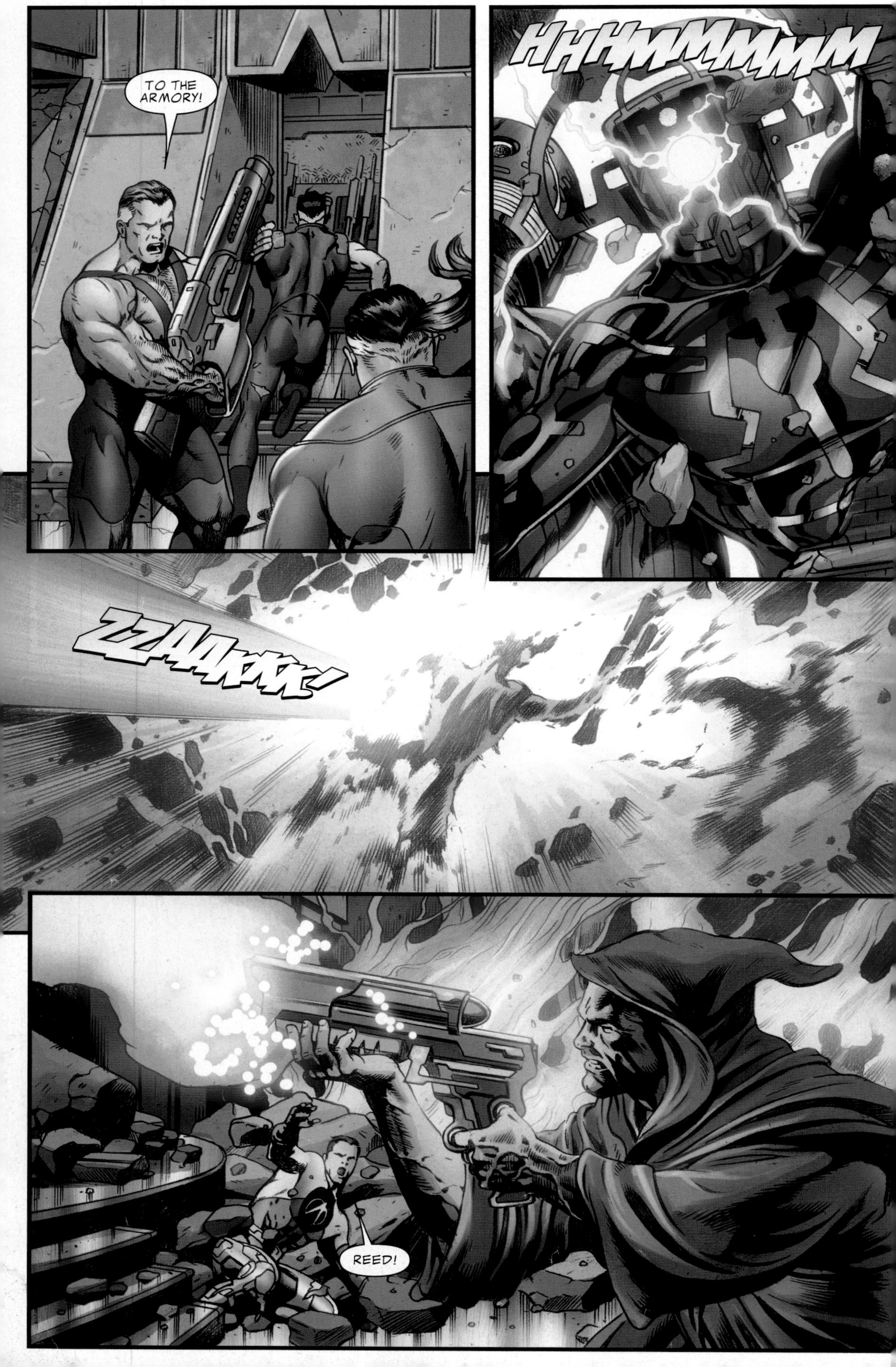
TO THE ARMORY!
HHHMMMMMM
ZZAAKKK!
REED!

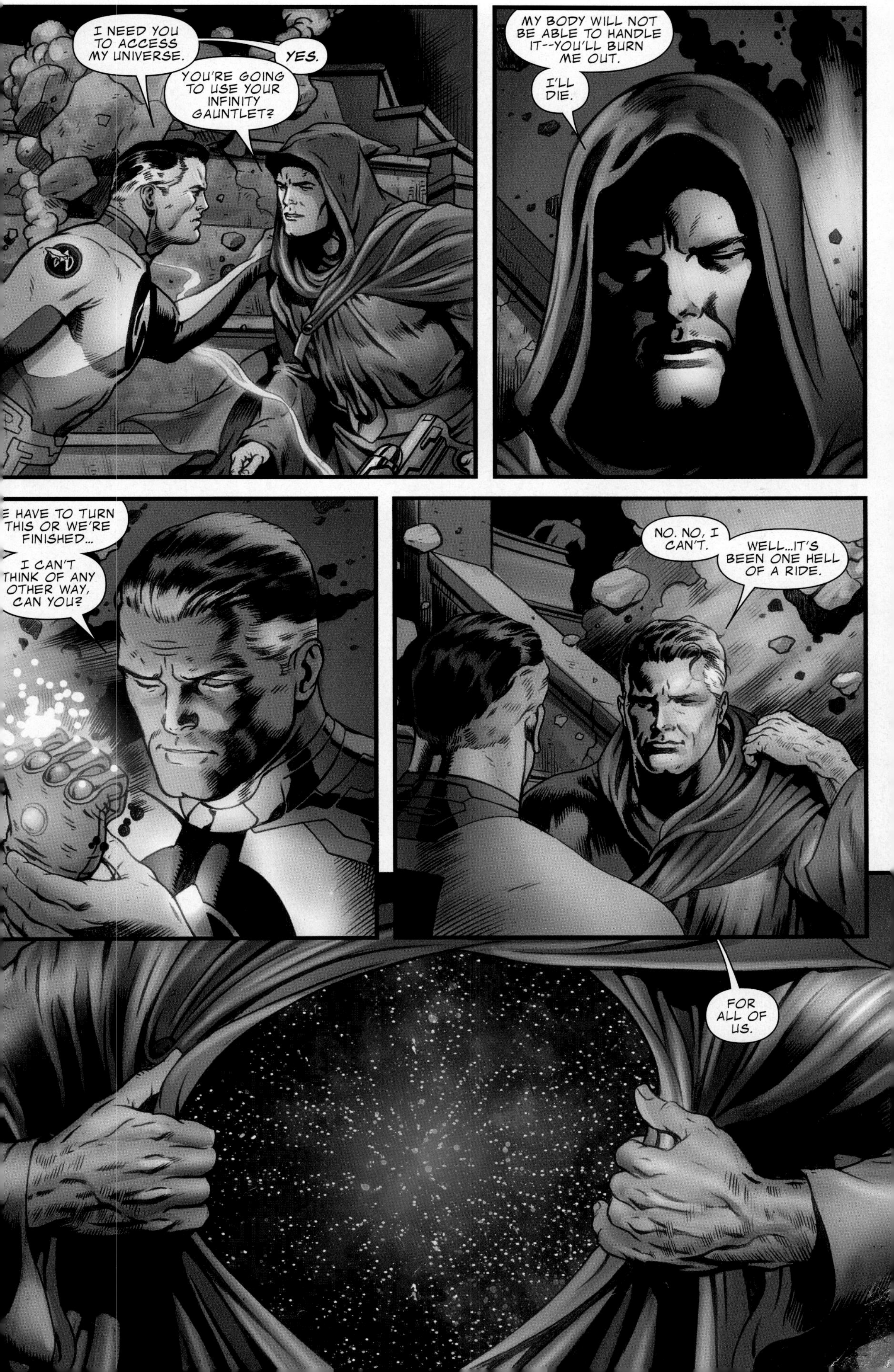
I NEED YOU TO ACCESS MY UNIVERSE.
YES.
YOU'RE GOING TO USE YOUR INFINITY GAUNTLET?
MY BODY WILL NOT BE ABLE TO HANDLE IT--YOU'LL BURN ME OUT.
I'LL DIE.
E HAVE TO TURN THIS OR WE'RE FINISHED...
I CAN'T THINK OF ANY OTHER WAY, CAN YOU?
NO. NO, I CAN'T.
WELL...IT'S BEEN ONE HELL OF A RIDE.
FOR ALL OF US.

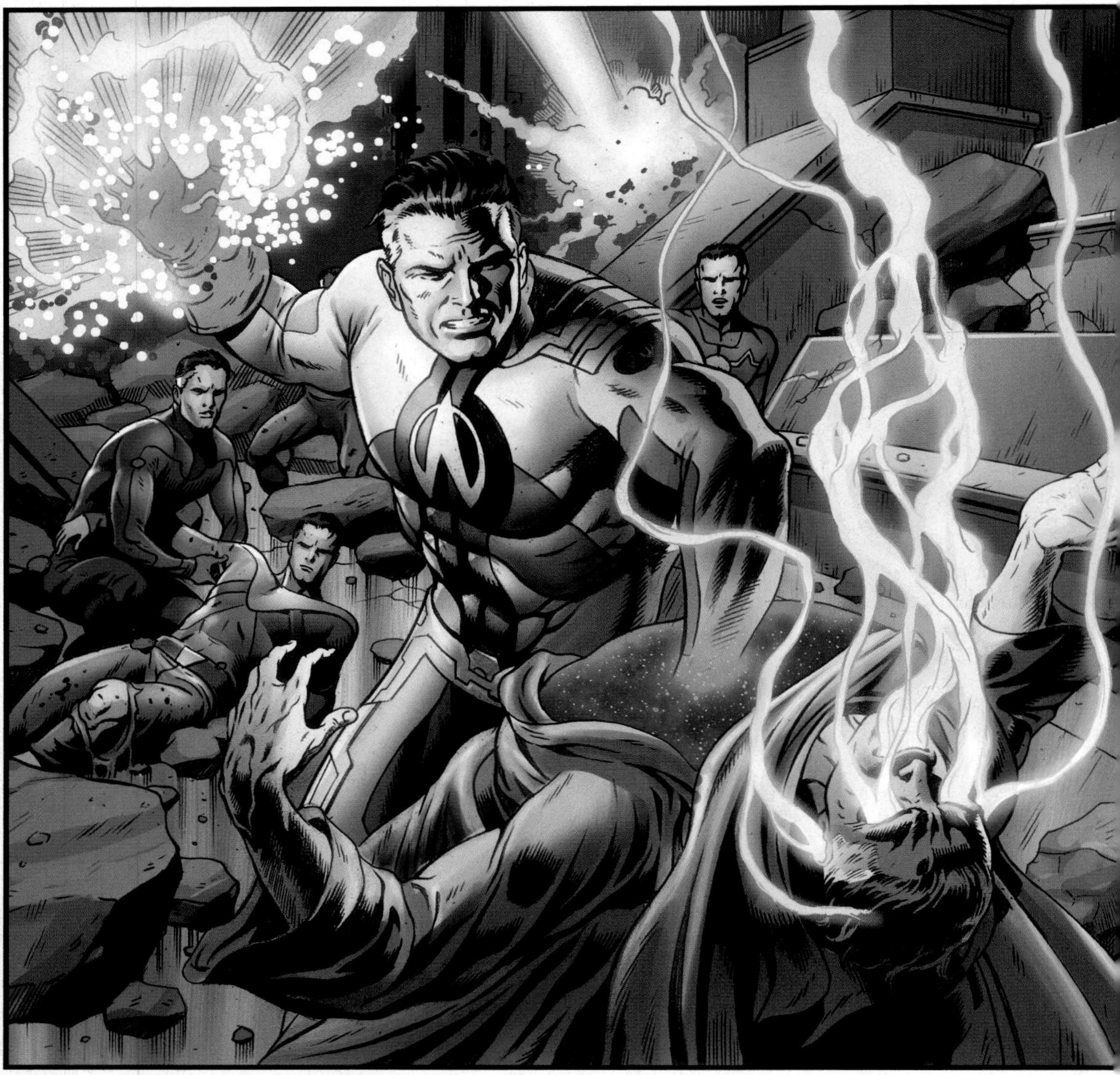
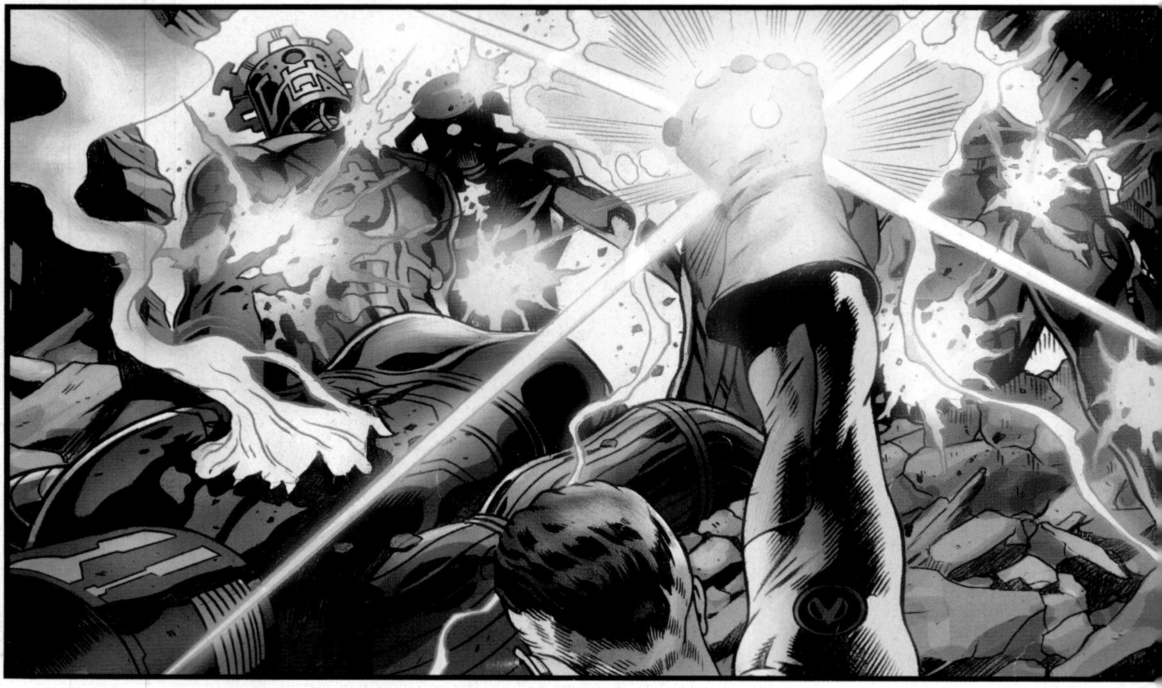

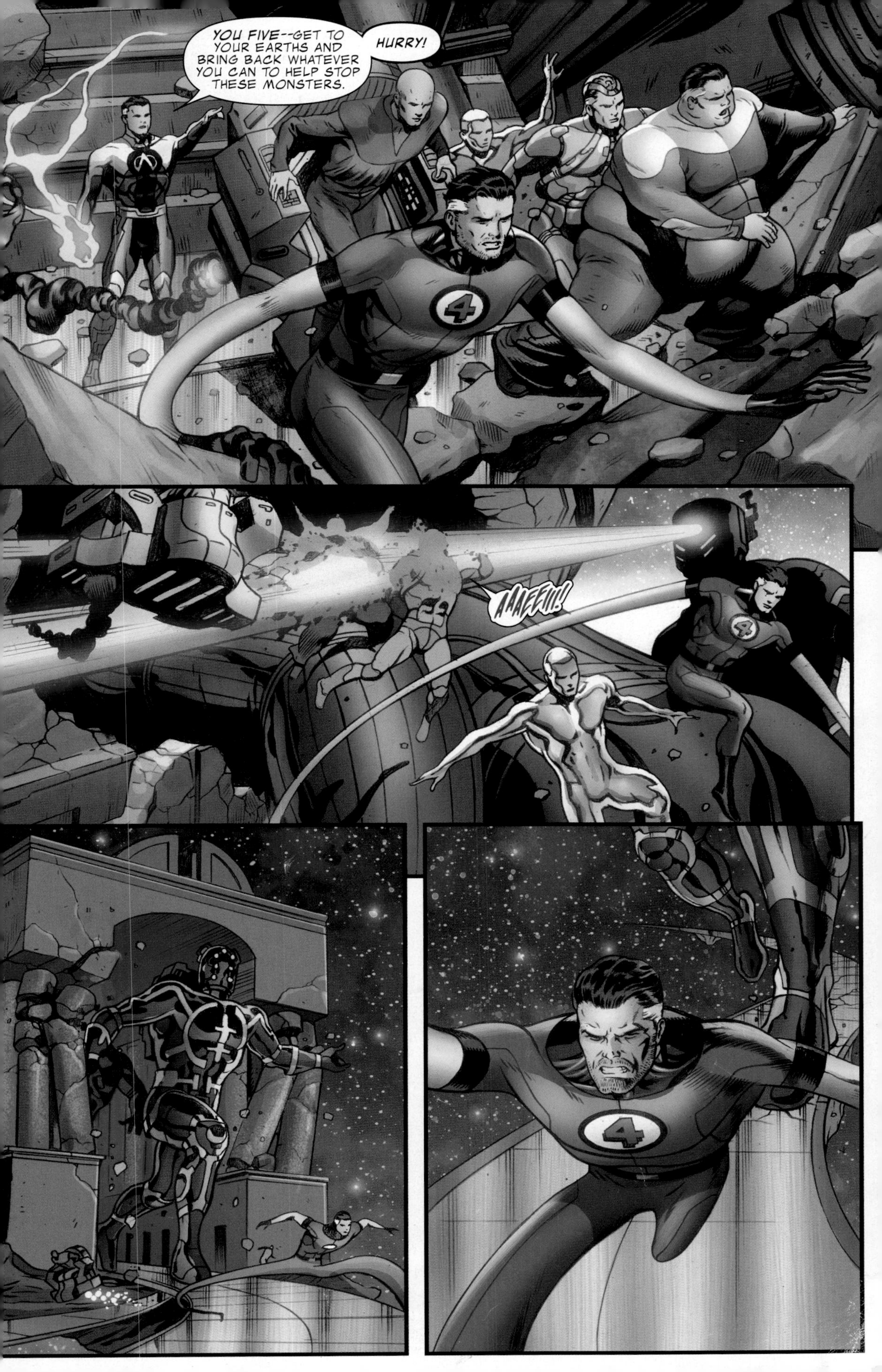
YOU FIVE--GET TO YOUR EARTHS AND BRING BACK WHATEVER YOU CAN TO HELP STOP THESE MONSTERS.
HURRY!
AAAEEIII!

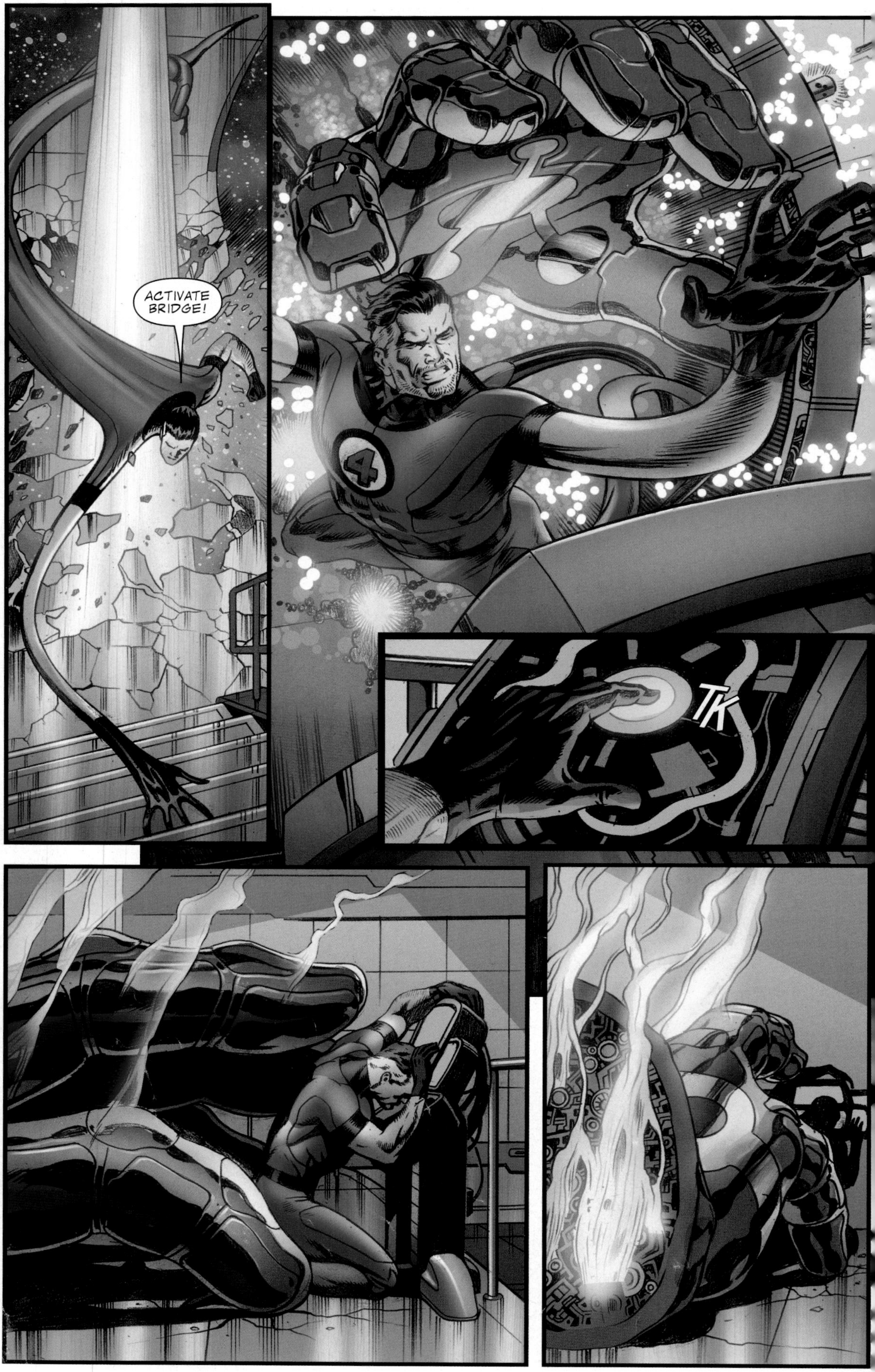
ACTIVATE BRIDGE!
TK

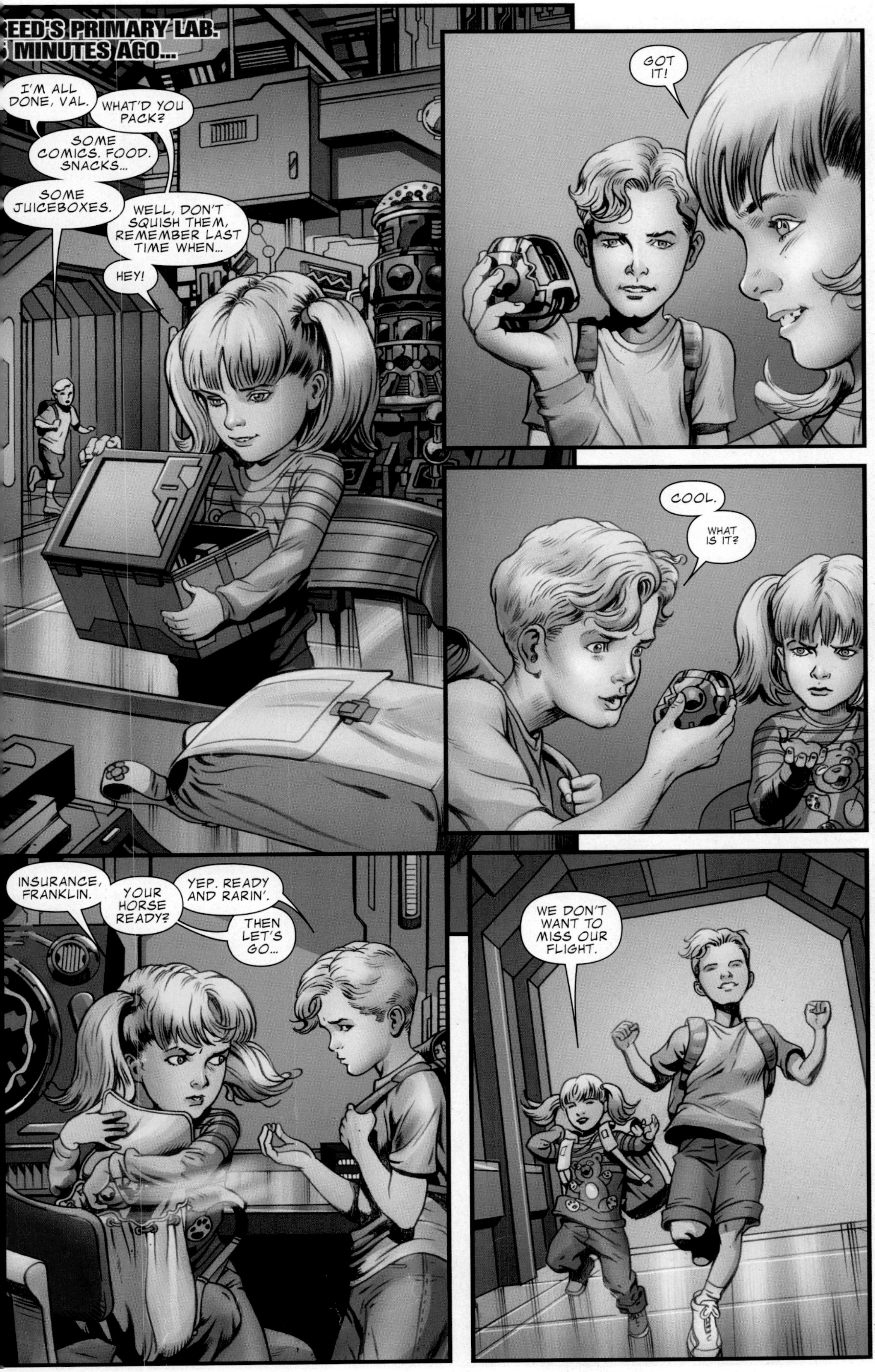
REED'S PRIMARY LAB. 5 MINUTES AGO...
I'M ALL DONE, VAL.
WHAT'D YOU PACK?
SOME COMICS. FOOD. SNACKS...
SOME JUICEBOXES.
WELL, DON'T SQUISH THEM, REMEMBER LAST TIME WHEN...
HEY!
GOT IT!
COOL.
WHAT IS IT?
INSURANCE, FRANKLIN.
YOUR HORSE READY?
YEP. READY AND RARIN'.
THEN LET'S GO...
WE DON'T WANT TO MISS OUR FLIGHT.

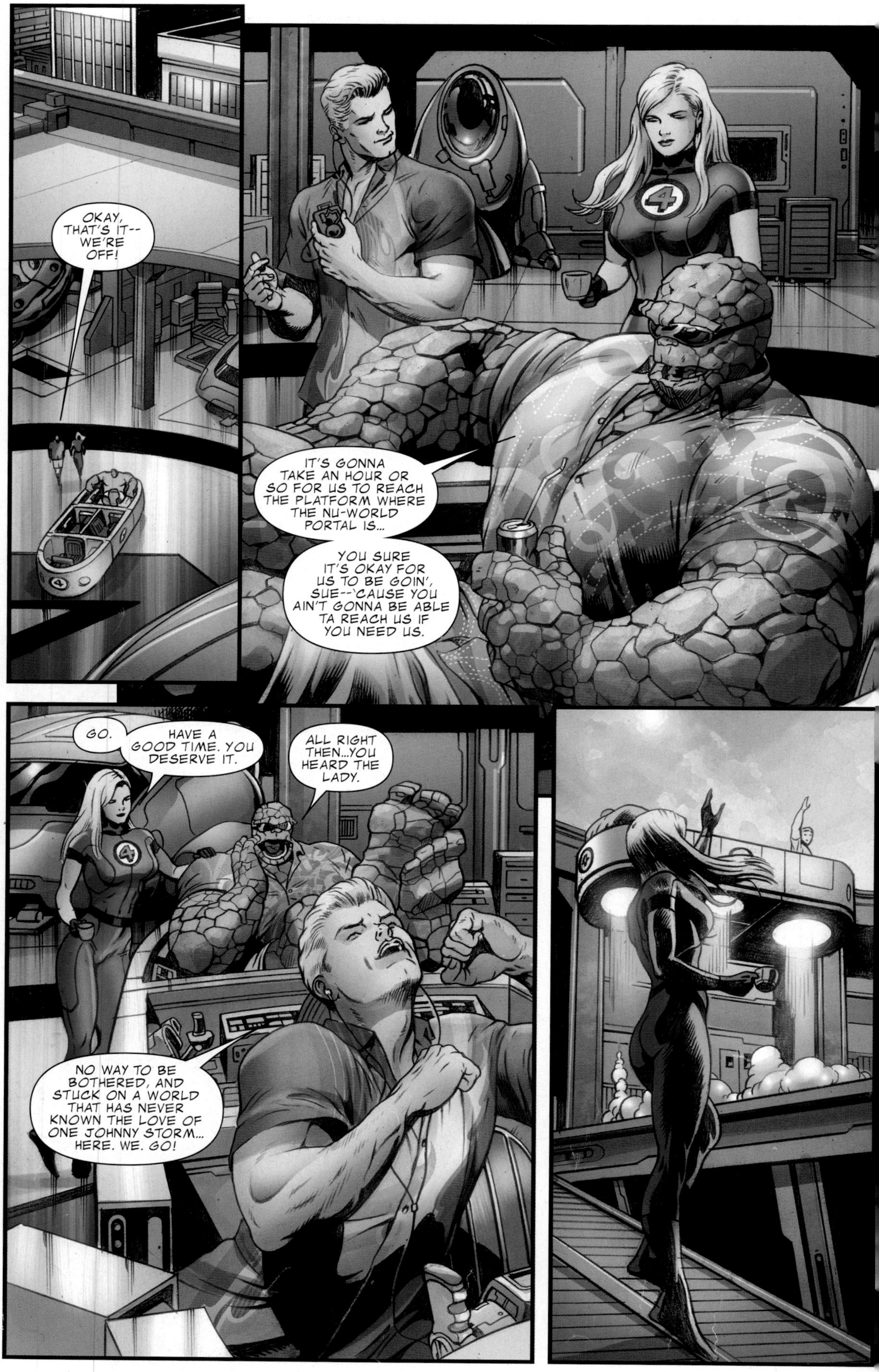
OKAY, THAT'S IT-- WE'RE OFF!
IT'S GONNA TAKE AN HOUR OR SO FOR US TO REACH THE PLATFORM WHERE THE NU-WORLD PORTAL IS...
YOU SURE IT'S OKAY FOR US TO BE GOIN', SUE--'CAUSE YOU AIN'T GONNA BE ABLE TA REACH US IF YOU NEED US.
GO.
HAVE A GOOD TIME. YOU DESERVE IT.
ALL RIGHT THEN...YOU HEARD THE LADY.
NO WAY TO BE BOTHERED, AND STUCK ON A WORLD THAT HAS NEVER KNOWN THE LOVE OF ONE JOHNNY STORM... HERE. WE. GO!

"HAT WAS IT YOU SAID?

"MOM, CAN WE PLEEEEEASE GO ON VACATION WITH UNCLE BEN AND UNCLE JOHNNY?"

"NO, ABSOLUTELY NOT," SHE SAID.

"MAYBE NEXT TIME--WHEN YOU'RE OLDER," SHE SAID.

AND WHAT DID WE THINK OF THAT?

IT DIDN'T SEEM FAIR.

IT WASN'T FAIR. NOT ONE BIT.

RIGHT... WAIT, WHY IS THAT AGAIN?

BECAUSE IT'S ALMOST YOUR BIRTHDAY.

RIIIGGHHT. THEN I WILL BE ONE YEAR OLDER.

FRANKLIN.

YEAH, VAL?

WE'RE GONNA HAVE TO ROUND UP.

I'M GONNA SHOOT THE THING NOW.

COOL.

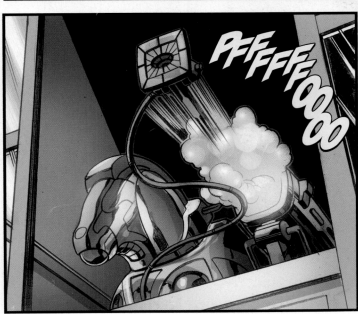

PFFFFFFOOOO

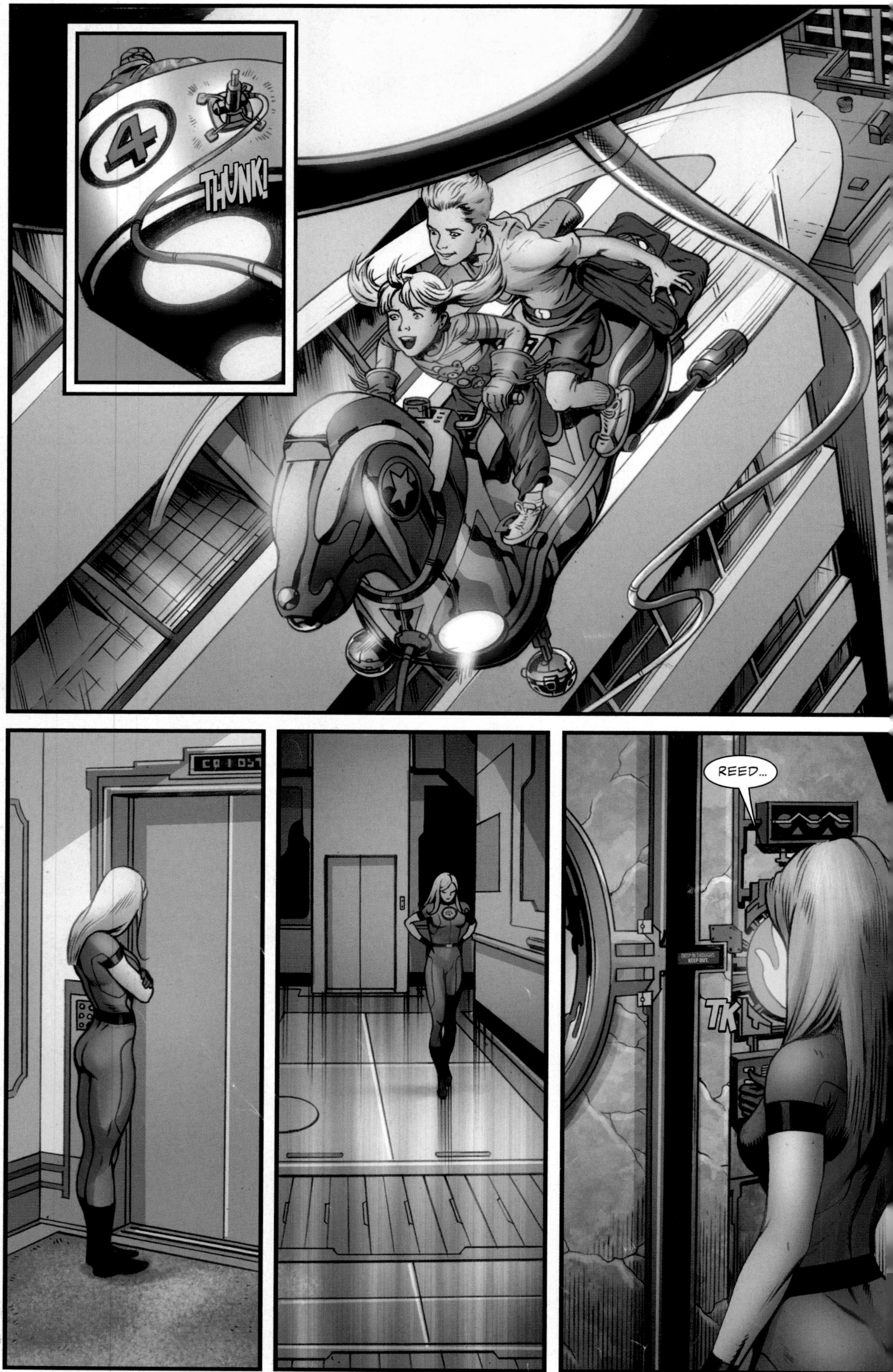
THUNK!
DEEP IN THOUGHT. KEEP OUT.
TK
REED...

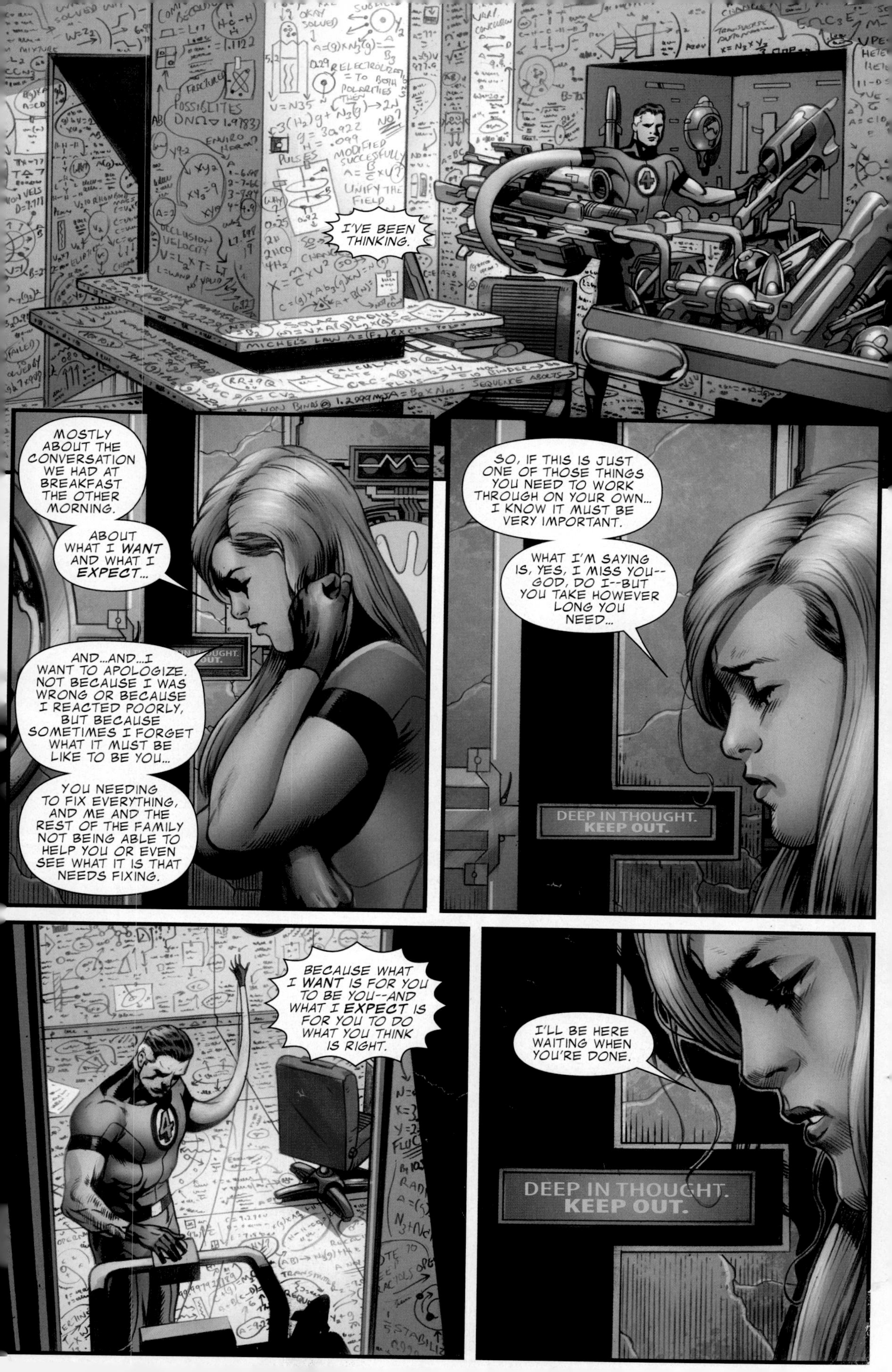
I'VE BEEN THINKING.
MOSTLY ABOUT THE CONVERSATION WE HAD AT BREAKFAST THE OTHER MORNING.
ABOUT WHAT I *WANT* AND WHAT I *EXPECT*...
AND...AND...I WANT TO APOLOGIZE. NOT BECAUSE I WAS WRONG OR BECAUSE I REACTED POORLY, BUT BECAUSE SOMETIMES I FORGET WHAT IT MUST BE LIKE TO BE YOU...
YOU NEEDING TO FIX EVERYTHING, AND ME AND THE REST OF THE FAMILY NOT BEING ABLE TO HELP YOU OR EVEN SEE WHAT IT IS THAT NEEDS FIXING.
SO, IF THIS IS JUST ONE OF THOSE THINGS YOU NEED TO WORK THROUGH ON YOUR OWN... I KNOW IT MUST BE VERY IMPORTANT.
WHAT I'M SAYING IS, YES, I MISS YOU--GOD, DO I--BUT YOU TAKE HOWEVER LONG YOU NEED...
DEEP IN THOUGHT.
KEEP OUT.
BECAUSE WHAT I *WANT* IS FOR YOU TO BE YOU--AND WHAT I *EXPECT* IS FOR YOU TO DO WHAT YOU THINK IS RIGHT.
I'LL BE HERE WAITING WHEN YOU'RE DONE.
DEEP IN THOUGHT.
KEEP OUT.

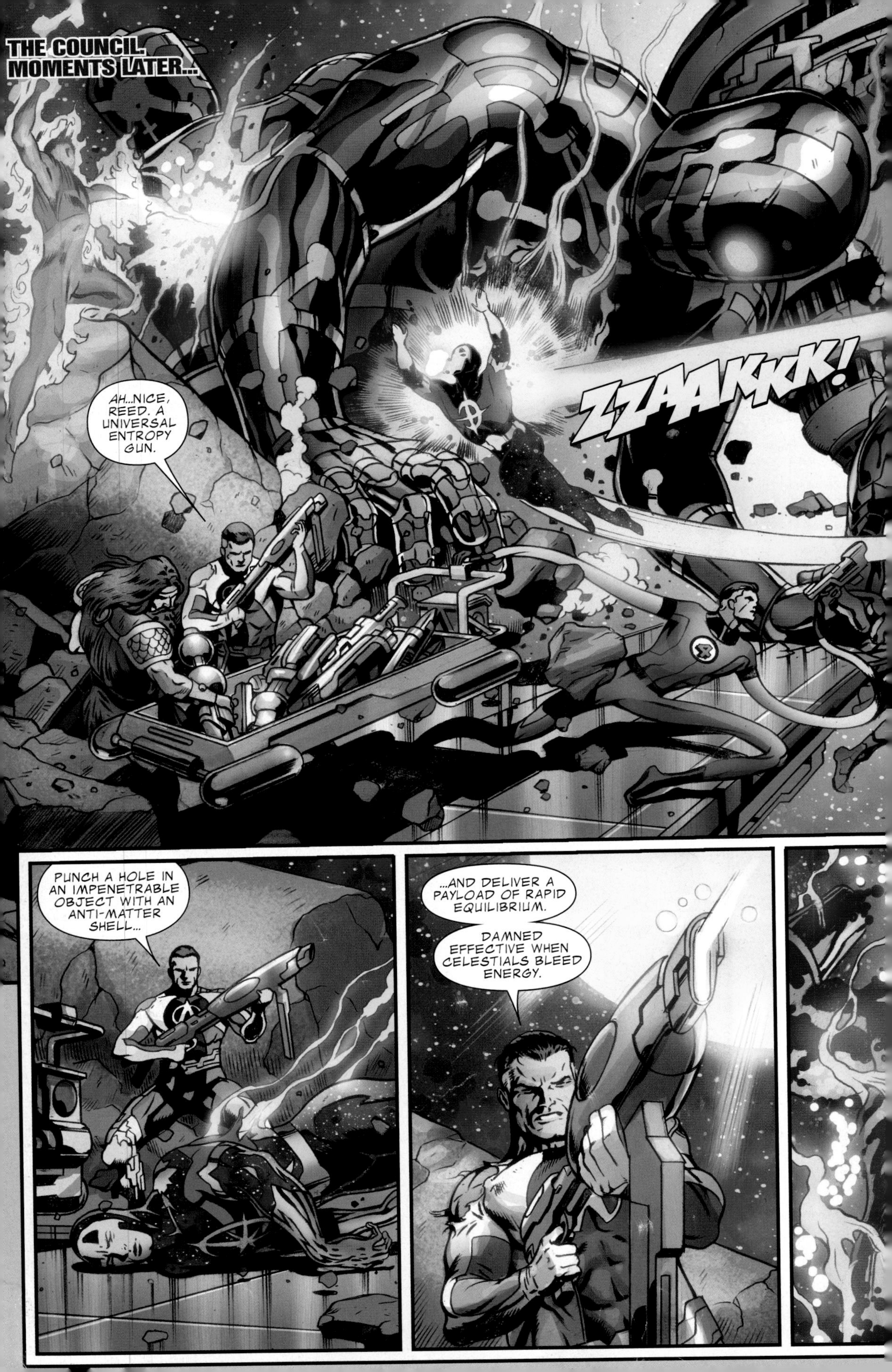
THE COUNCIL. MOMENTS LATER...
AH...NICE, REED. A UNIVERSAL ENTROPY GUN.
ZZAAKKK!
PUNCH A HOLE IN AN IMPENETRABLE OBJECT WITH AN ANTI-MATTER SHELL...
...AND DELIVER A PAYLOAD OF RAPID EQUILIBRIUM.
DAMNED EFFECTIVE WHEN CELESTIALS BLEED ENERGY.

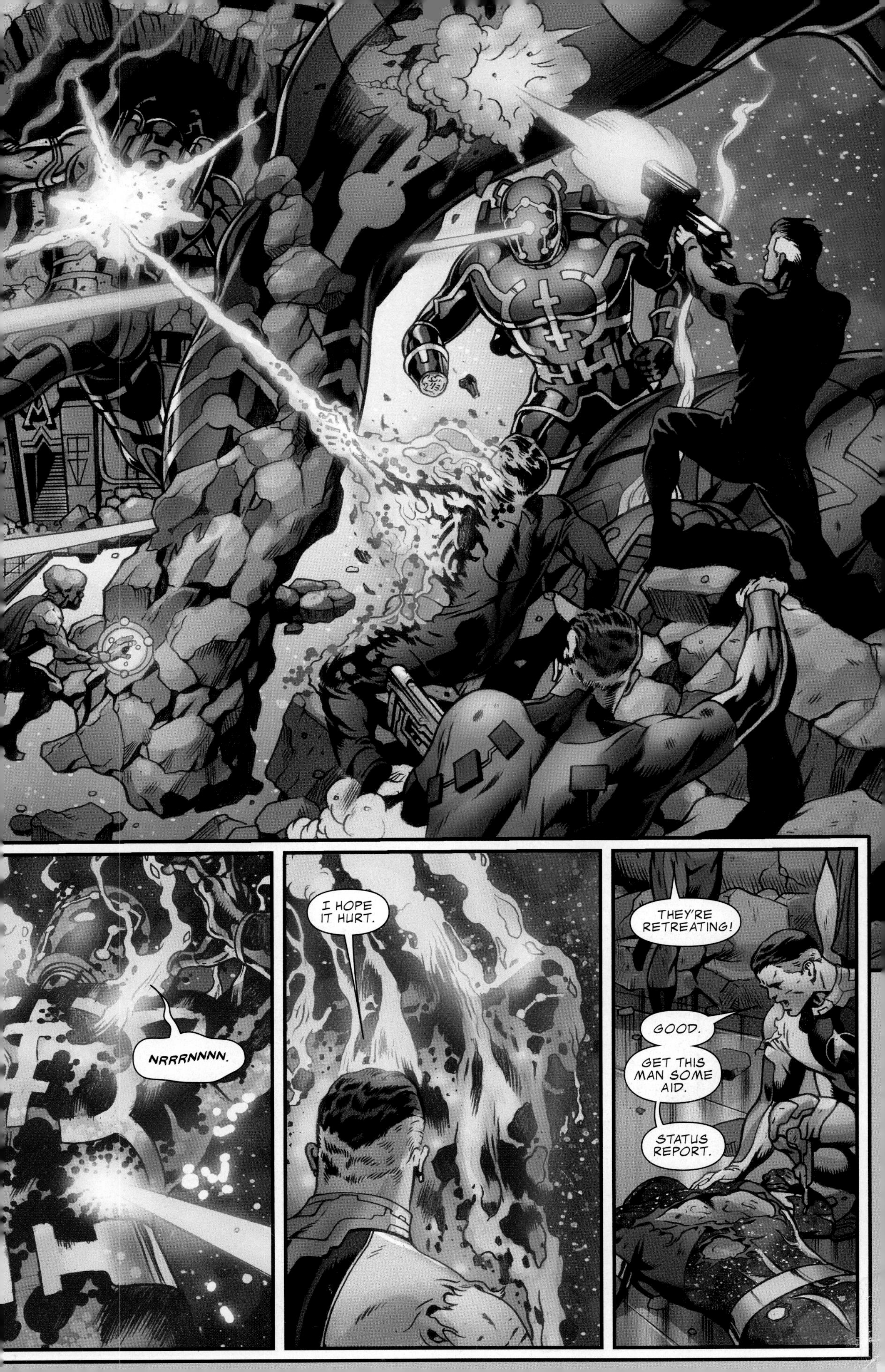
NRRRNNNN.
I HOPE IT HURT.
THEY'RE RETREATING!
GOOD.
GET THIS MAN SOME AID.
STATUS REPORT.

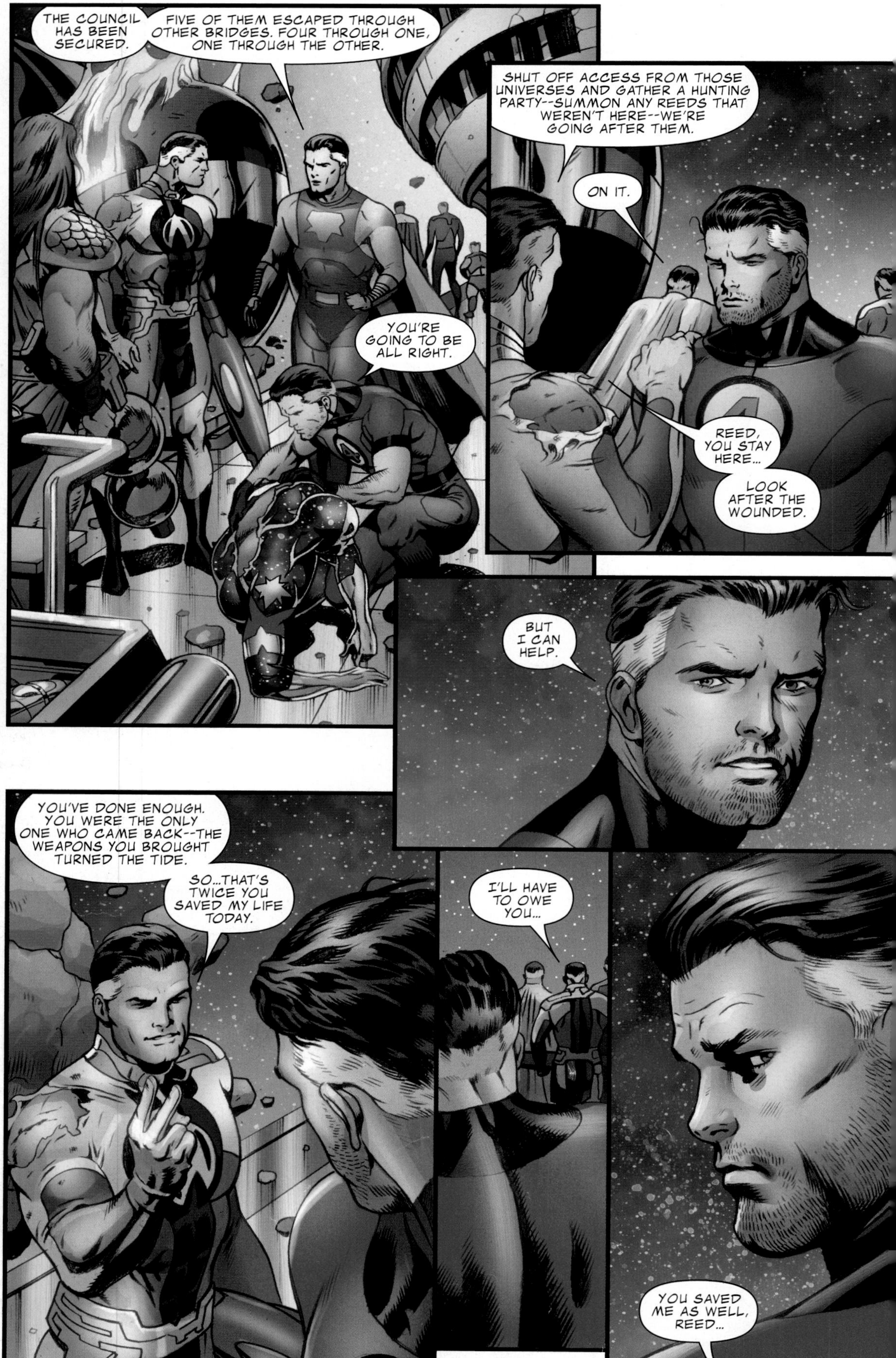
THE COUNCIL HAS BEEN SECURED.
FIVE OF THEM ESCAPED THROUGH OTHER BRIDGES. FOUR THROUGH ONE, ONE THROUGH THE OTHER.
YOU'RE GOING TO BE ALL RIGHT.
SHUT OFF ACCESS FROM THOSE UNIVERSES AND GATHER A HUNTING PARTY--SUMMON ANY REEDS THAT WEREN'T HERE--WE'RE GOING AFTER THEM.
ON IT.
REED, YOU STAY HERE...
LOOK AFTER THE WOUNDED.
BUT I CAN HELP.
YOU'VE DONE ENOUGH. YOU WERE THE ONLY ONE WHO CAME BACK--THE WEAPONS YOU BROUGHT TURNED THE TIDE.
SO...THAT'S TWICE YOU SAVED MY LIFE TODAY.
I'LL HAVE TO OWE YOU...
YOU SAVED ME AS WELL, REED...

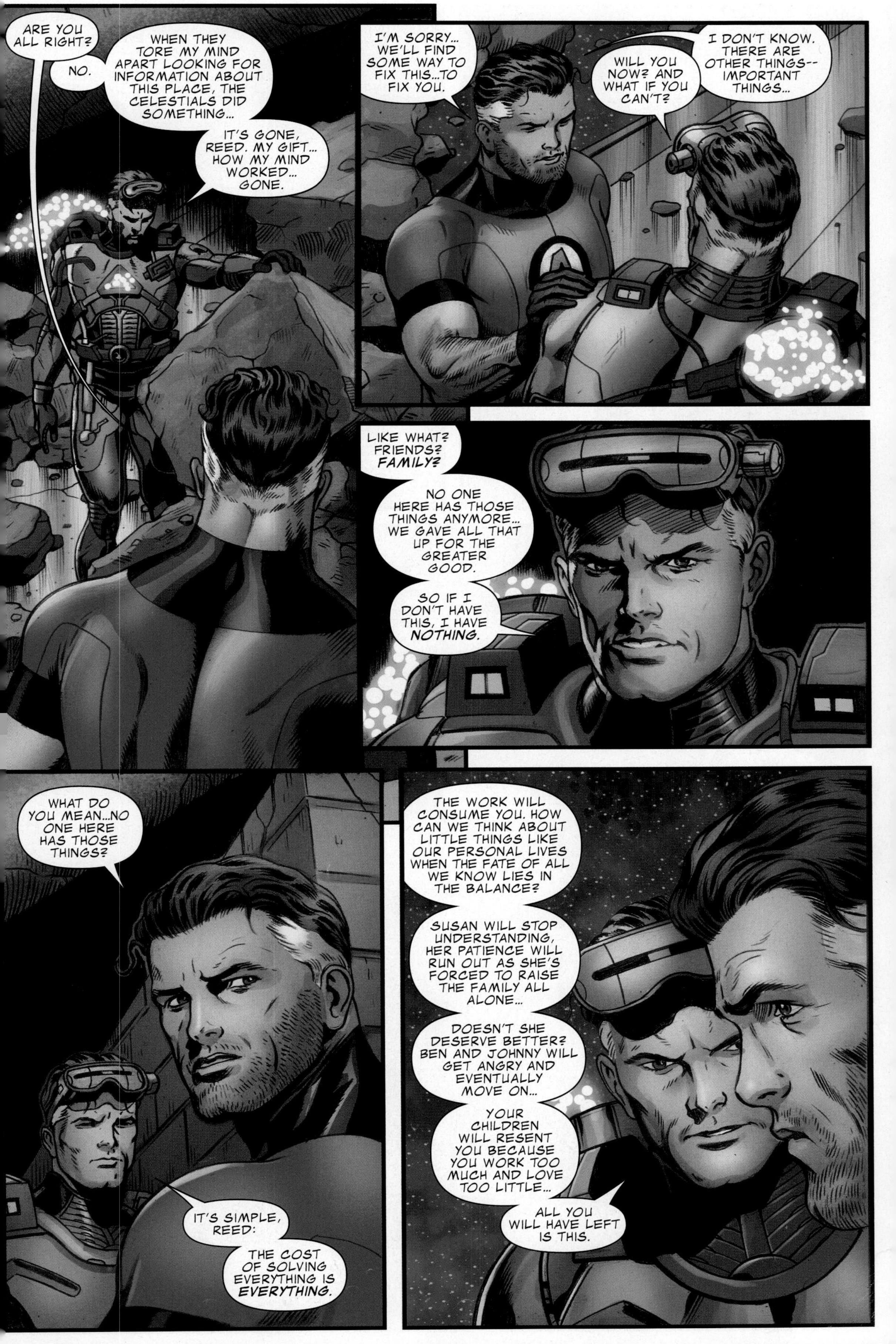

ARE YOU ALL RIGHT?
NO.
WHEN THEY TORE MY MIND APART LOOKING FOR INFORMATION ABOUT THIS PLACE, THE CELESTIALS DID SOMETHING...
IT'S GONE, REED. MY GIFT... HOW MY MIND WORKED... GONE.
I'M SORRY... WE'LL FIND SOME WAY TO FIX THIS...TO FIX YOU.
WILL YOU NOW? AND WHAT IF YOU CAN'T?
I DON'T KNOW. THERE ARE OTHER THINGS-- IMPORTANT THINGS...
LIKE WHAT? FRIENDS? *FAMILY?*
NO ONE HERE HAS THOSE THINGS ANYMORE... WE GAVE ALL THAT UP FOR THE GREATER GOOD.
SO IF I DON'T HAVE THIS, I HAVE *NOTHING*.
WHAT DO YOU MEAN...NO ONE HERE HAS THOSE THINGS?
IT'S SIMPLE, REED:
THE COST OF SOLVING EVERYTHING IS *EVERYTHING*.
THE WORK WILL CONSUME YOU. HOW CAN WE THINK ABOUT LITTLE THINGS LIKE OUR PERSONAL LIVES WHEN THE FATE OF ALL WE KNOW LIES IN THE BALANCE?
SUSAN WILL STOP UNDERSTANDING, HER PATIENCE WILL RUN OUT AS SHE'S FORCED TO RAISE THE FAMILY ALL ALONE...
DOESN'T SHE DESERVE BETTER? BEN AND JOHNNY WILL GET ANGRY AND EVENTUALLY MOVE ON...
YOUR CHILDREN WILL RESENT YOU BECAUSE YOU WORK TOO MUCH AND LOVE TOO LITTLE...
ALL YOU WILL HAVE LEFT IS THIS.

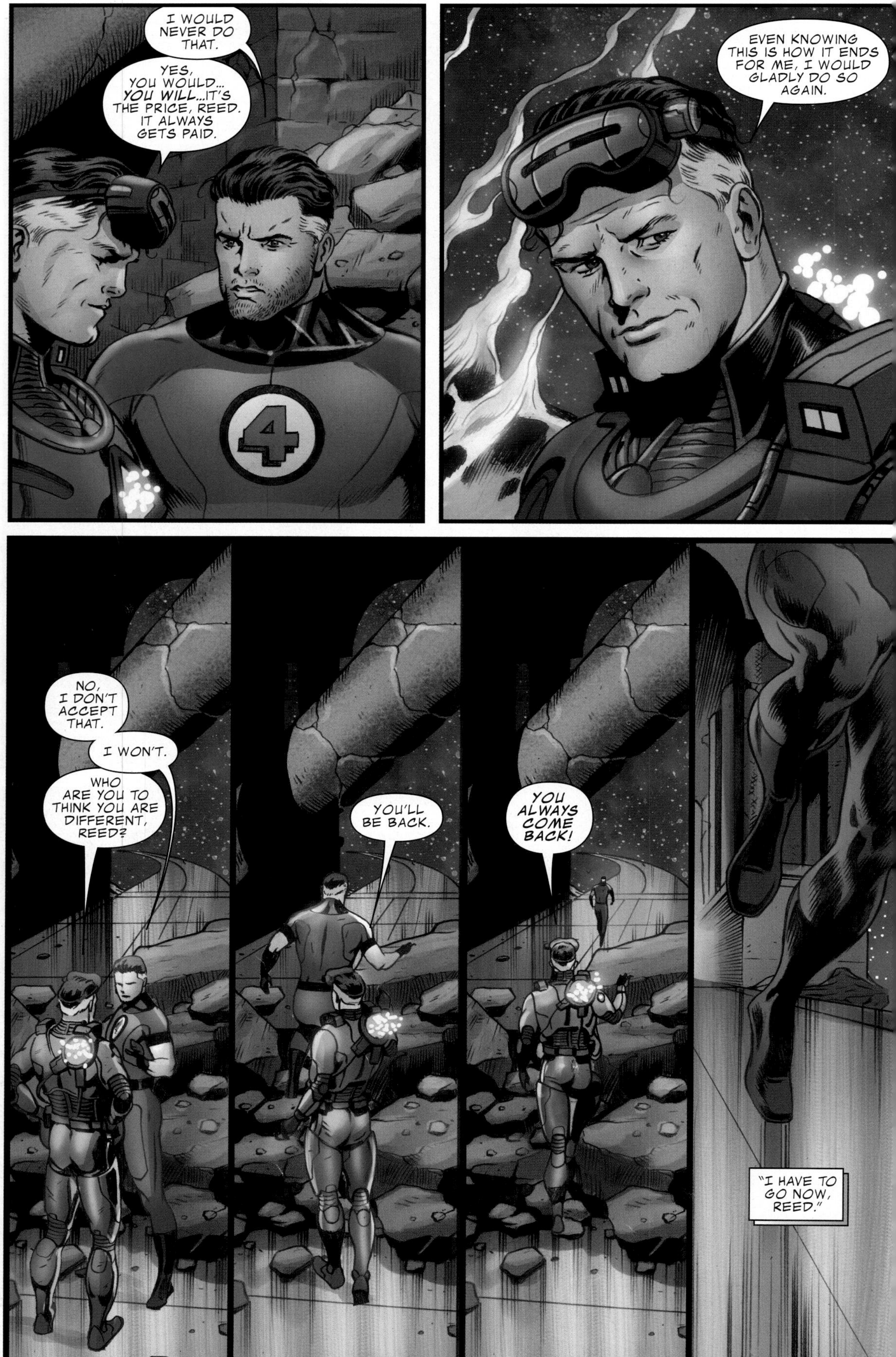
I WOULD NEVER DO THAT.
YES, YOU WOULD... *YOU WILL*...IT'S THE PRICE, REED. IT ALWAYS GETS PAID.
EVEN KNOWING THIS IS HOW IT ENDS FOR ME, I WOULD GLADLY DO SO AGAIN.
NO, I DON'T ACCEPT THAT.
I WON'T.
WHO ARE YOU TO THINK YOU ARE DIFFERENT, REED?
YOU'LL BE BACK.
YOU ALWAYS COME BACK!
"I HAVE TO GO NOW, REED."

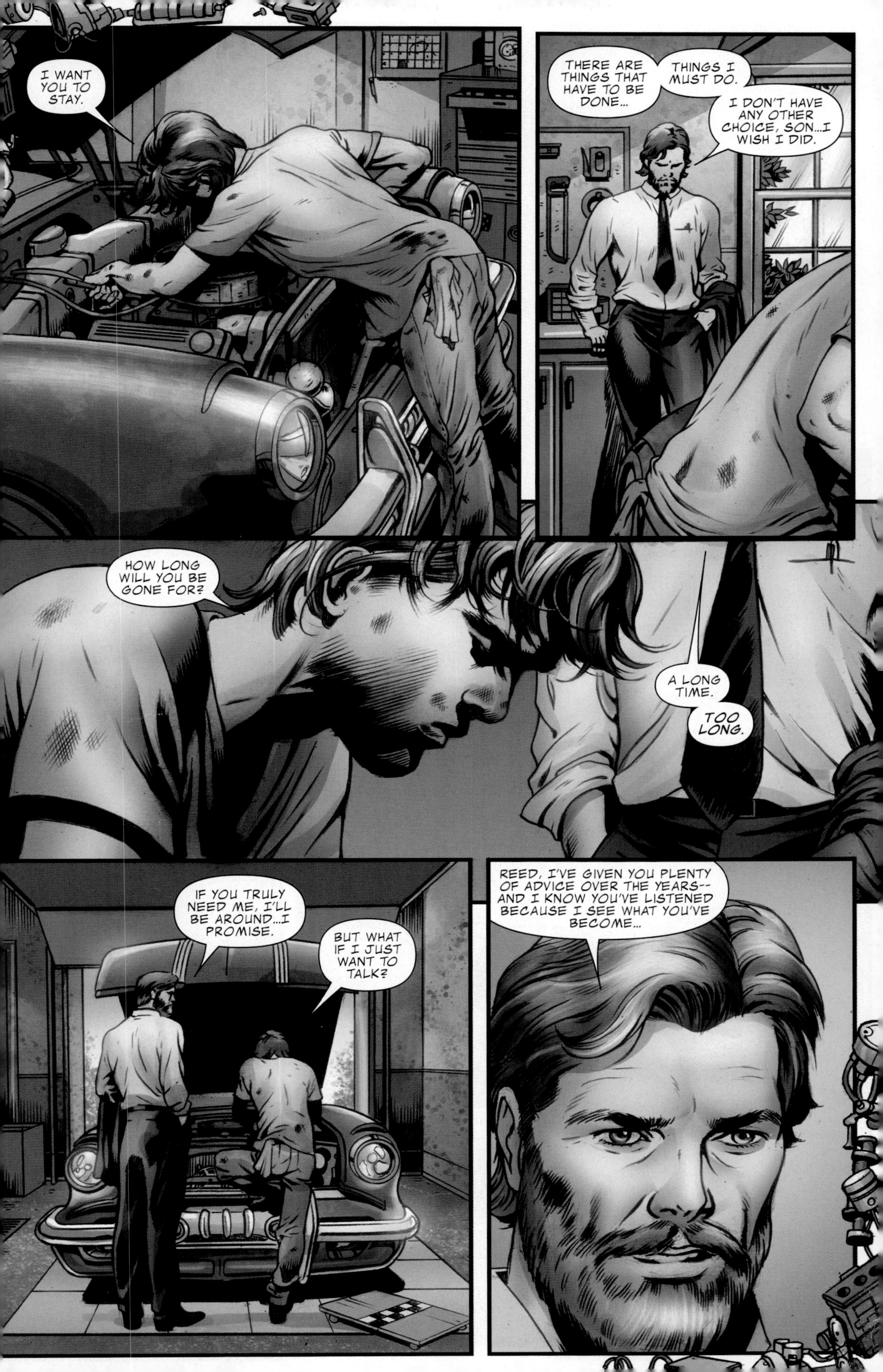
I WANT YOU TO STAY.
THERE ARE THINGS THAT HAVE TO BE DONE...
THINGS I MUST DO.
I DON'T HAVE ANY OTHER CHOICE, SON...I WISH I DID.
HOW LONG WILL YOU BE GONE FOR?
A LONG TIME.
TOO LONG.
IF YOU TRULY NEED ME, I'LL BE AROUND...I PROMISE.
BUT WHAT IF I JUST WANT TO TALK?
REED, I'VE GIVEN YOU PLENTY OF ADVICE OVER THE YEARS--AND I KNOW YOU'VE LISTENED BECAUSE I SEE WHAT YOU'VE BECOME...

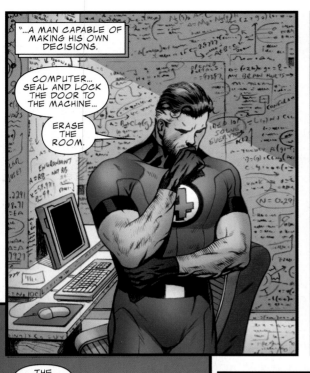

"...A MAN CAPABLE OF MAKING HIS OWN DECISIONS.

COMPUTER... SEAL AND LOCK THE DOOR TO THE MACHINE...

ERASE THE ROOM.

"BUT I WANT YOU TO REMEMBER ONE LAST THING BEFORE I GO..."

THE WORLD IS UGLY.

IT SHOULD NOT BE, BUT IT IS. IT WILL FORCE YOU TO DO THINGS YOU KNOW YOU SHOULD NOT DO--TO COMPROMISE--SIMPLY BECAUSE YOU FEEL LIKE YOU HAVE NO OTHER CHOICE.

THIS WEAKENS US. IT MAKES MEN LESS THAN WHAT WE SHOULD BE, AND IT WILL BE EVEN MORE DIFFICULT FOR YOU BECAUSE YOU HAVE AN EXTRA BURDEN...

BECAUSE YOU HAVE A GIFT THAT WILL AFFECT MANY PEOPLE.

BUT THIS...

...WITHOUT THIS...

...MEANS NOTHING.

IT'S A TERRIBLE THING FOR SOMEONE NOT TO REACH THEIR FULL POTENTIAL...

I KNOW.

AS I'VE GROWN OLDER, I'VE REALIZED THAT I DO NOT HAVE THE CHARACTER TO BE BOTH GOOD AND GREAT AT THE SAME TIME.

BUT YOU DO, REED... AND AS SUCH, ALL OF MY HOPES AND DESIRES REST IN YOU BECOMING WHAT I AM NOT.

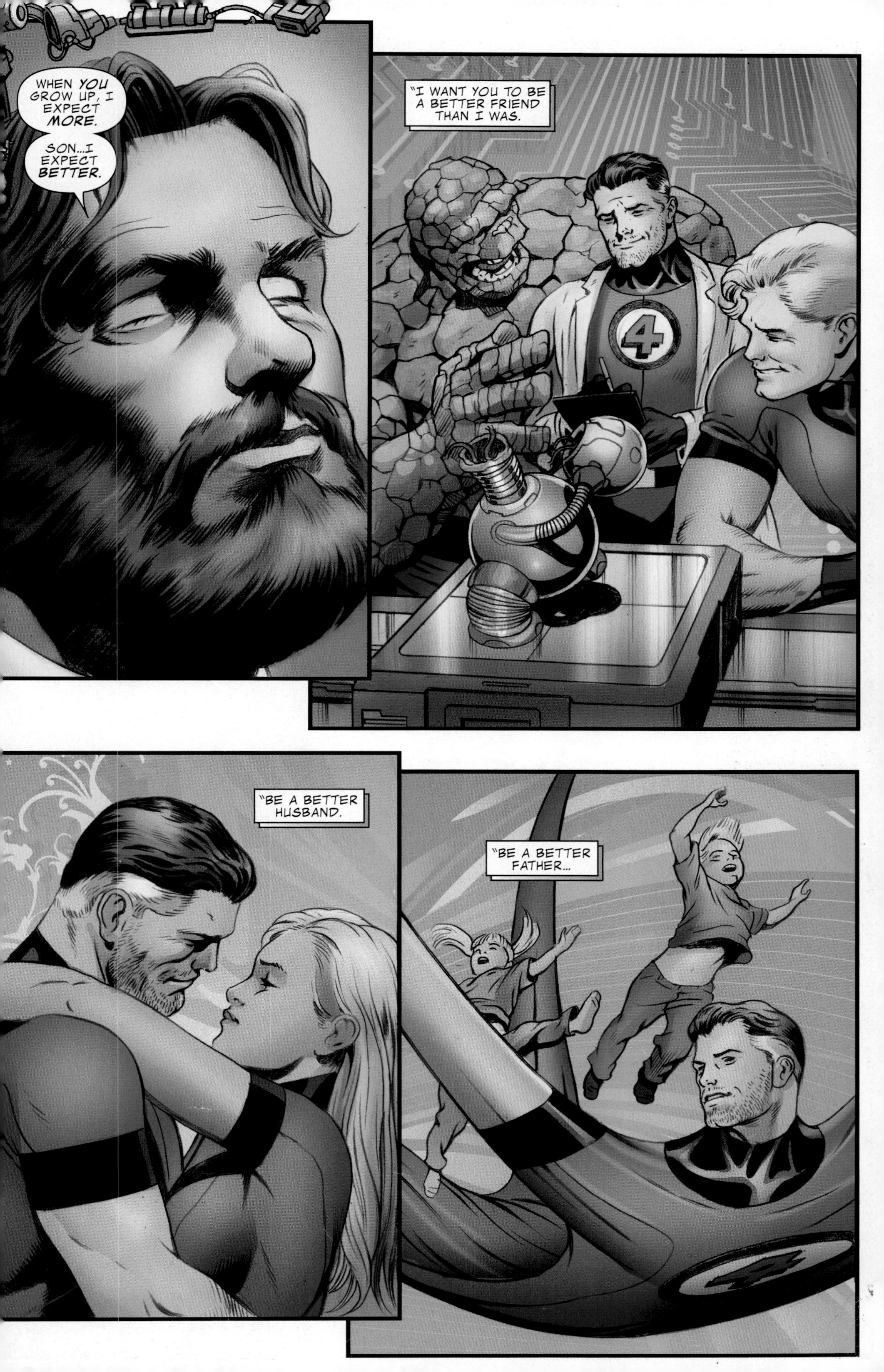
WHEN YOU GROW UP, I EXPECT MORE.
SON...I EXPECT BETTER.
"I WANT YOU TO BE A BETTER FRIEND THAN I WAS.
"BE A BETTER HUSBAND.
"BE A BETTER FATHER...

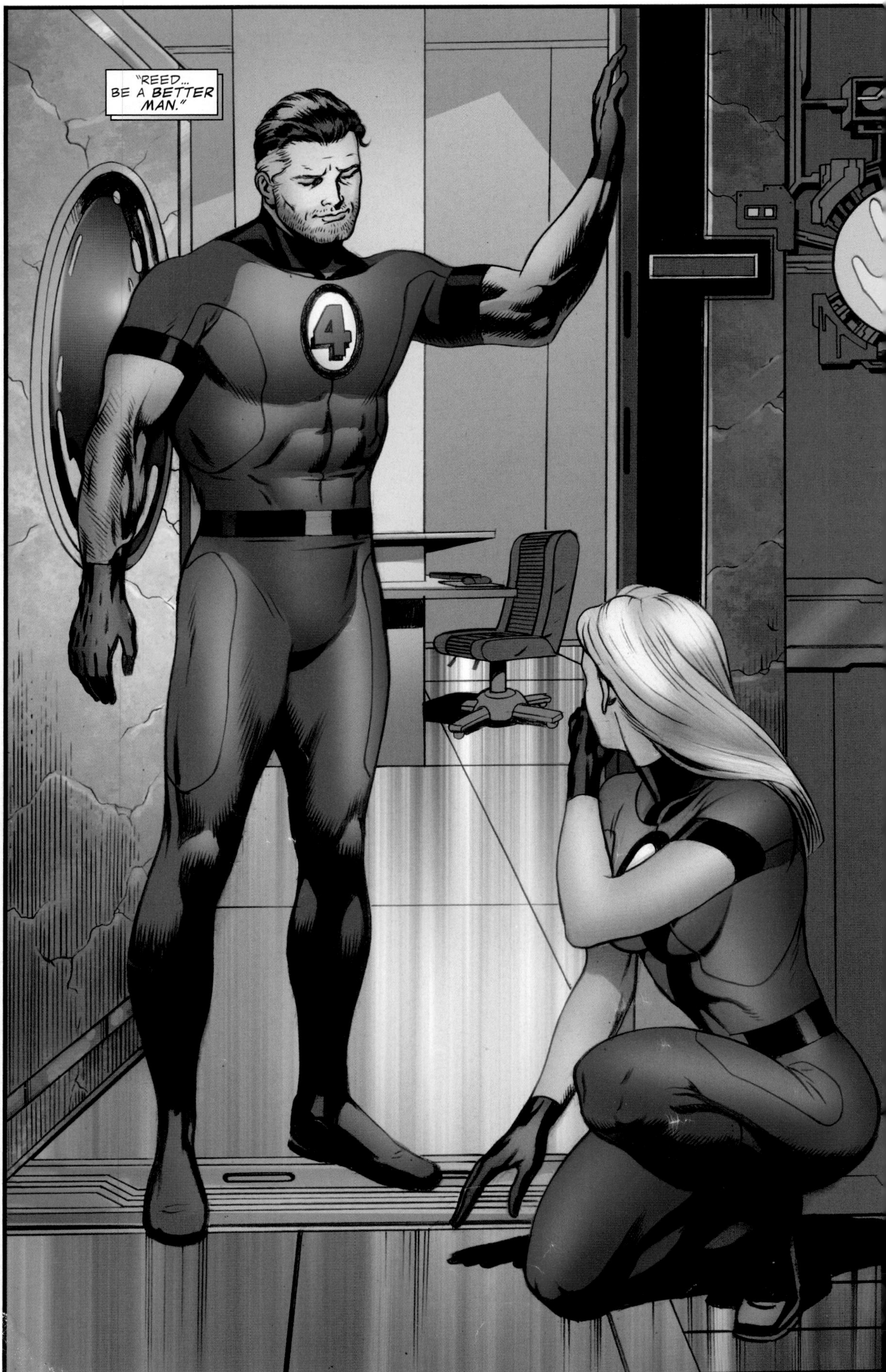
"REED... BE A BETTER MAN."

THESE ARE THE
END TIMES

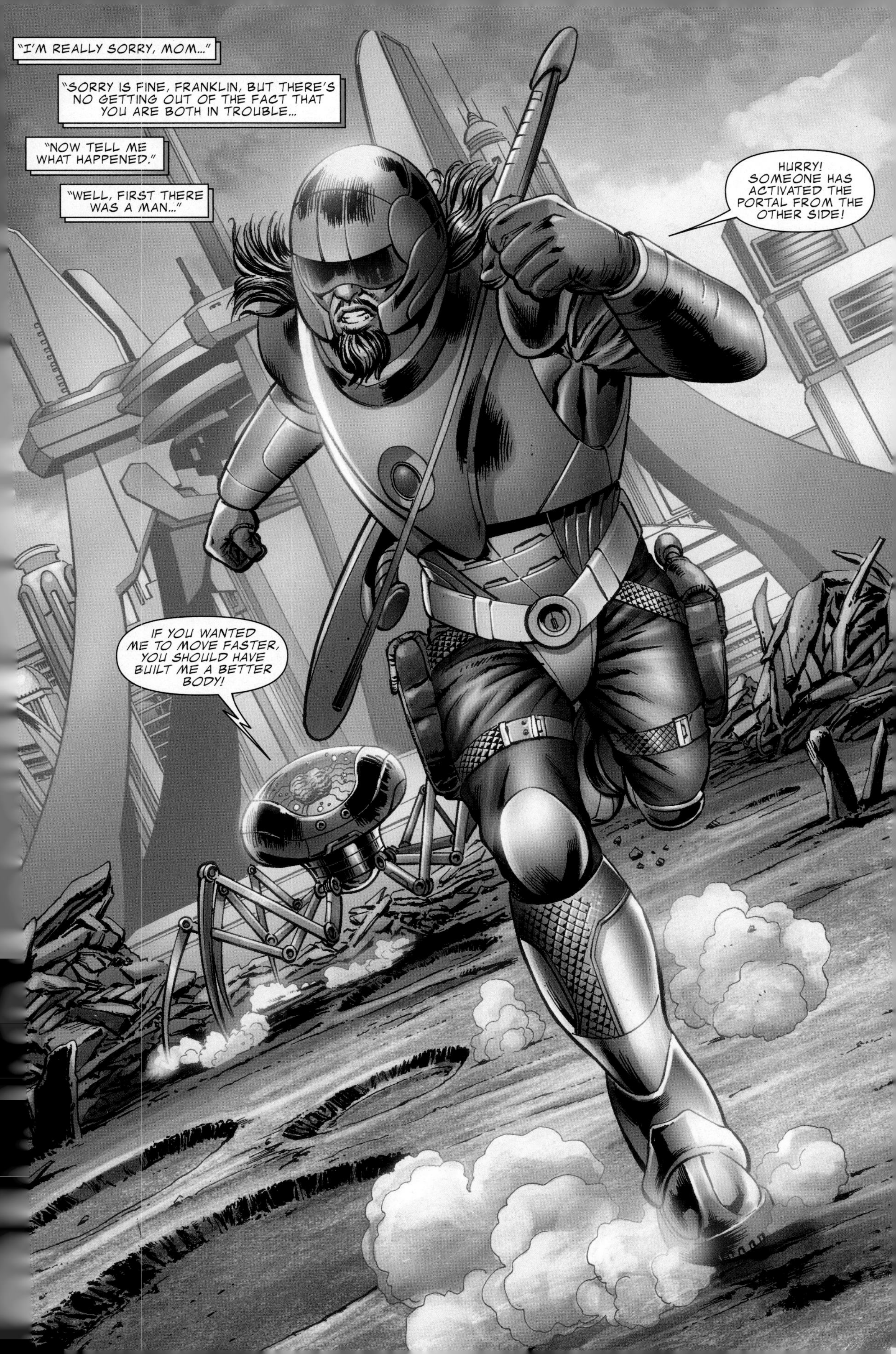
"I'M REALLY SORRY, MOM..."
"SORRY IS FINE, FRANKLIN, BUT THERE'S NO GETTING OUT OF THE FACT THAT YOU ARE BOTH IN TROUBLE...
"NOW TELL ME WHAT HAPPENED."
"WELL, FIRST THERE WAS A MAN..."
HURRY! SOMEONE HAS ACTIVATED THE PORTAL FROM THE OTHER SIDE!
IF YOU WANTED ME TO MOVE FASTER, YOU SHOULD HAVE BUILT ME A BETTER BODY!

ULTRON TERRITORY
I DID THE BEST I COULD WITH WHAT WAS AVAILABLE, ALYSSA. AT LEAST NOW YOU'RE NOT JUST A WELL-PRESERVED BRAIN ON A SHELF IN MY LAB.
NOW CONCENTRATE! WE HAVE TO GET TO THE GATEWAY BEFORE IT CLOSES OR WHOEVER COMES THROUGH WILL HAVE NO WAY BACK TO EARTH.
WOULD THAT BE SO BAD, TEDDY? I'M HAPPY HERE.
IF YOU HAD EYES, I WOULD TELL YOU TO USE THEM, LOVE.
THESE ARE THE END TIMES. THE SUN COLLAPSED AND FORMED A SINGULARITY. NOW WE'RE BEING SLOWLY SUCKED INSIDE.
SPACE-TIME IS BUCKLING!
YOUR HEART RATE IS ELEVATED, DEAR. PLEASE RELAX...YOU KNOW YOU HAVE A HISTORY OF HEART DISEASE IN YOUR FAMILY.
WE'RE TRAPPED IN A PETRI DISH OF UNNATURAL PROGRESS.
A FAKE WORLD FULL OF REFUGEES FROM 500 YEARS IN THE FUTURE UNDERGOING ABNORMAL EVOLUTIONARY ACCELERATION, THE CAUSE OF WHICH WILL EVENTUALLY KILL US ALL!
THIS IS **NOT** HOW THINGS WERE SUPPOSED TO BE!

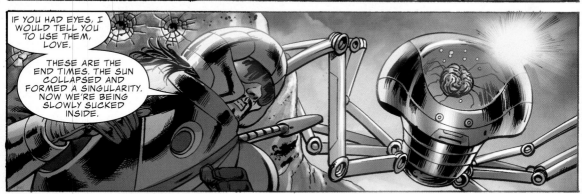

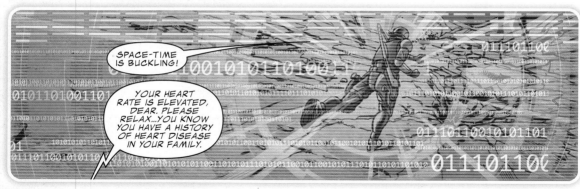

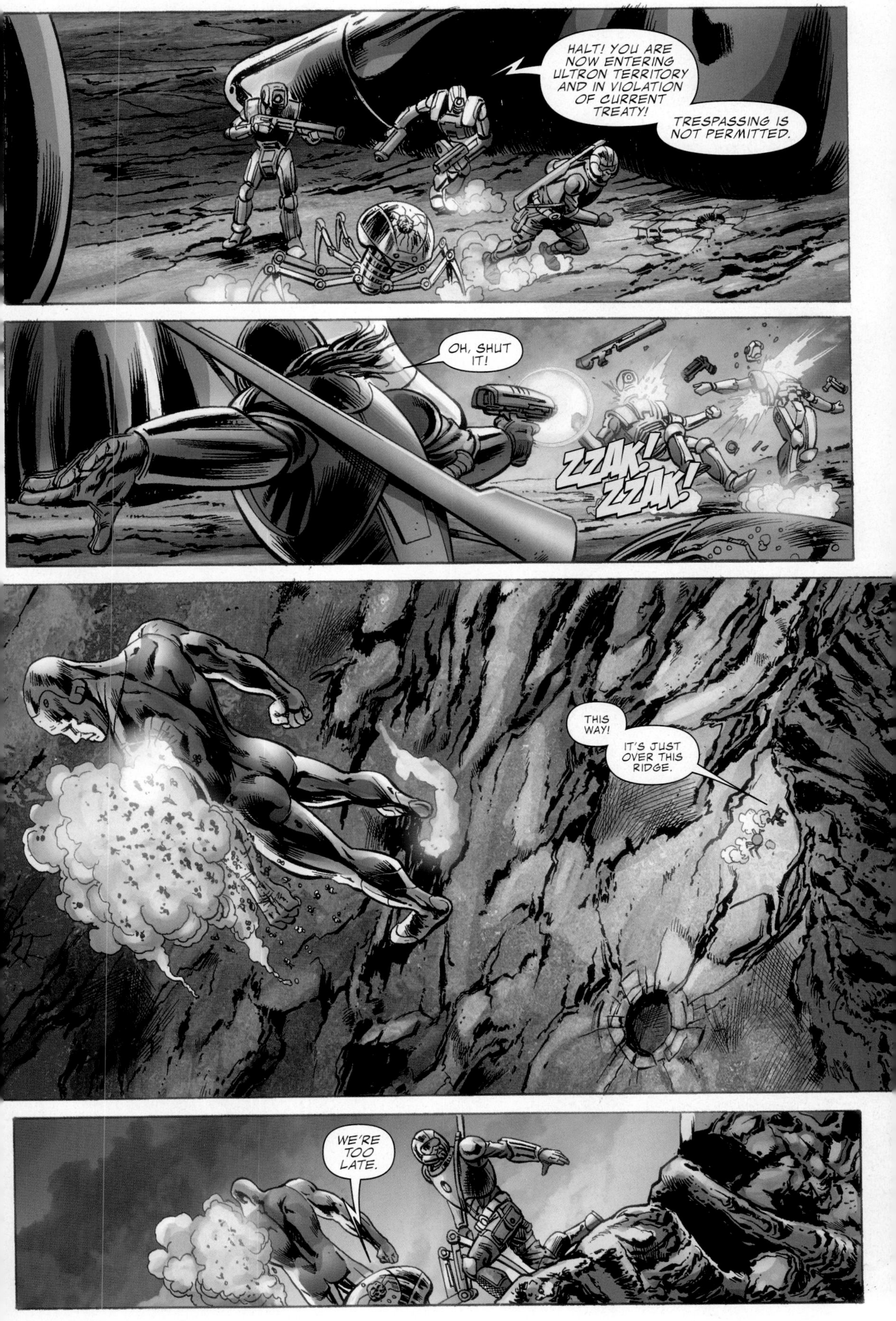
HALT! YOU ARE NOW ENTERING ULTRON TERRITORY AND IN VIOLATION OF CURRENT TREATY!
TRESPASSING IS NOT PERMITTED.
OH, SHUT IT!
ZZAK! ZZAK!
THIS WAY!
IT'S JUST OVER THIS RIDGE.
WE'RE TOO LATE.

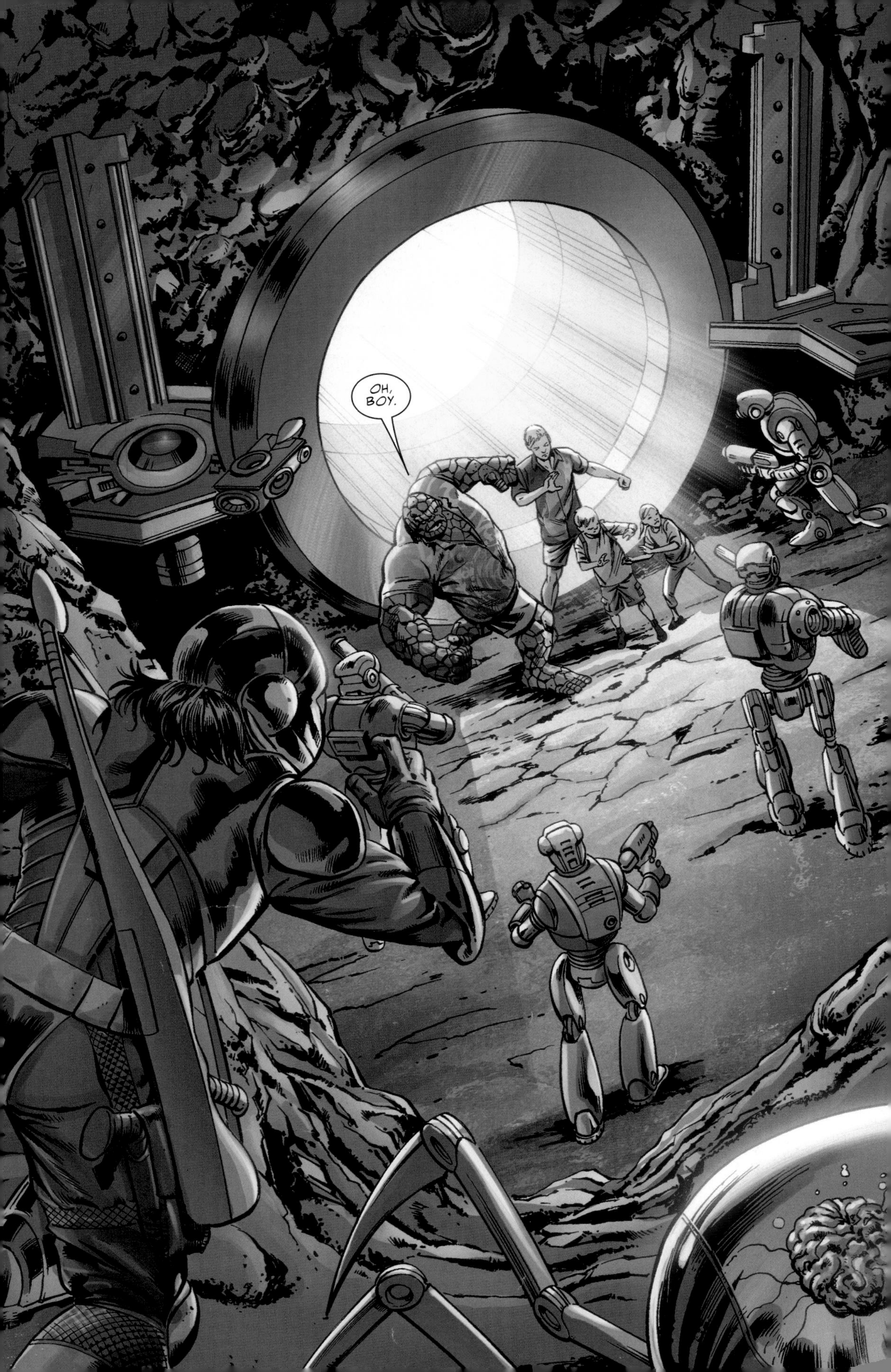
OH, BOY.

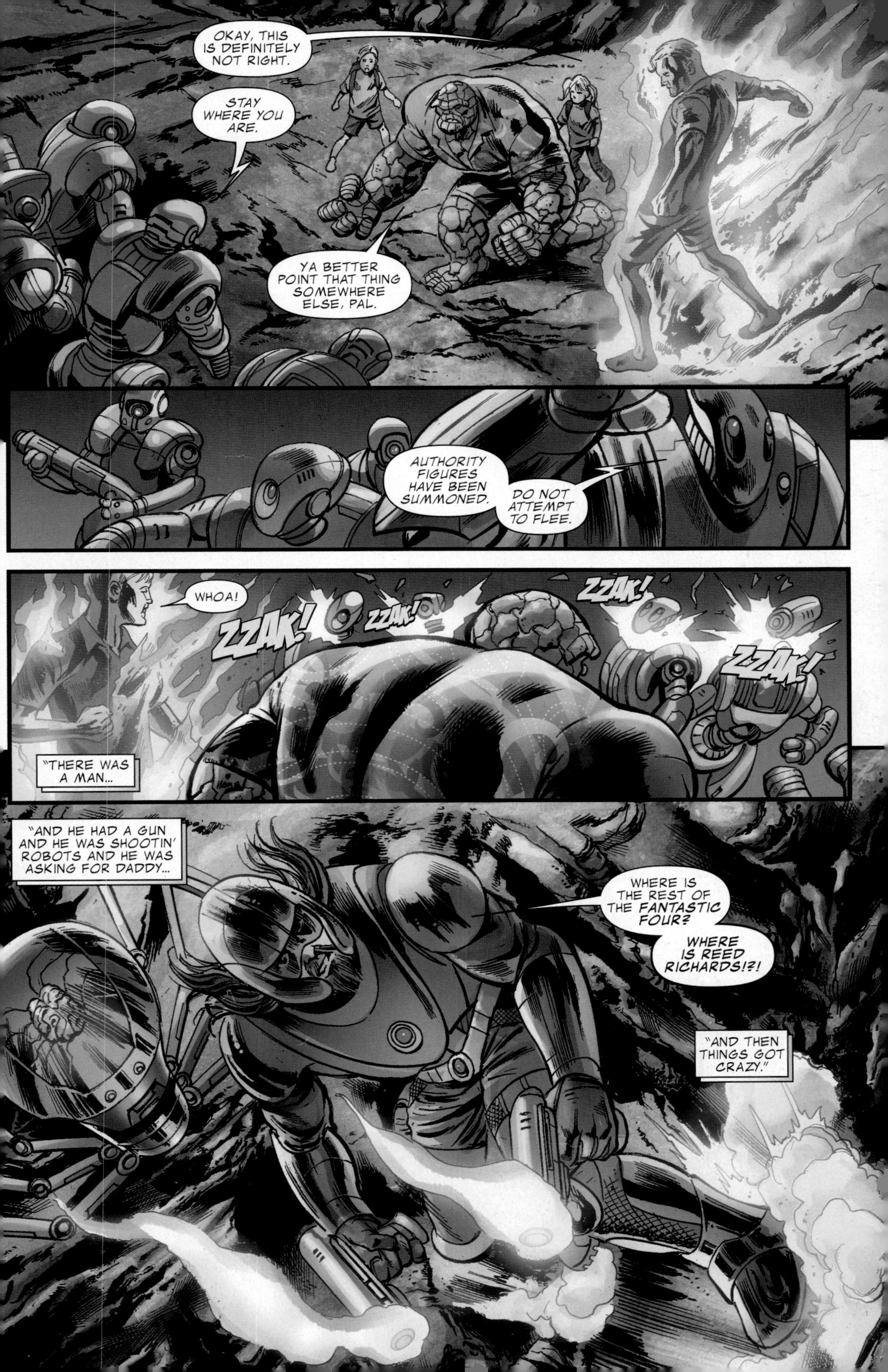
OKAY, THIS IS DEFINITELY NOT RIGHT.
STAY WHERE YOU ARE.
YA BETTER POINT THAT THING SOMEWHERE ELSE, PAL.
AUTHORITY FIGURES HAVE BEEN SUMMONED.
DO NOT ATTEMPT TO FLEE.
WHOA!
ZZAK!
ZZAK!
ZZAK!
ZZAK!
"THERE WAS A MAN...
"AND HE HAD A GUN AND HE WAS SHOOTIN' ROBOTS AND HE WAS ASKING FOR DADDY...
WHERE IS THE REST OF THE FANTASTIC FOUR?
WHERE IS REED RICHARDS!?!
"AND THEN THINGS GOT CRAZY."

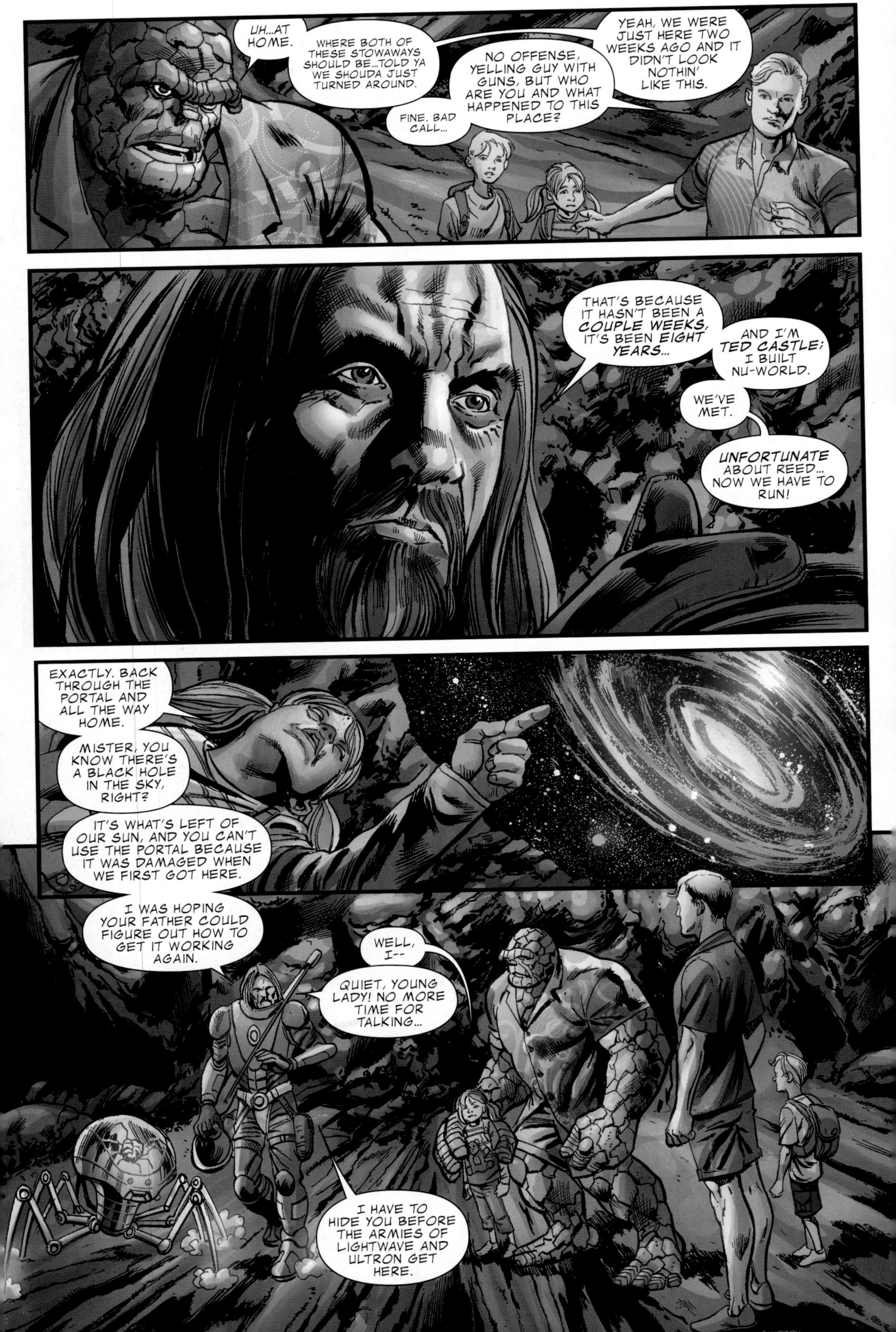

UH...AT HOME.
WHERE BOTH OF THESE STOWAWAYS SHOULD BE...TOLD YA WE SHOUDA JUST TURNED AROUND.
FINE. BAD CALL...
NO OFFENSE, YELLING GUY WITH GUNS, BUT WHO ARE YOU AND WHAT HAPPENED TO THIS PLACE?
YEAH, WE WERE JUST HERE TWO WEEKS AGO AND IT DIDN'T LOOK NOTHIN' LIKE THIS.
THAT'S BECAUSE IT HASN'T BEEN A COUPLE WEEKS, IT'S BEEN EIGHT YEARS...
AND I'M TED CASTLE; I BUILT NU-WORLD.
WE'VE MET.
UNFORTUNATE ABOUT REED... NOW WE HAVE TO RUN!
EXACTLY. BACK THROUGH THE PORTAL AND ALL THE WAY HOME.
MISTER, YOU KNOW THERE'S A BLACK HOLE IN THE SKY, RIGHT?
IT'S WHAT'S LEFT OF OUR SUN, AND YOU CAN'T USE THE PORTAL BECAUSE IT WAS DAMAGED WHEN WE FIRST GOT HERE.
I WAS HOPING YOUR FATHER COULD FIGURE OUT HOW TO GET IT WORKING AGAIN.
WELL, I--
QUIET, YOUNG LADY! NO MORE TIME FOR TALKING...
I HAVE TO HIDE YOU BEFORE THE ARMIES OF LIGHTWAVE AND ULTRON GET HERE.

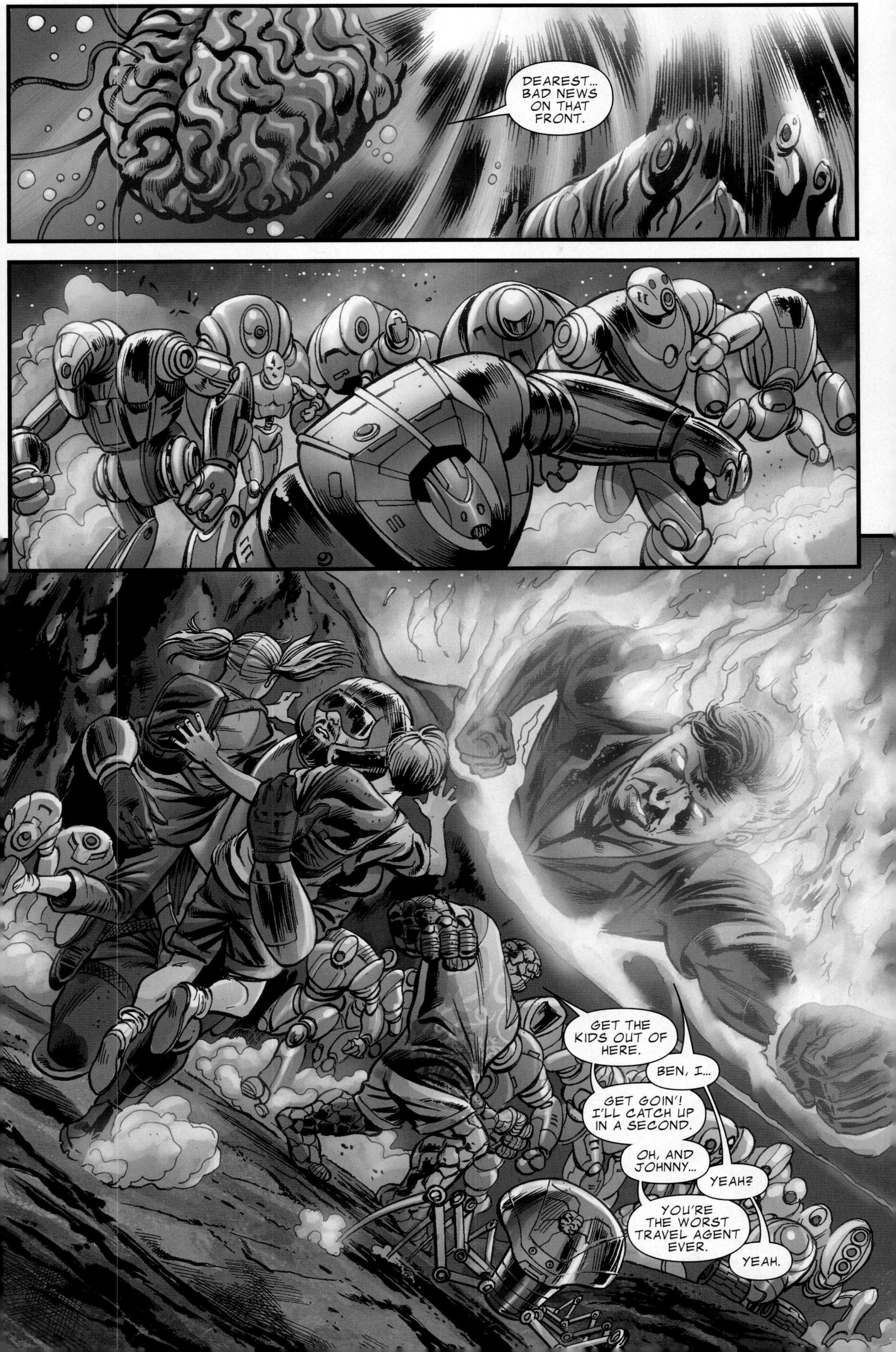
DEAREST... BAD NEWS ON THAT FRONT.
GET THE KIDS OUT OF HERE.
BEN, I...
GET GOIN'! I'LL CATCH UP IN A SECOND.
OH, AND JOHNNY...
YEAH?
YOU'RE THE WORST TRAVEL AGENT EVER.
YEAH.

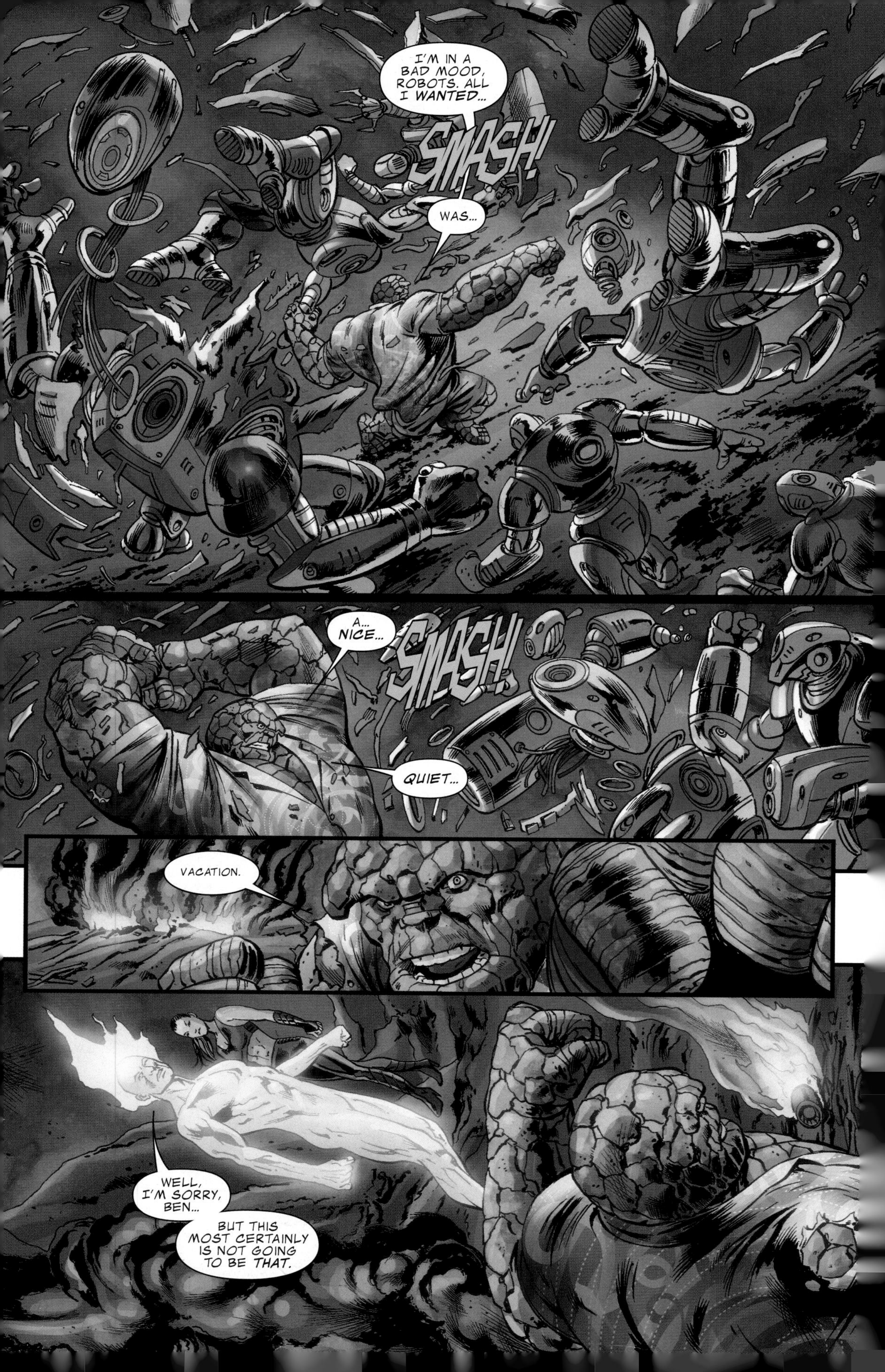
I'M IN A BAD MOOD, ROBOTS. ALL I WANTED...
SMASH!
WAS...
A... NICE...
SMASH!
QUIET...
VACATION.
WELL, I'M SORRY, BEN...
BUT THIS MOST CERTAINLY IS NOT GOING TO BE THAT.

BA-BOOOM!

UNCLE BEN!

MOVE! HE CAN TAKE CARE OF HIMSELF.

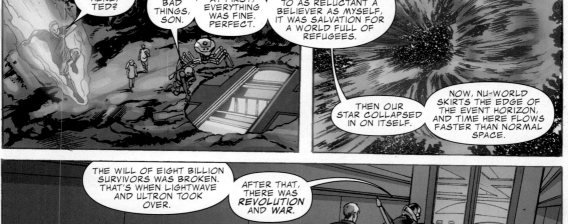

WHAT HAPPENED HERE, TED?

VERY BAD THINGS, SON.

AT FIRST, EVERYTHING WAS FINE. PERFECT.

A NEW GOVERNMENT...A NEW SOCIETY. EVEN TO AS RELUCTANT A BELIEVER AS MYSELF, IT WAS SALVATION FOR A WORLD FULL OF REFUGEES.

THEN OUR STAR COLLAPSED IN ON ITSELF.

NOW, NU-WORLD SKIRTS THE EDGE OF THE EVENT HORIZON, AND TIME HERE FLOWS FASTER THAN NORMAL SPACE.

THE WILL OF EIGHT BILLION SURVIVORS WAS BROKEN. THAT'S WHEN LIGHTWAVE AND ULTRON TOOK OVER.

AFTER THAT, THERE WAS REVOLUTION AND WAR.

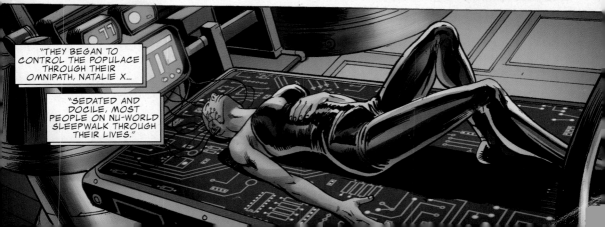

"THEY BEGAN TO CONTROL THE POPULACE THROUGH THEIR OMNIPATH, NATALIE X...

"SEDATED AND DOCILE, MOST PEOPLE ON NU-WORLD SLEEPWALK THROUGH THEIR LIVES."

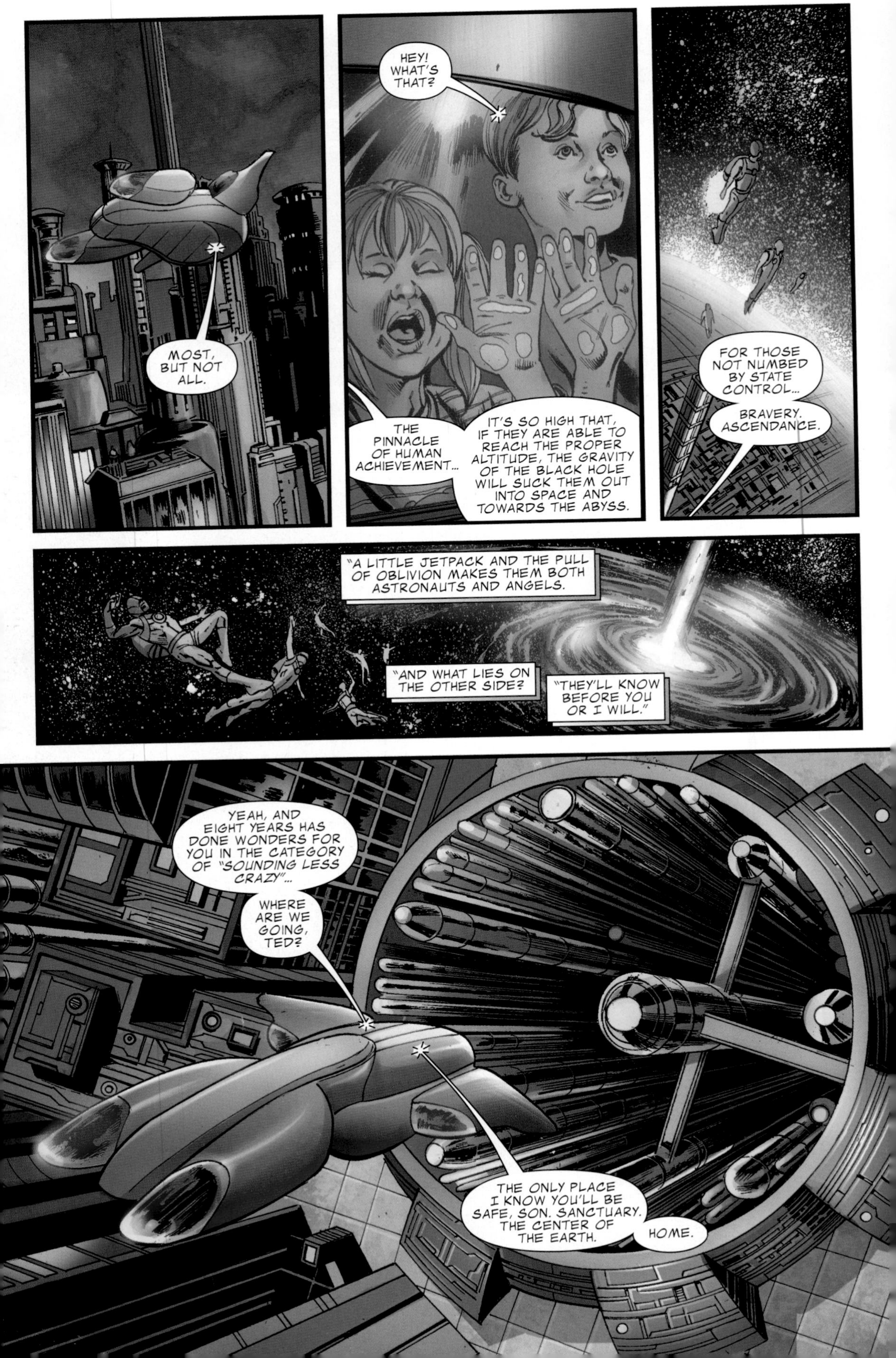
MOST, BUT NOT ALL.
HEY! WHAT'S THAT?
THE PINNACLE OF HUMAN ACHIEVEMENT...
IT'S SO HIGH THAT, IF THEY ARE ABLE TO REACH THE PROPER ALTITUDE, THE GRAVITY OF THE BLACK HOLE WILL SUCK THEM OUT INTO SPACE AND TOWARDS THE ABYSS.
FOR THOSE NOT NUMBED BY STATE CONTROL...
BRAVERY. ASCENDANCE.
"A LITTLE JETPACK AND THE PULL OF OBLIVION MAKES THEM BOTH ASTRONAUTS AND ANGELS.
"AND WHAT LIES ON THE OTHER SIDE?
"THEY'LL KNOW BEFORE YOU OR I WILL."
YEAH, AND EIGHT YEARS HAS DONE WONDERS FOR YOU IN THE CATEGORY OF "SOUNDING LESS CRAZY"...
WHERE ARE WE GOING, TED?
THE ONLY PLACE I KNOW YOU'LL BE SAFE, SON. SANCTUARY. THE CENTER OF THE EARTH.
HOME.

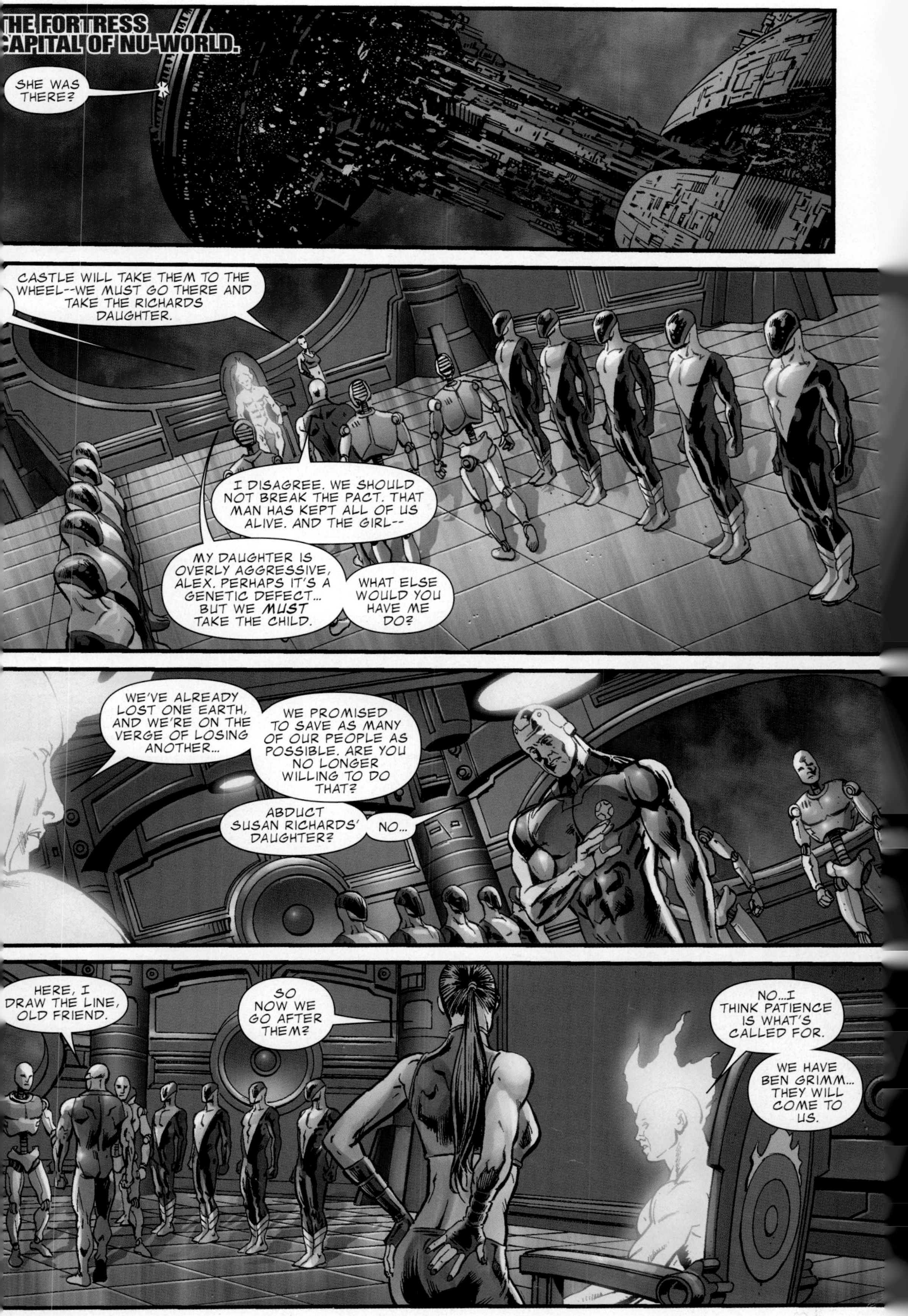
THE FORTRESS CAPITAL OF NU-WORLD.
SHE WAS THERE?
CASTLE WILL TAKE THEM TO THE WHEEL--WE MUST GO THERE AND TAKE THE RICHARDS DAUGHTER.
I DISAGREE. WE SHOULD NOT BREAK THE PACT. THAT MAN HAS KEPT ALL OF US ALIVE. AND THE GIRL--
MY DAUGHTER IS OVERLY AGGRESSIVE, ALEX. PERHAPS IT'S A GENETIC DEFECT... BUT WE MUST TAKE THE CHILD.
WHAT ELSE WOULD YOU HAVE ME DO?
WE'VE ALREADY LOST ONE EARTH, AND WE'RE ON THE VERGE OF LOSING ANOTHER...
WE PROMISED TO SAVE AS MANY OF OUR PEOPLE AS POSSIBLE. ARE YOU NO LONGER WILLING TO DO THAT?
ABDUCT SUSAN RICHARDS' DAUGHTER?
NO...
HERE, I DRAW THE LINE, OLD FRIEND.
SO NOW WE GO AFTER THEM?
NO...I THINK PATIENCE IS WHAT'S CALLED FOR.
WE HAVE BEN GRIMM... THEY WILL COME TO US.

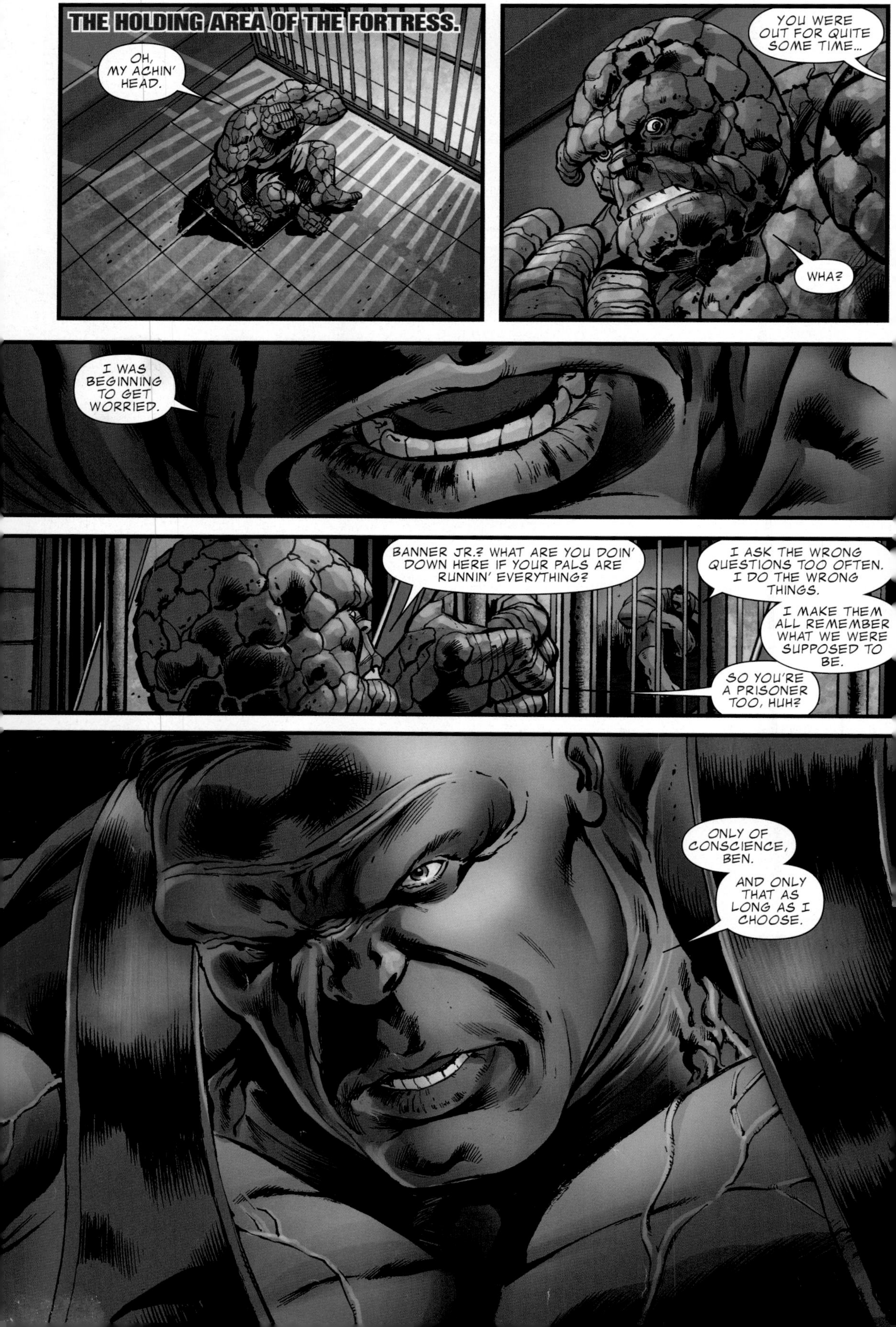
THE HOLDING AREA OF THE FORTRESS.
OH, MY ACHIN' HEAD.
YOU WERE OUT FOR QUITE SOME TIME...
WHA?
I WAS BEGINNING TO GET WORRIED.
BANNER JR.? WHAT ARE YOU DOIN' DOWN HERE IF YOUR PALS ARE RUNNIN' EVERYTHING?
I ASK THE WRONG QUESTIONS TOO OFTEN. I DO THE WRONG THINGS.
I MAKE THEM ALL REMEMBER WHAT WE WERE SUPPOSED TO BE.
SO YOU'RE A PRISONER TOO, HUH?
ONLY OF CONSCIENCE, BEN.
AND ONLY THAT AS LONG AS I CHOOSE.

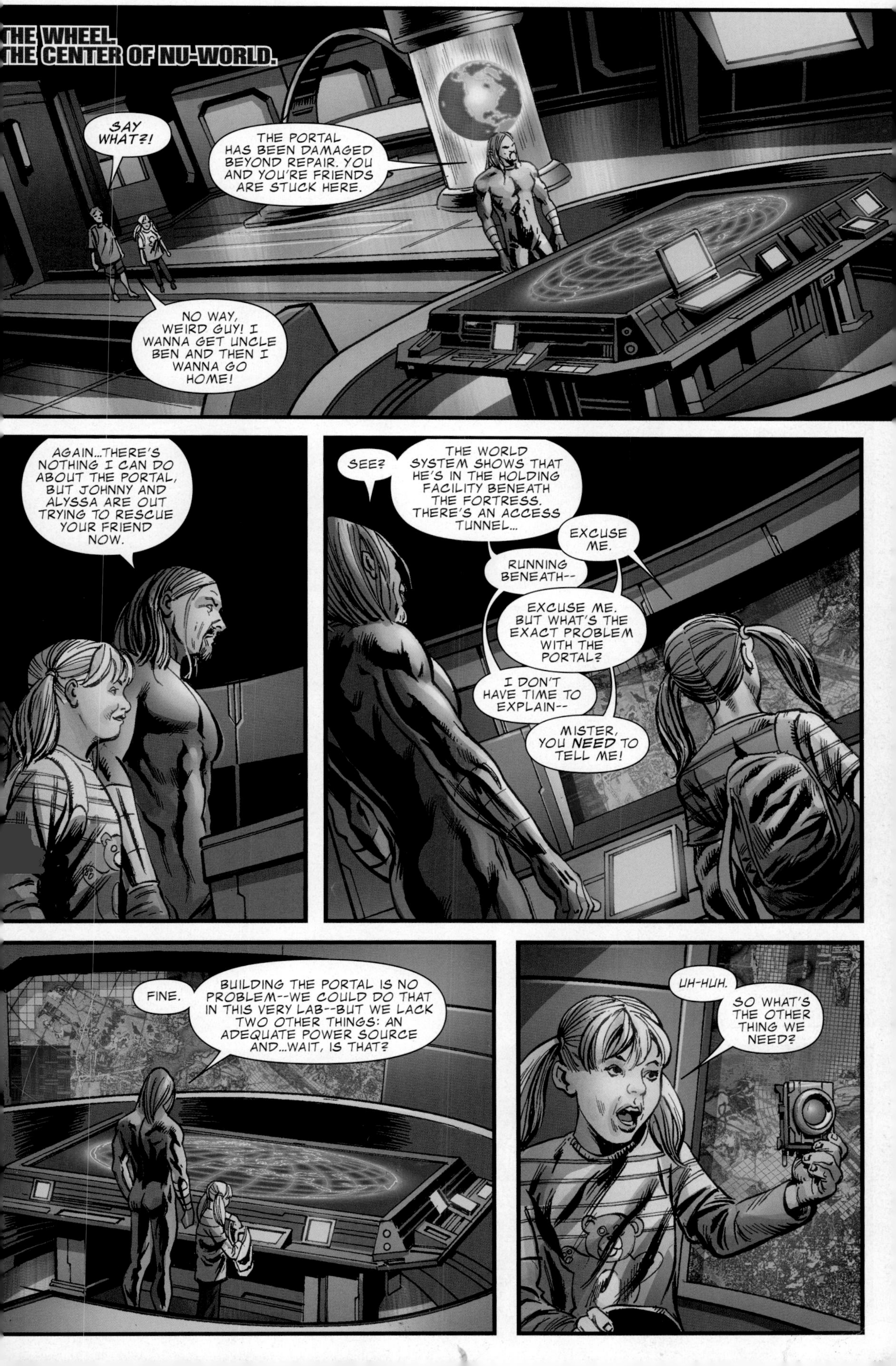
THE WHEEL.
THE CENTER OF NU-WORLD.
SAY WHAT?!
THE PORTAL HAS BEEN DAMAGED BEYOND REPAIR. YOU AND YOU'RE FRIENDS ARE STUCK HERE.
NO WAY, WEIRD GUY! I WANNA GET UNCLE BEN AND THEN I WANNA GO HOME!
AGAIN...THERE'S NOTHING I CAN DO ABOUT THE PORTAL, BUT JOHNNY AND ALYSSA ARE OUT TRYING TO RESCUE YOUR FRIEND NOW.
SEE?
THE WORLD SYSTEM SHOWS THAT HE'S IN THE HOLDING FACILITY BENEATH THE FORTRESS. THERE'S AN ACCESS TUNNEL...
EXCUSE ME.
RUNNING BENEATH--
EXCUSE ME. BUT WHAT'S THE EXACT PROBLEM WITH THE PORTAL?
I DON'T HAVE TIME TO EXPLAIN--
MISTER, YOU NEED TO TELL ME!
FINE.
BUILDING THE PORTAL IS NO PROBLEM--WE COULD DO THAT IN THIS VERY LAB--BUT WE LACK TWO OTHER THINGS: AN ADEQUATE POWER SOURCE AND...WAIT, IS THAT?
UH-HUH.
SO WHAT'S THE OTHER THING WE NEED?

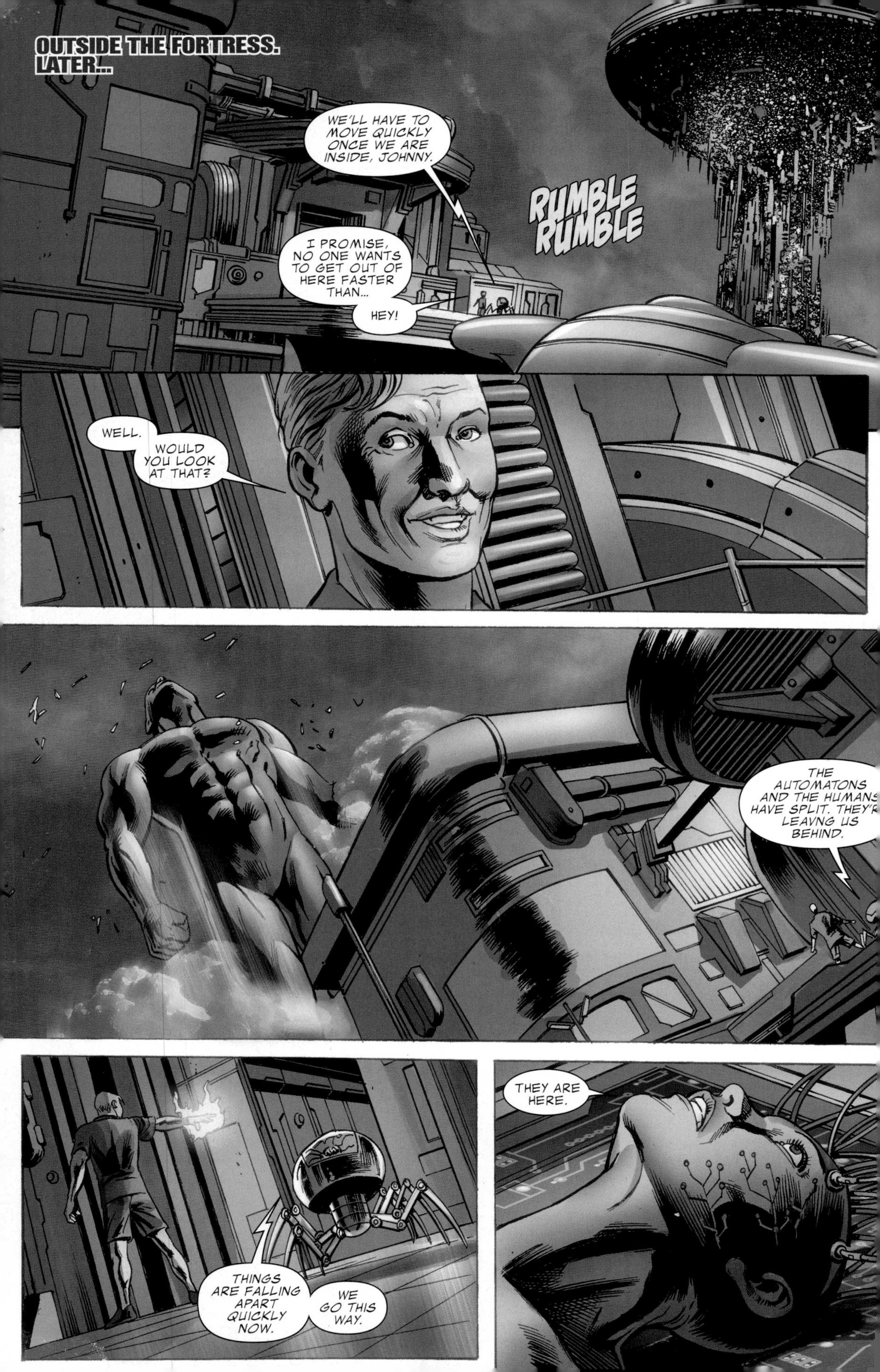
OUTSIDE THE FORTRESS. LATER...
WE'LL HAVE TO MOVE QUICKLY ONCE WE ARE INSIDE, JOHNNY.
RUMBLE RUMBLE
I PROMISE, NO ONE WANTS TO GET OUT OF HERE FASTER THAN...
HEY!
WELL.
WOULD YOU LOOK AT THAT?
THE AUTOMATONS AND THE HUMANS HAVE SPLIT. THEY'RE LEAVNG US BEHIND.
THINGS ARE FALLING APART QUICKLY NOW.
WE GO THIS WAY.
THEY ARE HERE.

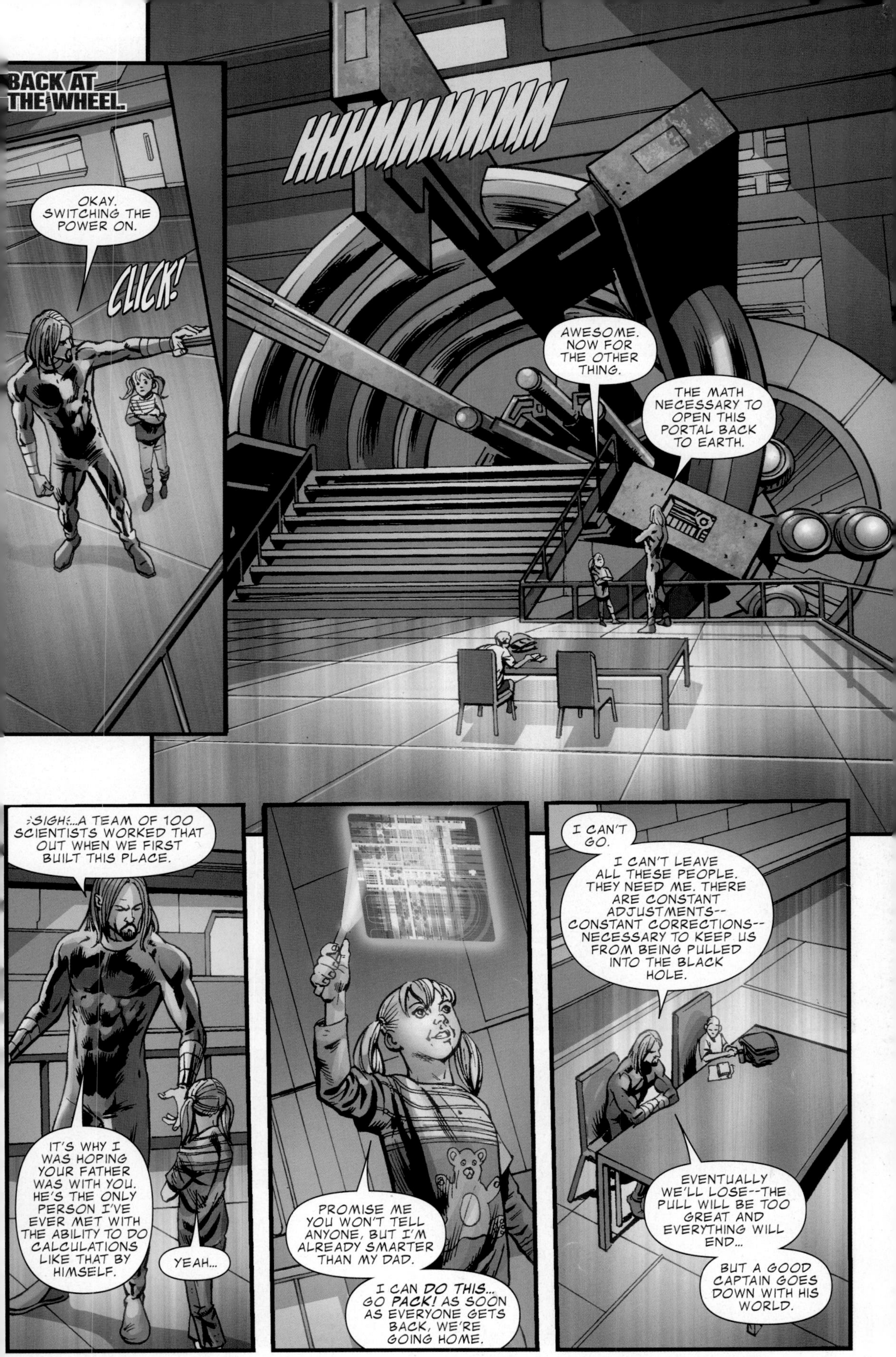
BACK AT THE WHEEL.
HHHMMMMMMM
OKAY. SWITCHING THE POWER ON.
CLICK!
AWESOME. NOW FOR THE OTHER THING.
THE MATH NECESSARY TO OPEN THIS PORTAL BACK TO EARTH.
SIGH...A TEAM OF 100 SCIENTISTS WORKED THAT OUT WHEN WE FIRST BUILT THIS PLACE.
IT'S WHY I WAS HOPING YOUR FATHER WAS WITH YOU. HE'S THE ONLY PERSON I'VE EVER MET WITH THE ABILITY TO DO CALCULATIONS LIKE THAT BY HIMSELF.
YEAH...
PROMISE ME YOU WON'T TELL ANYONE, BUT I'M ALREADY SMARTER THAN MY DAD.
I CAN DO THIS... GO PACK! AS SOON AS EVERYONE GETS BACK, WE'RE GOING HOME.
I CAN'T GO.
I CAN'T LEAVE ALL THESE PEOPLE. THEY NEED ME. THERE ARE CONSTANT ADJUSTMENTS-- CONSTANT CORRECTIONS-- NECESSARY TO KEEP US FROM BEING PULLED INTO THE BLACK HOLE.
EVENTUALLY WE'LL LOSE--THE PULL WILL BE TOO GREAT AND EVERYTHING WILL END...
BUT A GOOD CAPTAIN GOES DOWN WITH HIS WORLD.

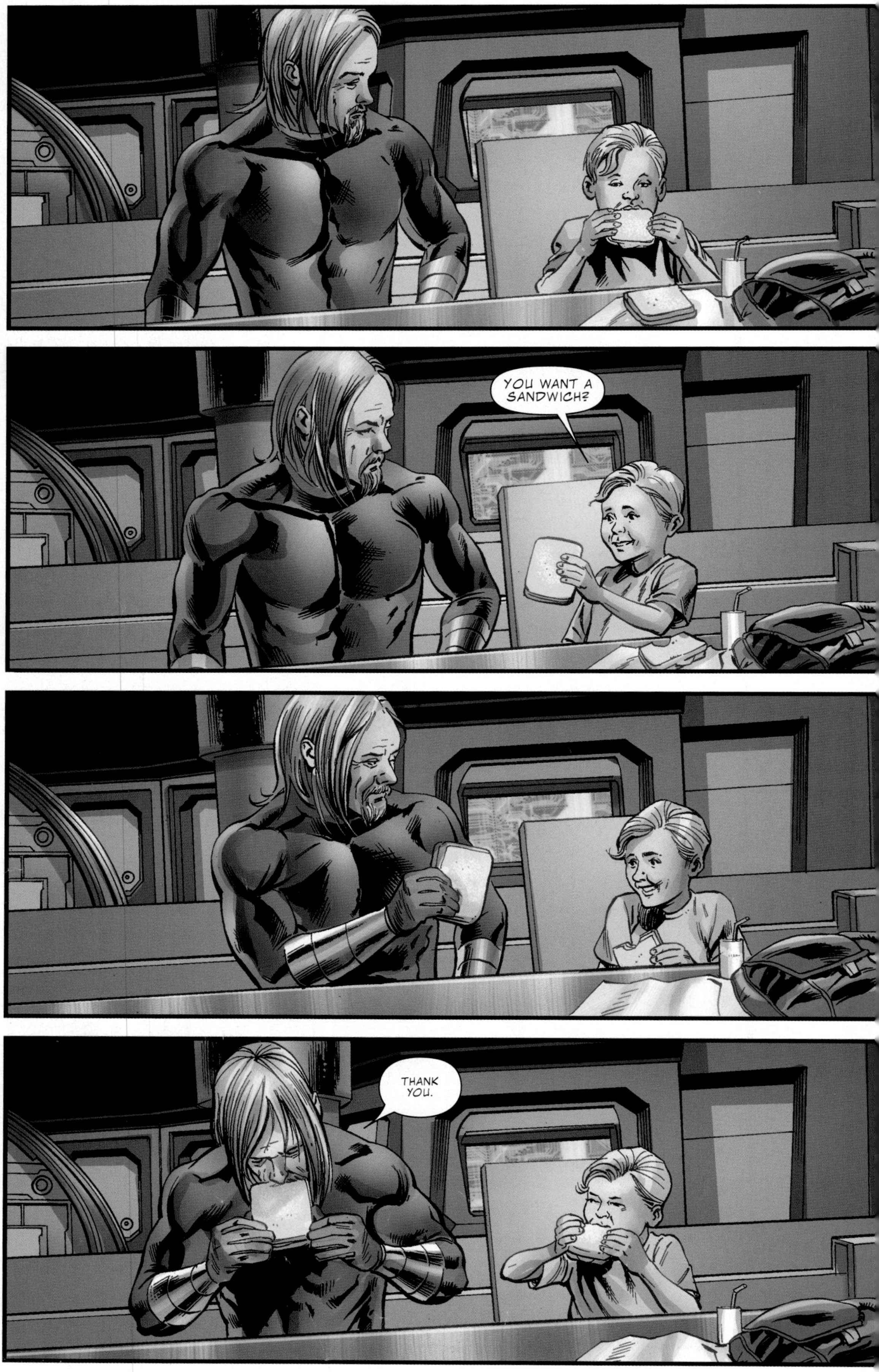
YOU WANT A SANDWICH?
THANK YOU.

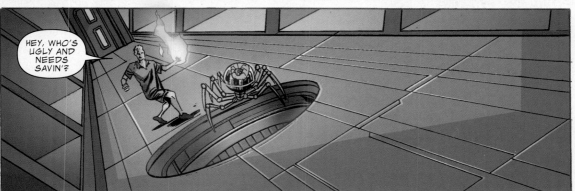

HEY, WHO'S UGLY AND NEEDS SAVIN'?

KIDDO, I BEEN BEATIN' ON THESE BARS FOR THE LAST HOUR...

YOU GET ME OUTTA HERE AND I TAKE BACK EVERYTHING BAD I'VE EVER SAID ABOUT YOU.

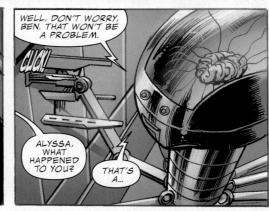

WELL, DON'T WORRY, BEN. THAT WON'T BE A PROBLEM.

CLICK!

ALYSSA, WHAT HAPPENED TO YOU?

THAT'S A...

A...

OH.

I CAN'T... <BZZT>

I CAN'T FEEL... <BZZT> MY... <BZZT> LEGS.

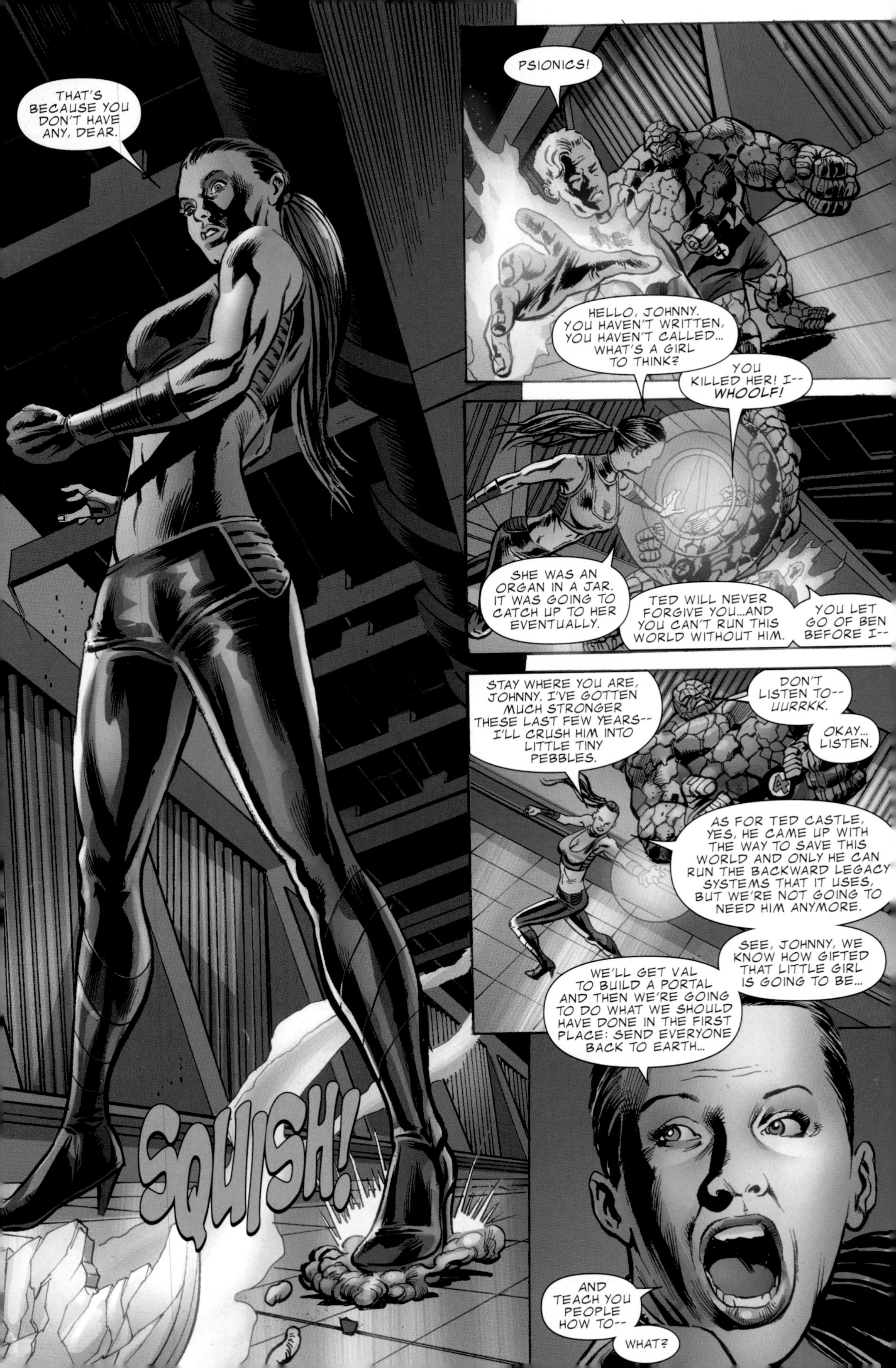
THAT'S BECAUSE YOU DON'T HAVE ANY, DEAR.
PSIONICS!
HELLO, JOHNNY. YOU HAVEN'T WRITTEN, YOU HAVEN'T CALLED... WHAT'S A GIRL TO THINK?
YOU KILLED HER! I-- WHOOLF!
SHE WAS AN ORGAN IN A JAR. IT WAS GOING TO CATCH UP TO HER EVENTUALLY.
TED WILL NEVER FORGIVE YOU...AND YOU CAN'T RUN THIS WORLD WITHOUT HIM.
YOU LET GO OF BEN BEFORE I--
STAY WHERE YOU ARE, JOHNNY. I'VE GOTTEN MUCH STRONGER THESE LAST FEW YEARS-- I'LL CRUSH HIM INTO LITTLE TINY PEBBLES.
DON'T LISTEN TO-- UURRKK.
OKAY... LISTEN.
AS FOR TED CASTLE, YES, HE CAME UP WITH THE WAY TO SAVE THIS WORLD AND ONLY HE CAN RUN THE BACKWARD LEGACY SYSTEMS THAT IT USES, BUT WE'RE NOT GOING TO NEED HIM ANYMORE.
SEE, JOHNNY, WE KNOW HOW GIFTED THAT LITTLE GIRL IS GOING TO BE...
WE'LL GET VAL TO BUILD A PORTAL AND THEN WE'RE GOING TO DO WHAT WE SHOULD HAVE DONE IN THE FIRST PLACE: SEND EVERYONE BACK TO EARTH...
SQUISH!
AND TEACH YOU PEOPLE HOW TO--
WHAT?

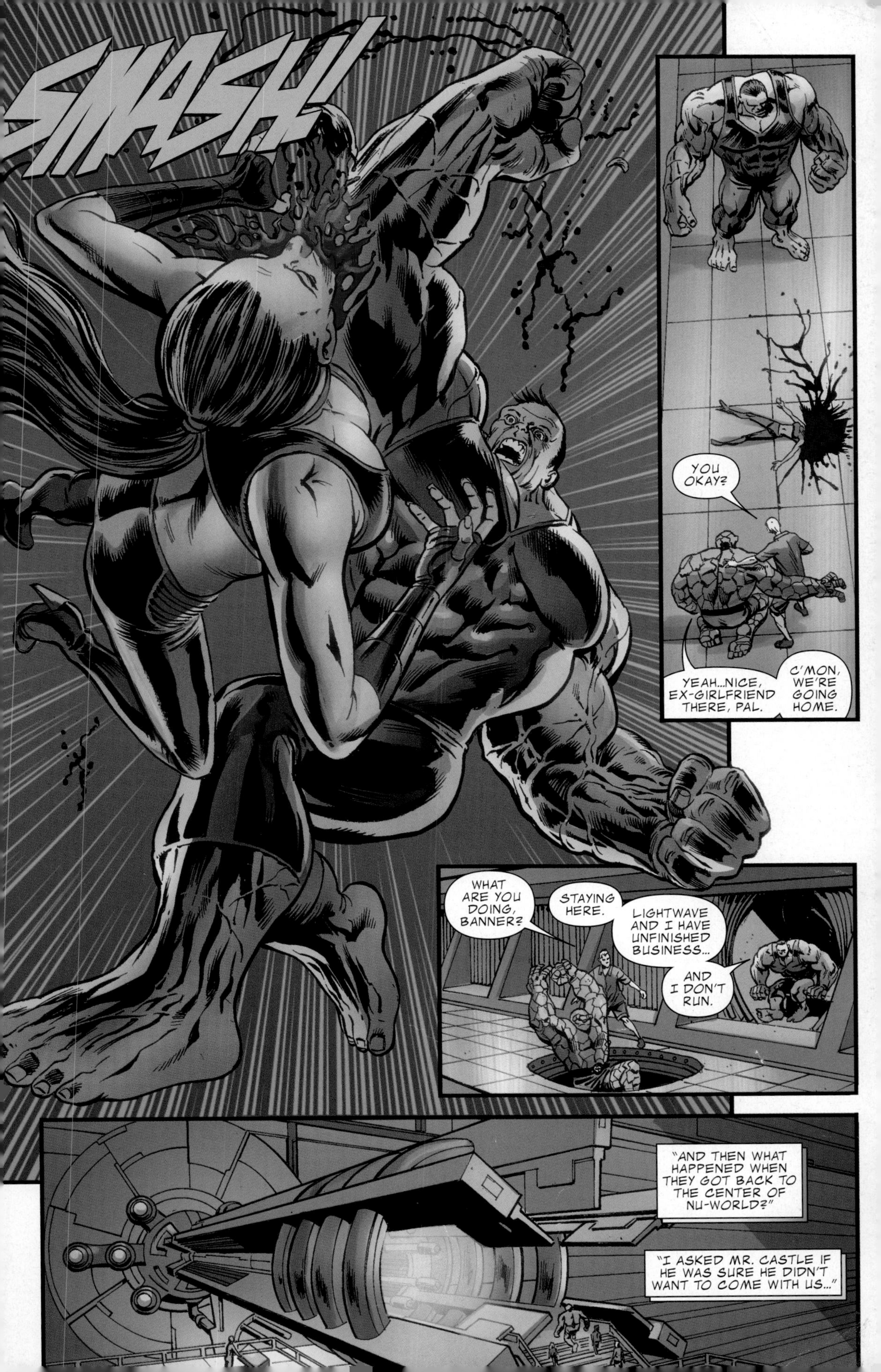
SMASH!
YOU OKAY?
YEAH...NICE, EX-GIRLFRIEND THERE, PAL.
C'MON, WE'RE GOING HOME.
WHAT ARE YOU DOING, BANNER?
STAYING HERE.
LIGHTWAVE AND I HAVE UNFINISHED BUSINESS...
AND I DON'T RUN.
"AND THEN WHAT HAPPENED WHEN THEY GOT BACK TO THE CENTER OF NU-WORLD?"
"I ASKED MR. CASTLE IF HE WAS SURE HE DIDN'T WANT TO COME WITH US..."

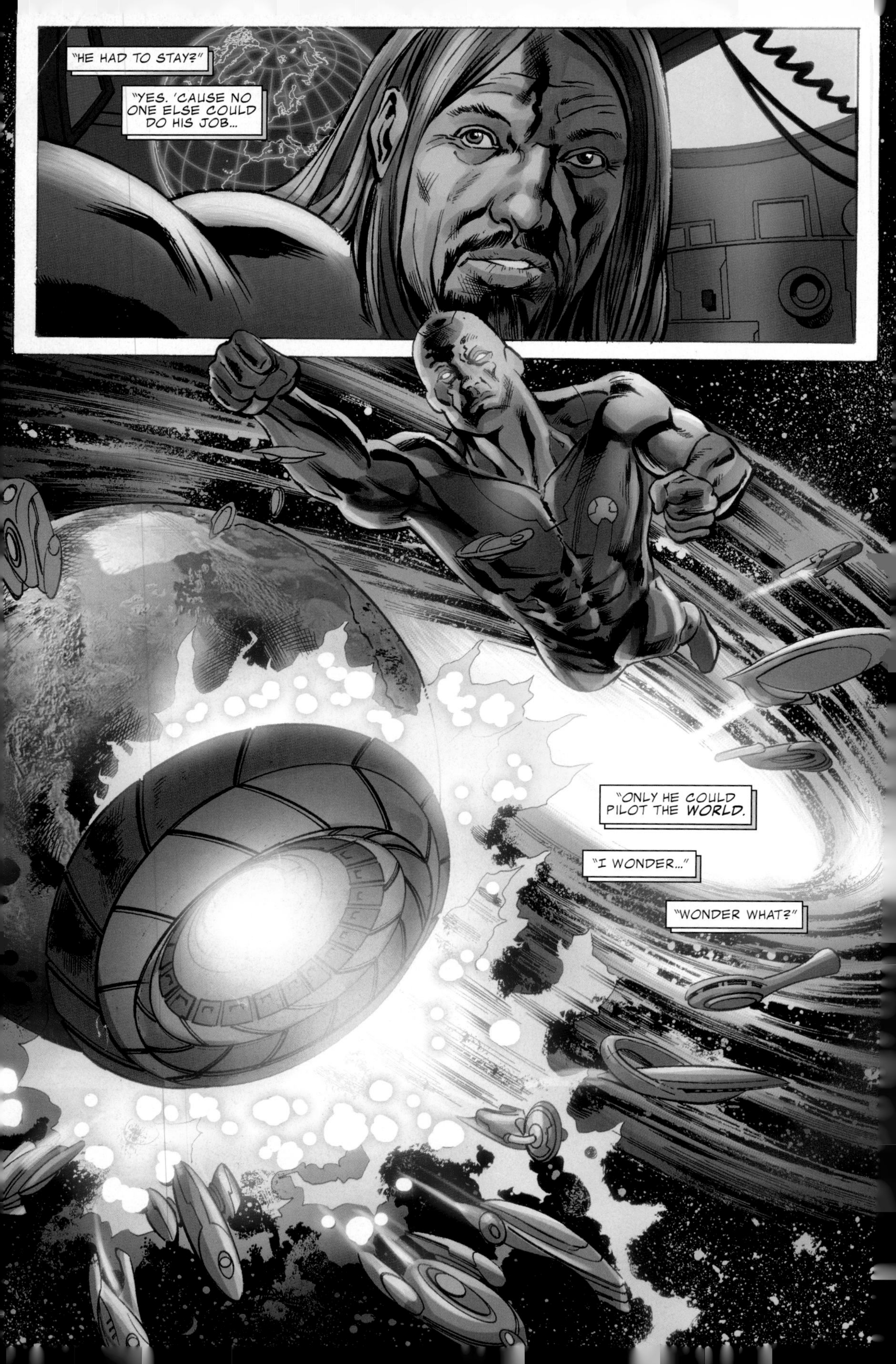
"HE HAD TO STAY?"
"YES. 'CAUSE NO ONE ELSE COULD DO HIS JOB...
"ONLY HE COULD PILOT THE WORLD.
"I WONDER..."
"WONDER WHAT?"

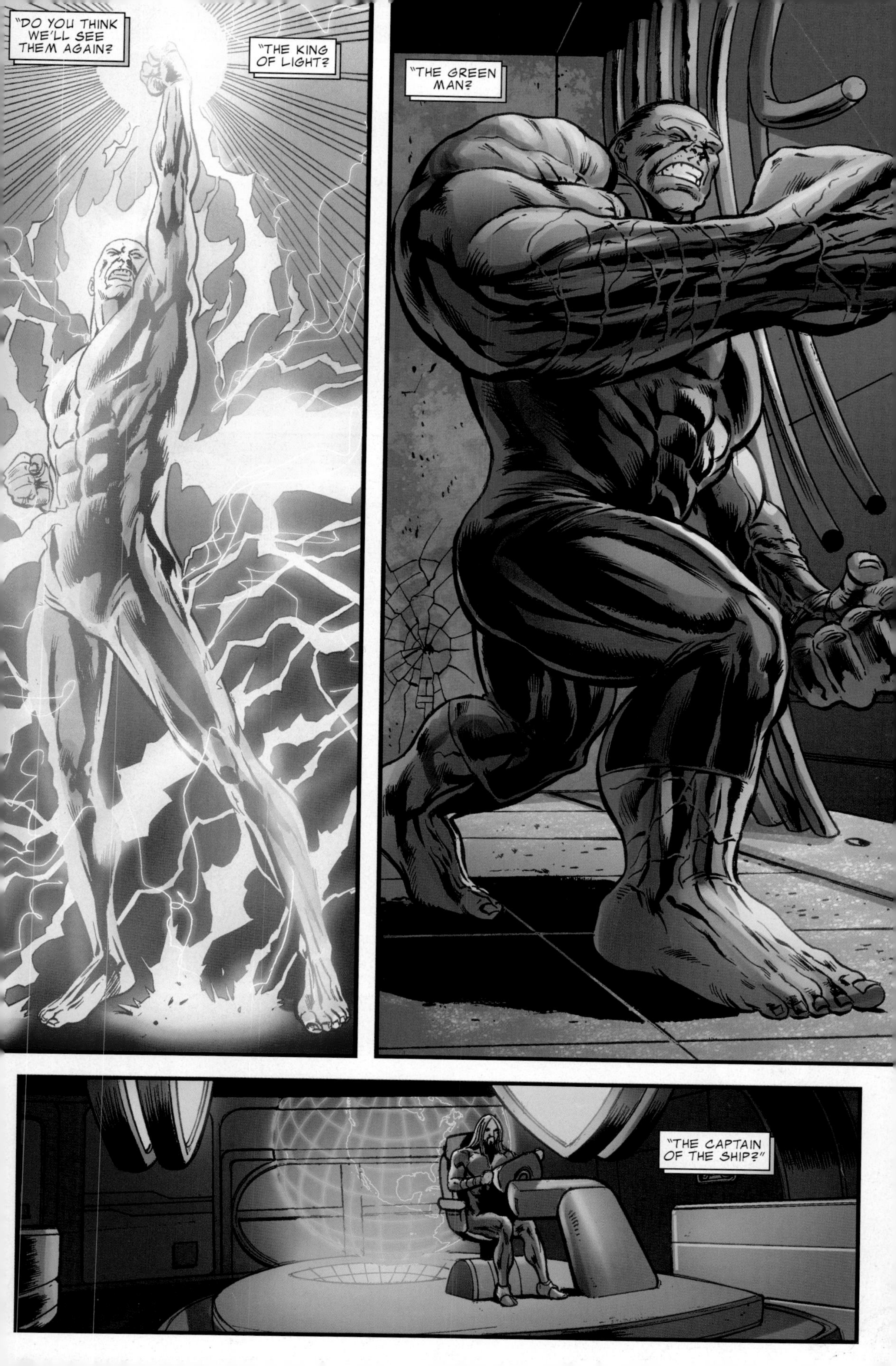
"DO YOU THINK WE'LL SEE THEM AGAIN?
"THE KING OF LIGHT?
"THE GREEN MAN?
"THE CAPTAIN OF THE SHIP?"

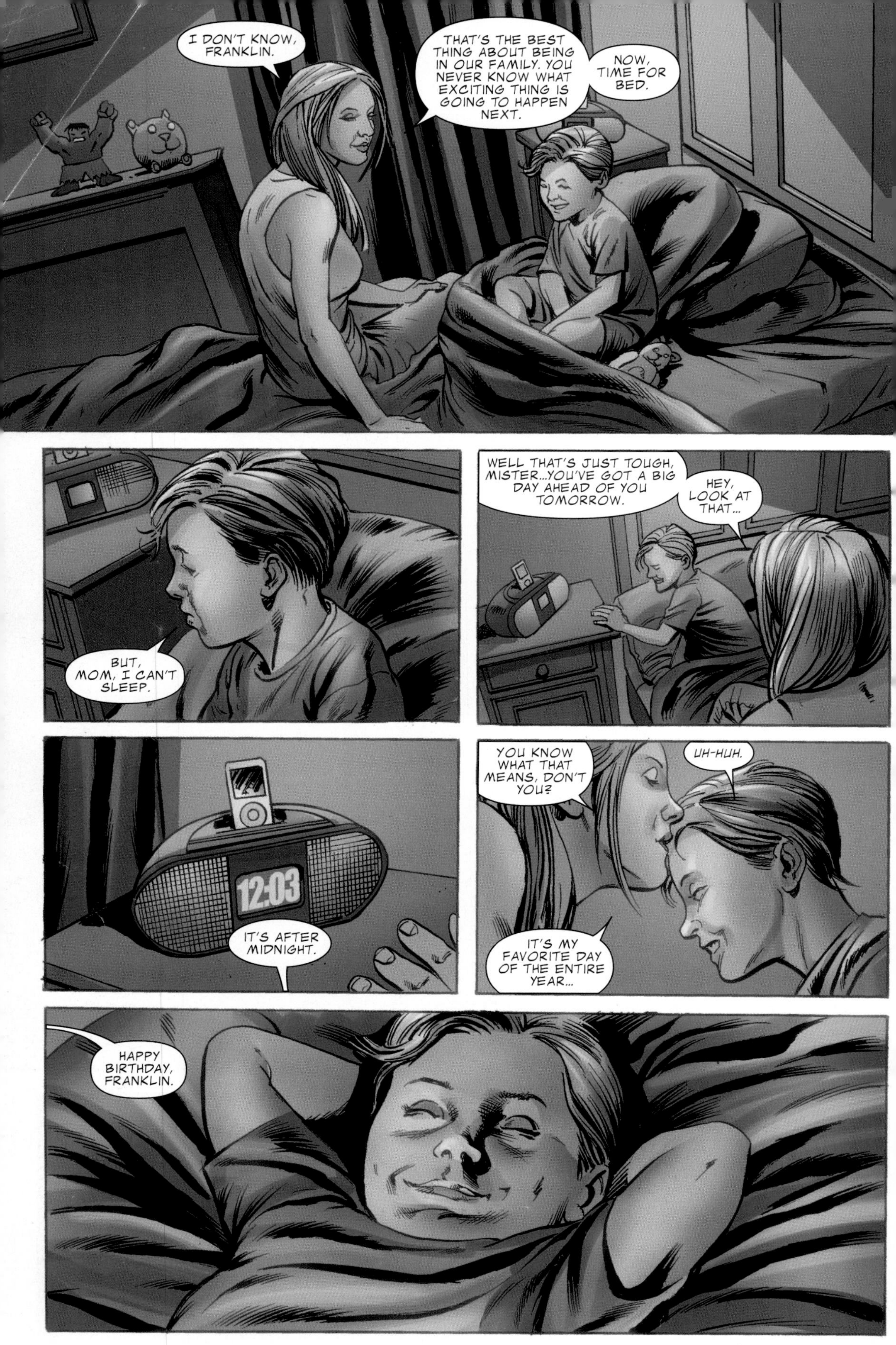
I DON'T KNOW, FRANKLIN.
THAT'S THE BEST THING ABOUT BEING IN OUR FAMILY. YOU NEVER KNOW WHAT EXCITING THING IS GOING TO HAPPEN NEXT.
NOW, TIME FOR BED.
BUT, MOM, I CAN'T SLEEP.
WELL THAT'S JUST TOUGH, MISTER...YOU'VE GOT A BIG DAY AHEAD OF YOU TOMORROW.
HEY, LOOK AT THAT...
12:03
IT'S AFTER MIDNIGHT.
YOU KNOW WHAT THAT MEANS, DON'T YOU?
UH-HUH.
IT'S MY FAVORITE DAY OF THE ENTIRE YEAR...
HAPPY BIRTHDAY, FRANKLIN.

ALL HOPE LIES WITH DOOM

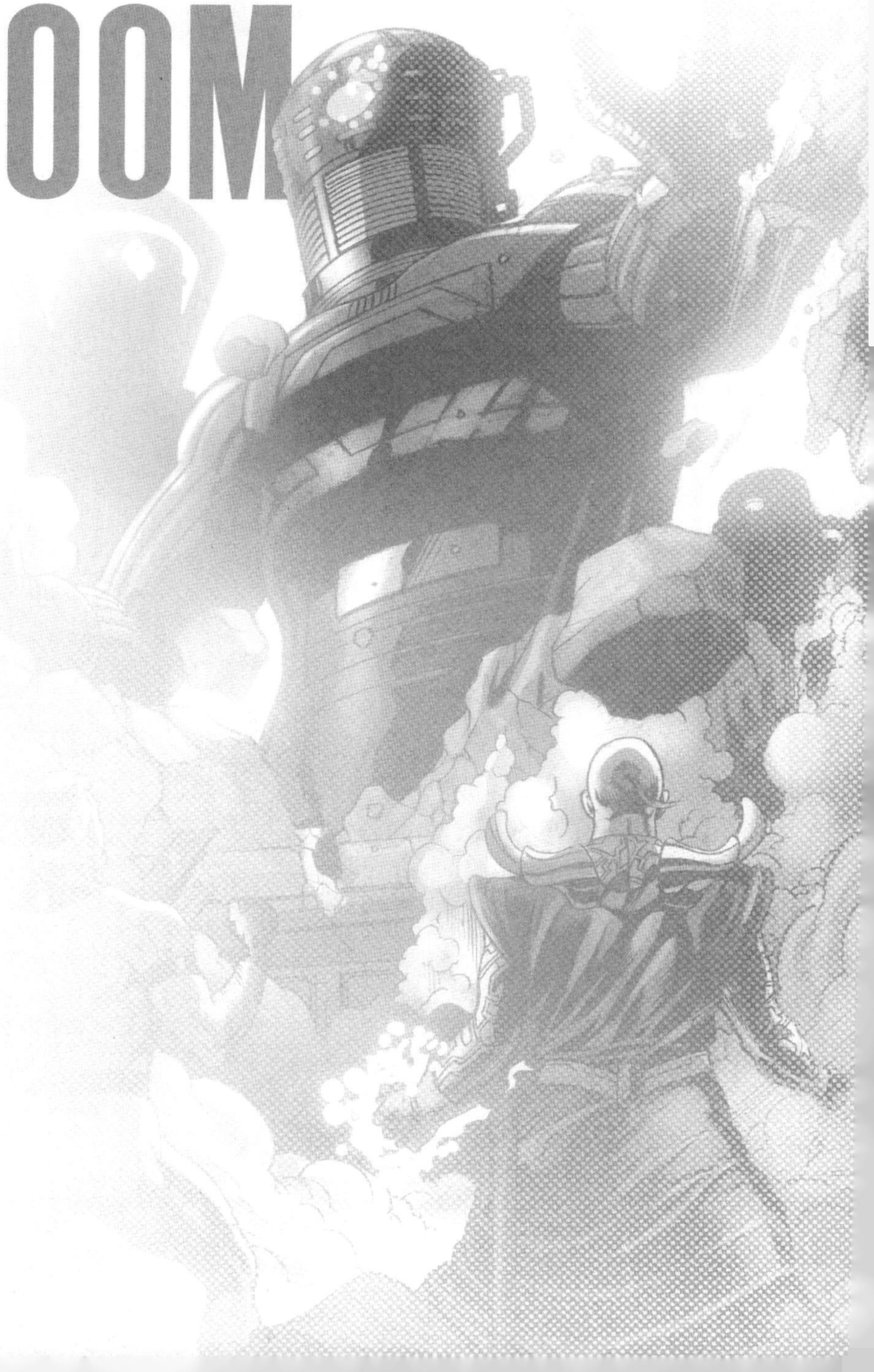

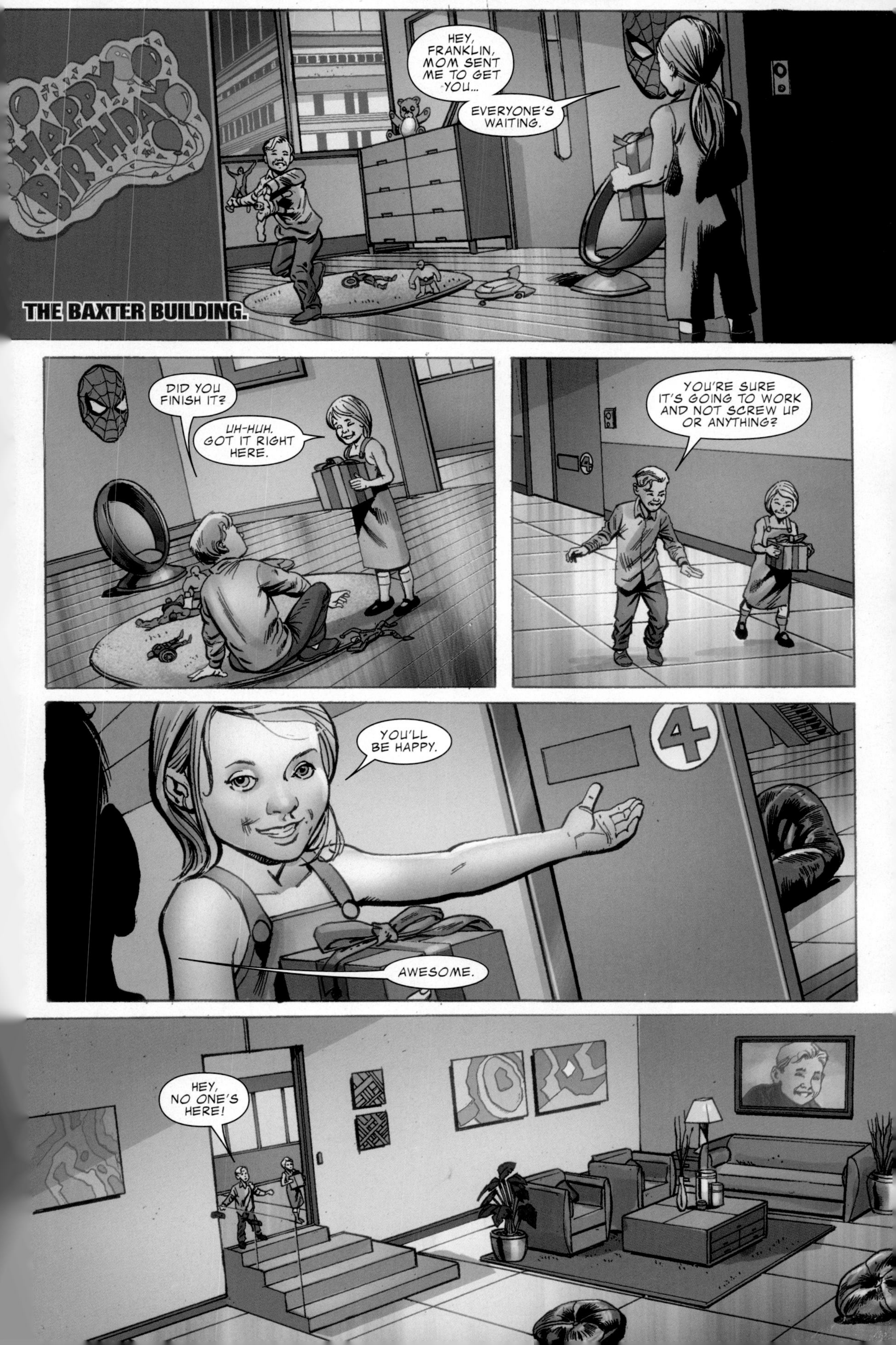
HAPPY BIRTHDAY
THE BAXTER BUILDING.
HEY, FRANKLIN, MOM SENT ME TO GET YOU...
EVERYONE'S WAITING.
DID YOU FINISH IT?
UH-HUH. GOT IT RIGHT HERE.
YOU'RE SURE IT'S GOING TO WORK AND NOT SCREW UP OR ANYTHING?
YOU'LL BE HAPPY.
AWESOME.
HEY, NO ONE'S HERE!

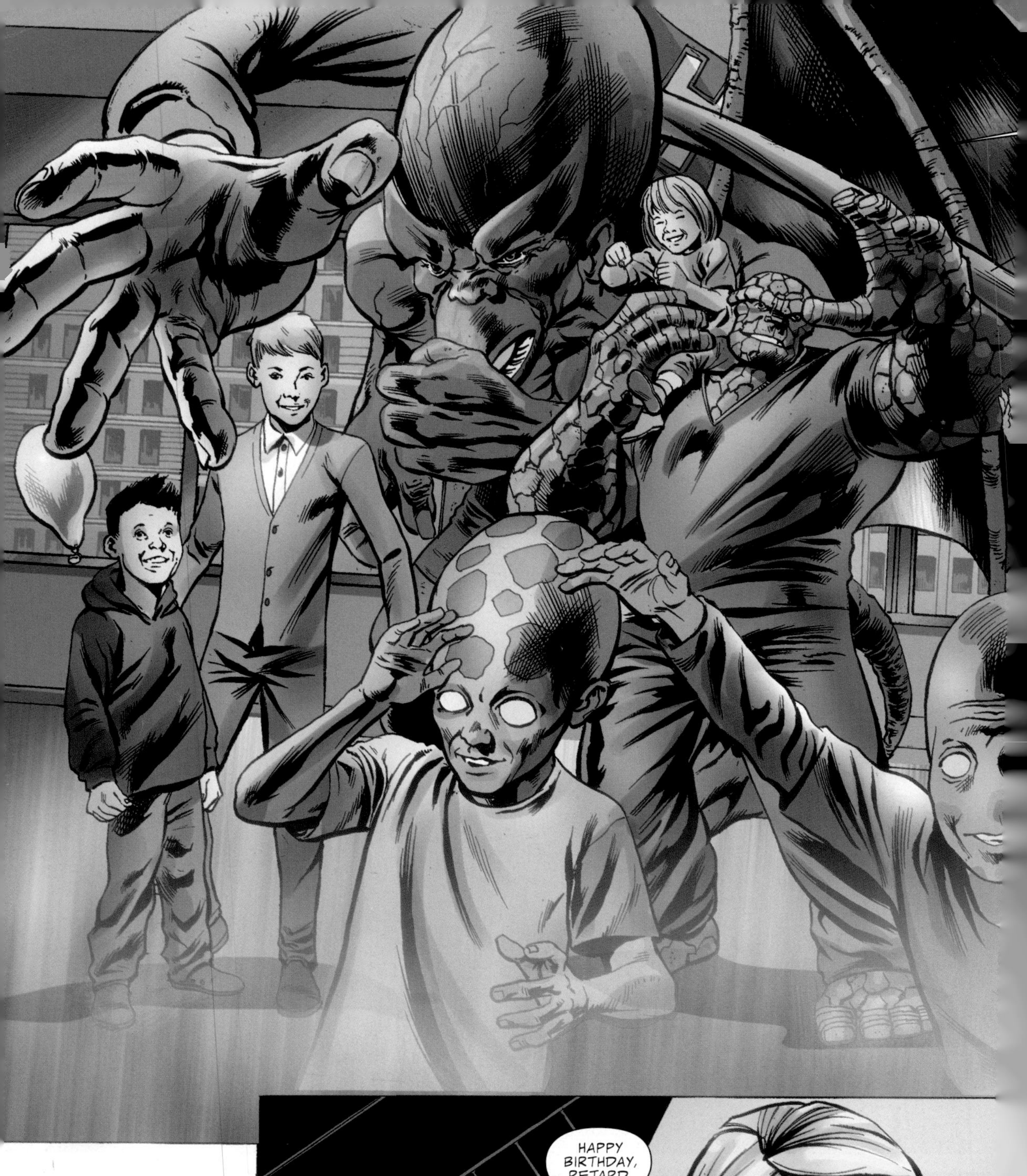

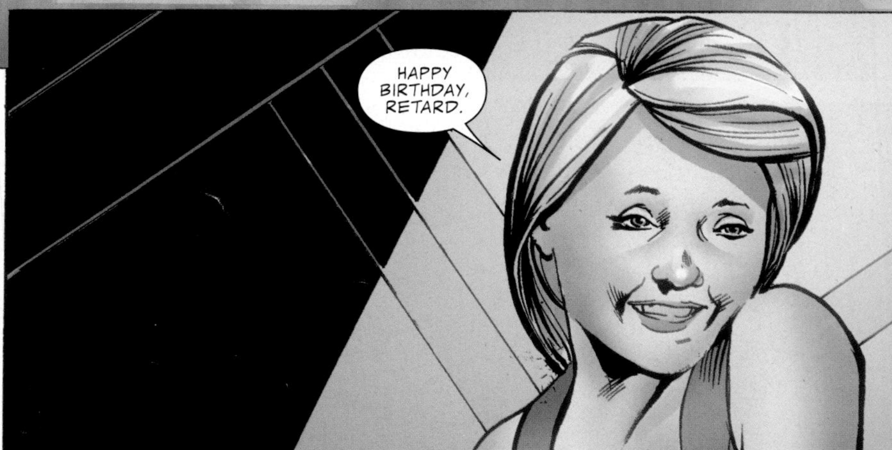
HAPPY BIRTHDAY, RETARD.

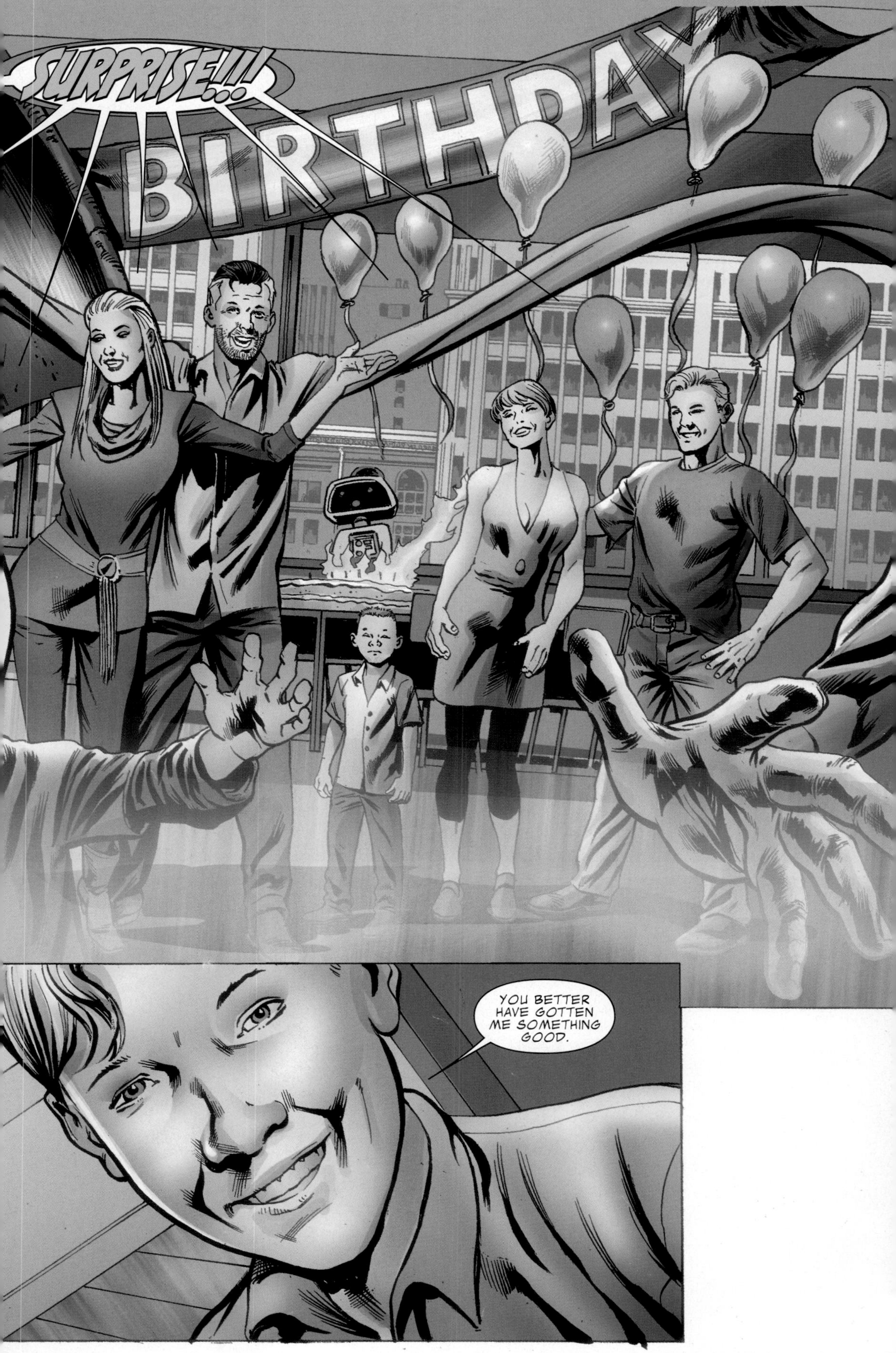
SURPRISE!!!
BIRTHDAY
YOU BETTER HAVE GOTTEN ME SOMETHING GOOD.

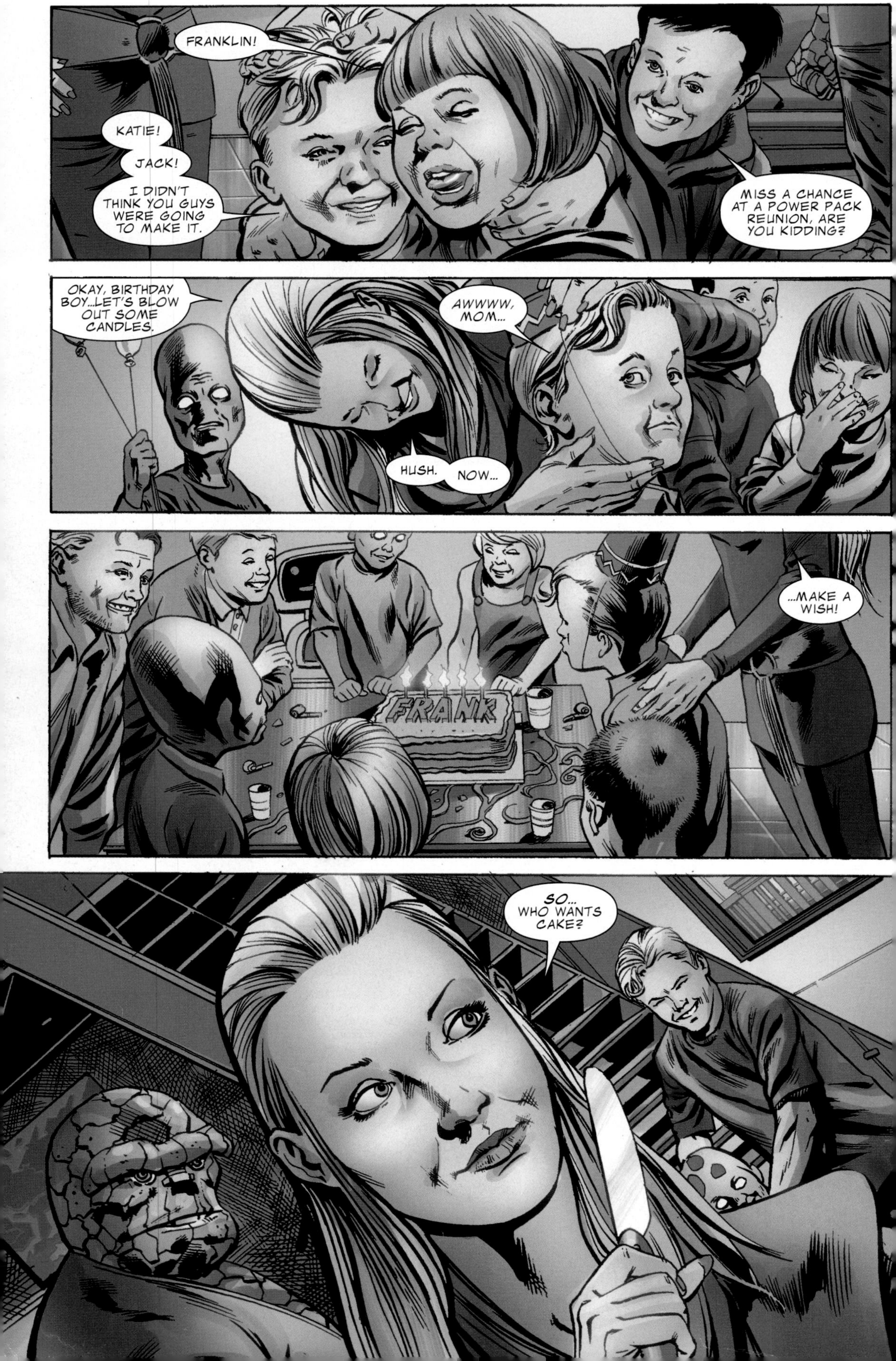
FRANKLIN!
KATIE!
JACK!
I DIDN'T THINK YOU GUYS WERE GOING TO MAKE IT.
MISS A CHANCE AT A POWER PACK REUNION, ARE YOU KIDDING?
OKAY, BIRTHDAY BOY...LET'S BLOW OUT SOME CANDLES.
AWWWW, MOM...
HUSH.
NOW...
FRANK
...MAKE A WISH!
SO... WHO WANTS CAKE?

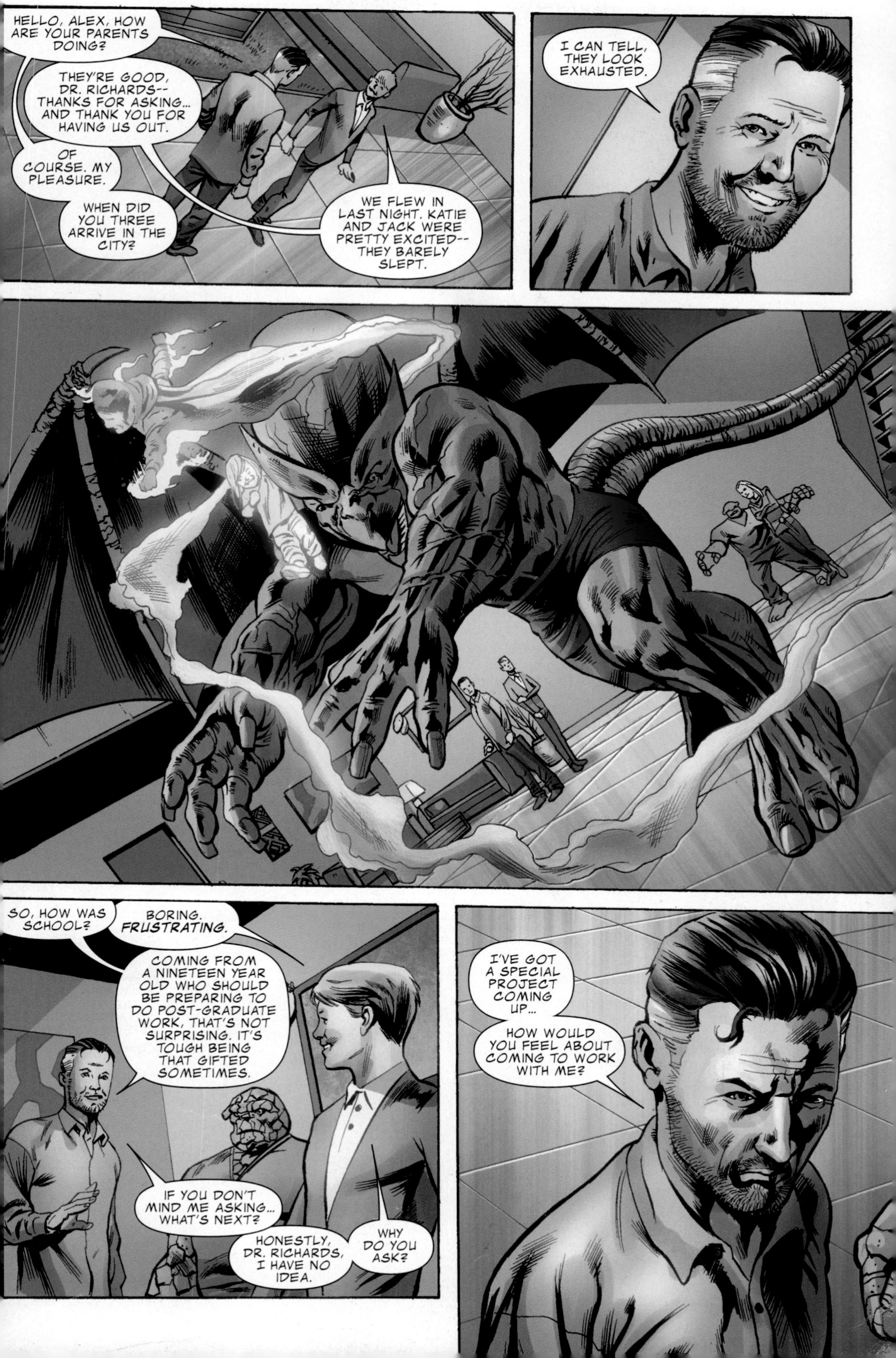
HELLO, ALEX, HOW ARE YOUR PARENTS DOING?
THEY'RE GOOD, DR. RICHARDS-- THANKS FOR ASKING... AND THANK YOU FOR HAVING US OUT.
OF COURSE. MY PLEASURE.
WHEN DID YOU THREE ARRIVE IN THE CITY?
WE FLEW IN LAST NIGHT. KATIE AND JACK WERE PRETTY EXCITED-- THEY BARELY SLEPT.
I CAN TELL, THEY LOOK EXHAUSTED.
SO, HOW WAS SCHOOL?
BORING. *FRUSTRATING.*
COMING FROM A NINETEEN YEAR OLD WHO SHOULD BE PREPARING TO DO POST-GRADUATE WORK, THAT'S NOT SURPRISING. IT'S TOUGH BEING THAT GIFTED SOMETIMES.
IF YOU DON'T MIND ME ASKING... WHAT'S NEXT?
HONESTLY, DR. RICHARDS, I HAVE NO IDEA.
WHY DO YOU ASK?
I'VE GOT A SPECIAL PROJECT COMING UP...
HOW WOULD YOU FEEL ABOUT COMING TO WORK WITH ME?

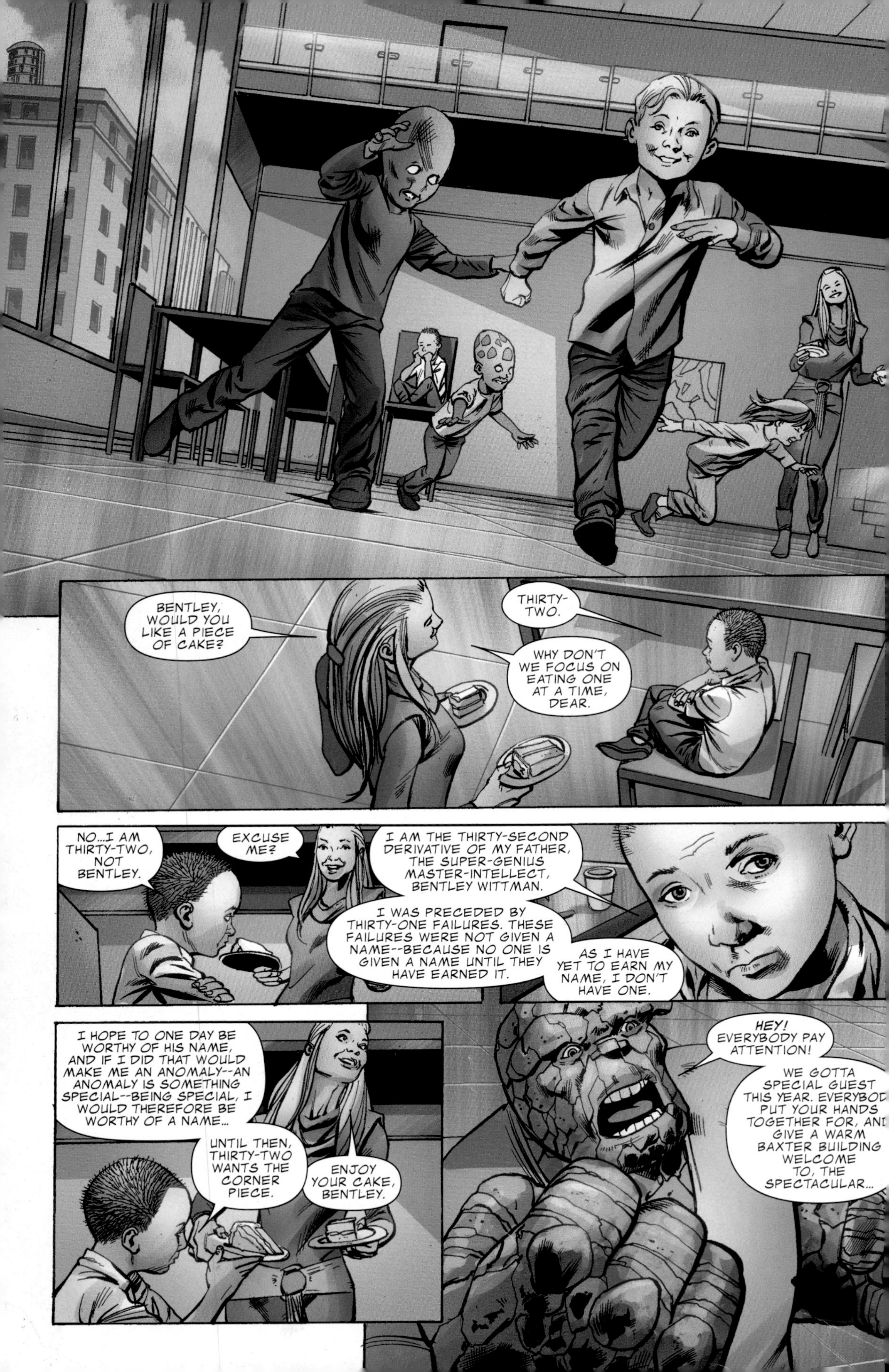
BENTLEY, WOULD YOU LIKE A PIECE OF CAKE?
THIRTY-TWO.
WHY DON'T WE FOCUS ON EATING ONE AT A TIME, DEAR.
NO...I AM THIRTY-TWO, NOT BENTLEY.
EXCUSE ME?
I AM THE THIRTY-SECOND DERIVATIVE OF MY FATHER, THE SUPER-GENIUS MASTER-INTELLECT, BENTLEY WITTMAN.
I WAS PRECEDED BY THIRTY-ONE FAILURES. THESE FAILURES WERE NOT GIVEN A NAME--BECAUSE NO ONE IS GIVEN A NAME UNTIL THEY HAVE EARNED IT.
AS I HAVE YET TO EARN MY NAME, I DON'T HAVE ONE.
I HOPE TO ONE DAY BE WORTHY OF HIS NAME, AND IF I DID THAT WOULD MAKE ME AN ANOMALY--AN ANOMALY IS SOMETHING SPECIAL--BEING SPECIAL, I WOULD THEREFORE BE WORTHY OF A NAME...
UNTIL THEN, THIRTY-TWO WANTS THE CORNER PIECE.
ENJOY YOUR CAKE, BENTLEY.
HEY! EVERYBODY PAY ATTENTION!
WE GOTTA SPECIAL GUEST THIS YEAR. EVERYBOD PUT YOUR HANDS TOGETHER FOR, ANI GIVE A WARM BAXTER BUILDING WELCOME TO, THE SPECTACULAR...

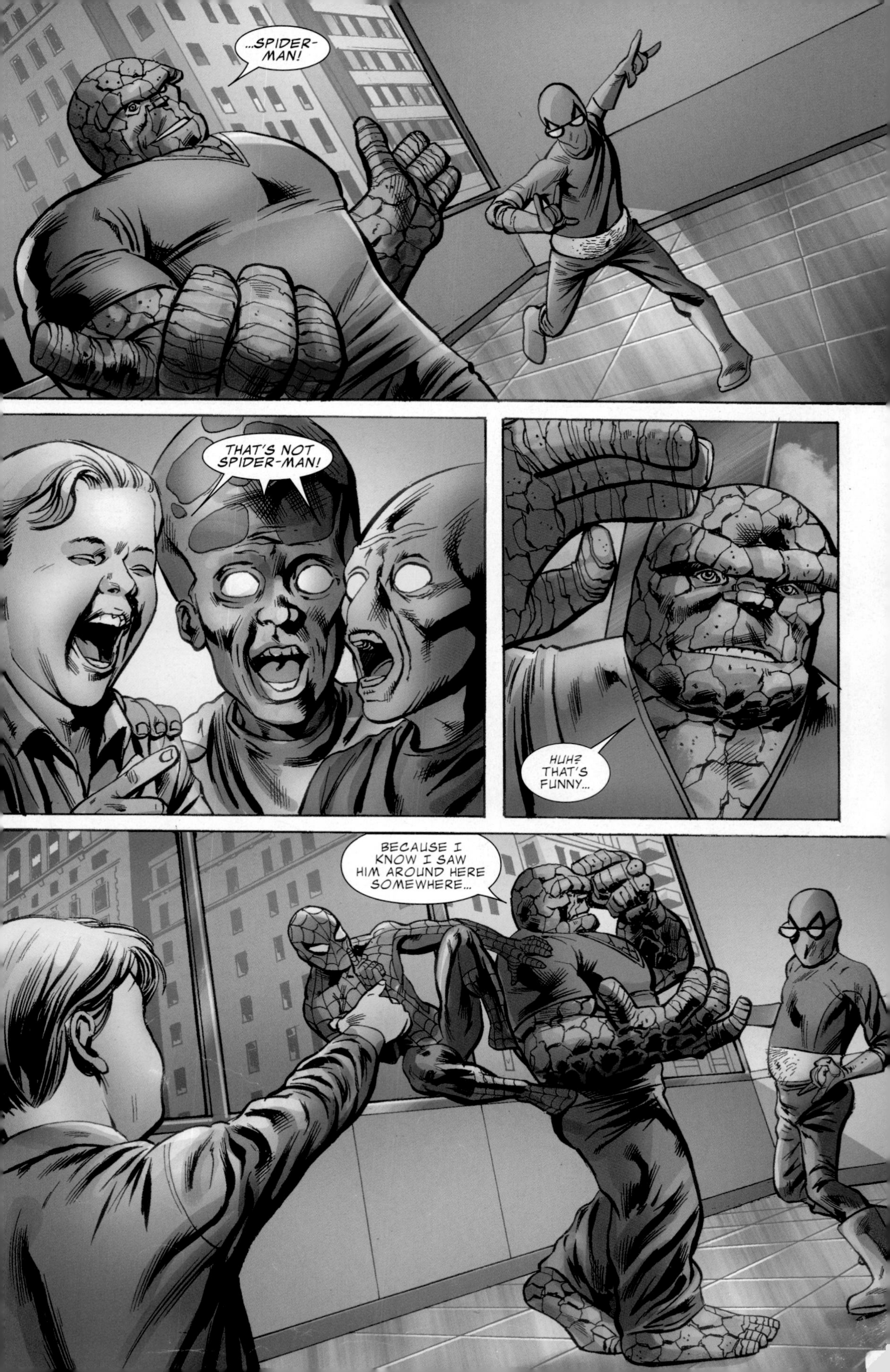
...SPIDER-MAN!
THAT'S NOT SPIDER-MAN!
HUH? THAT'S FUNNY...
BECAUSE I KNOW I SAW HIM AROUND HERE SOMEWHERE...

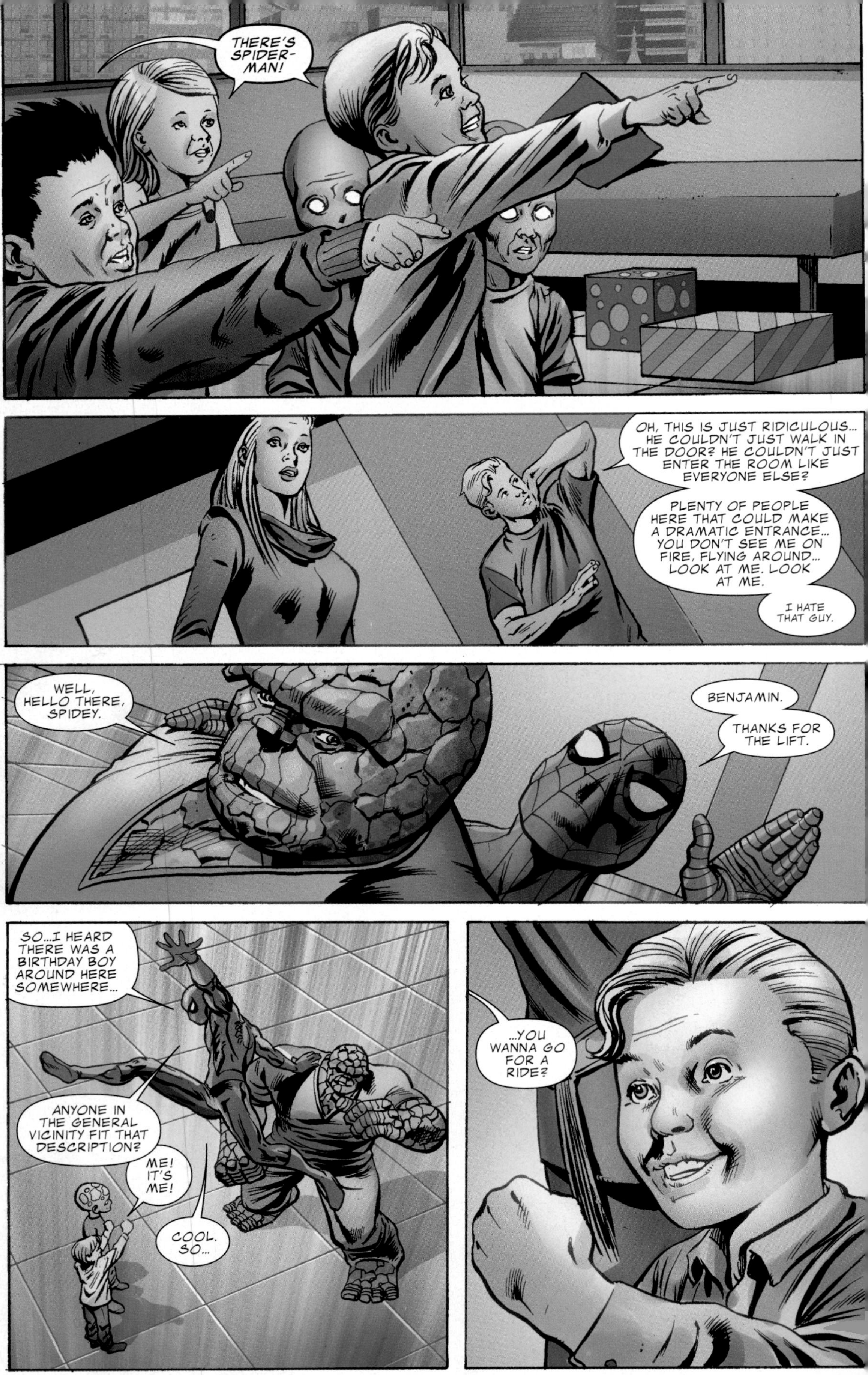
THERE'S SPIDER-MAN!
OH, THIS IS JUST RIDICULOUS... HE COULDN'T JUST WALK IN THE DOOR? HE COULDN'T JUST ENTER THE ROOM LIKE EVERYONE ELSE?
PLENTY OF PEOPLE HERE THAT COULD MAKE A DRAMATIC ENTRANCE... YOU DON'T SEE ME ON FIRE, FLYING AROUND... LOOK AT ME. LOOK AT ME.
I HATE THAT GUY.
WELL, HELLO THERE, SPIDEY.
BENJAMIN.
THANKS FOR THE LIFT.
SO...I HEARD THERE WAS A BIRTHDAY BOY AROUND HERE SOMEWHERE...
ANYONE IN THE GENERAL VICINITY FIT THAT DESCRIPTION?
ME! IT'S ME!
COOL. SO...
...YOU WANNA GO FOR A RIDE?

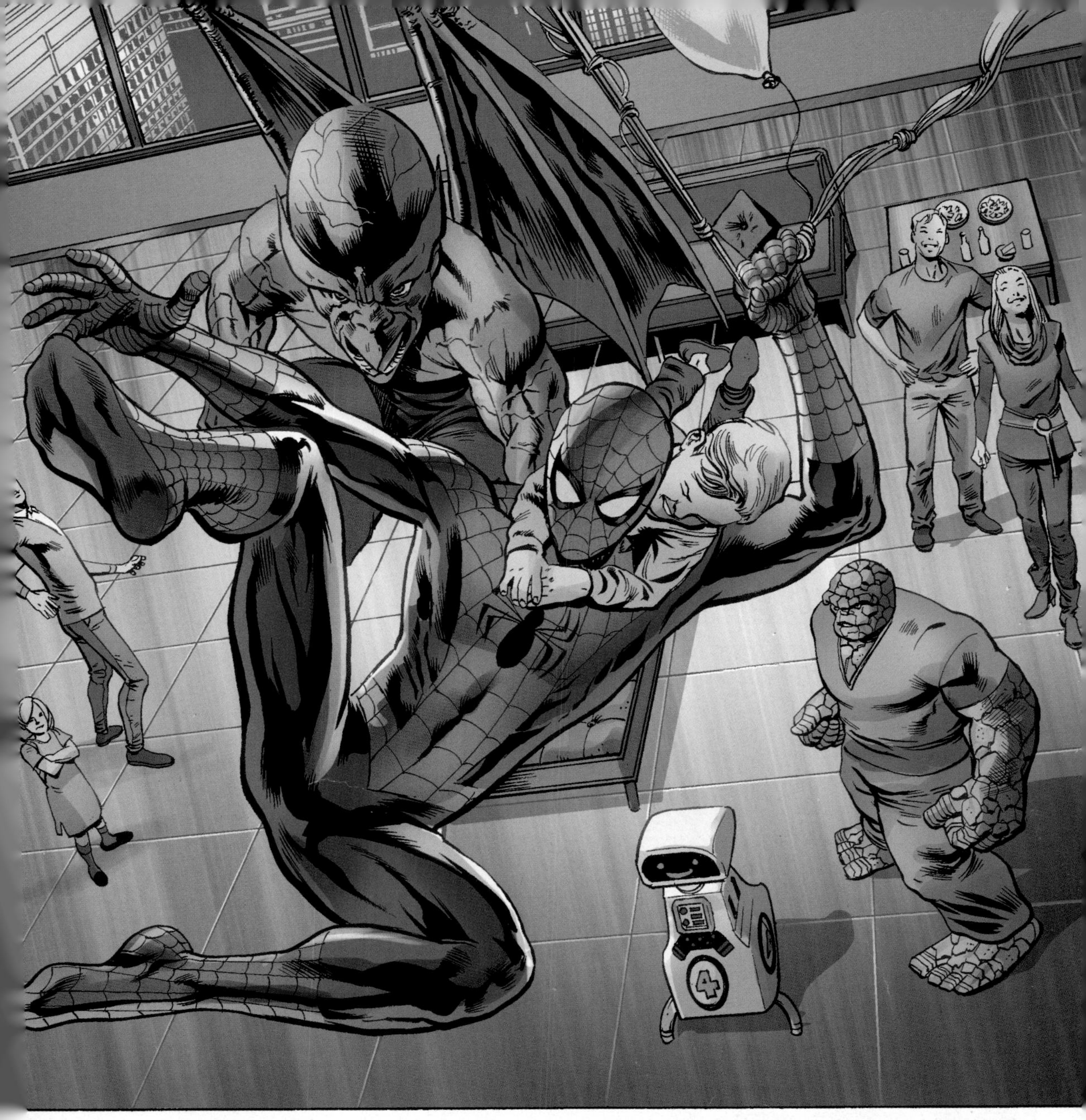

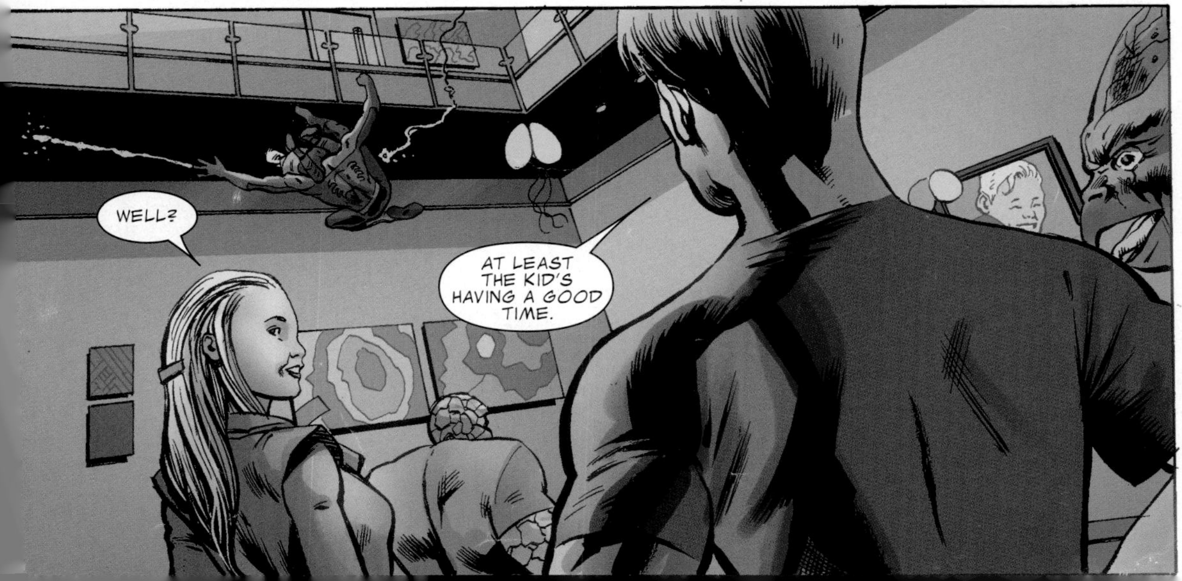
WELL?
AT LEAST THE KID'S HAVING A GOOD TIME.

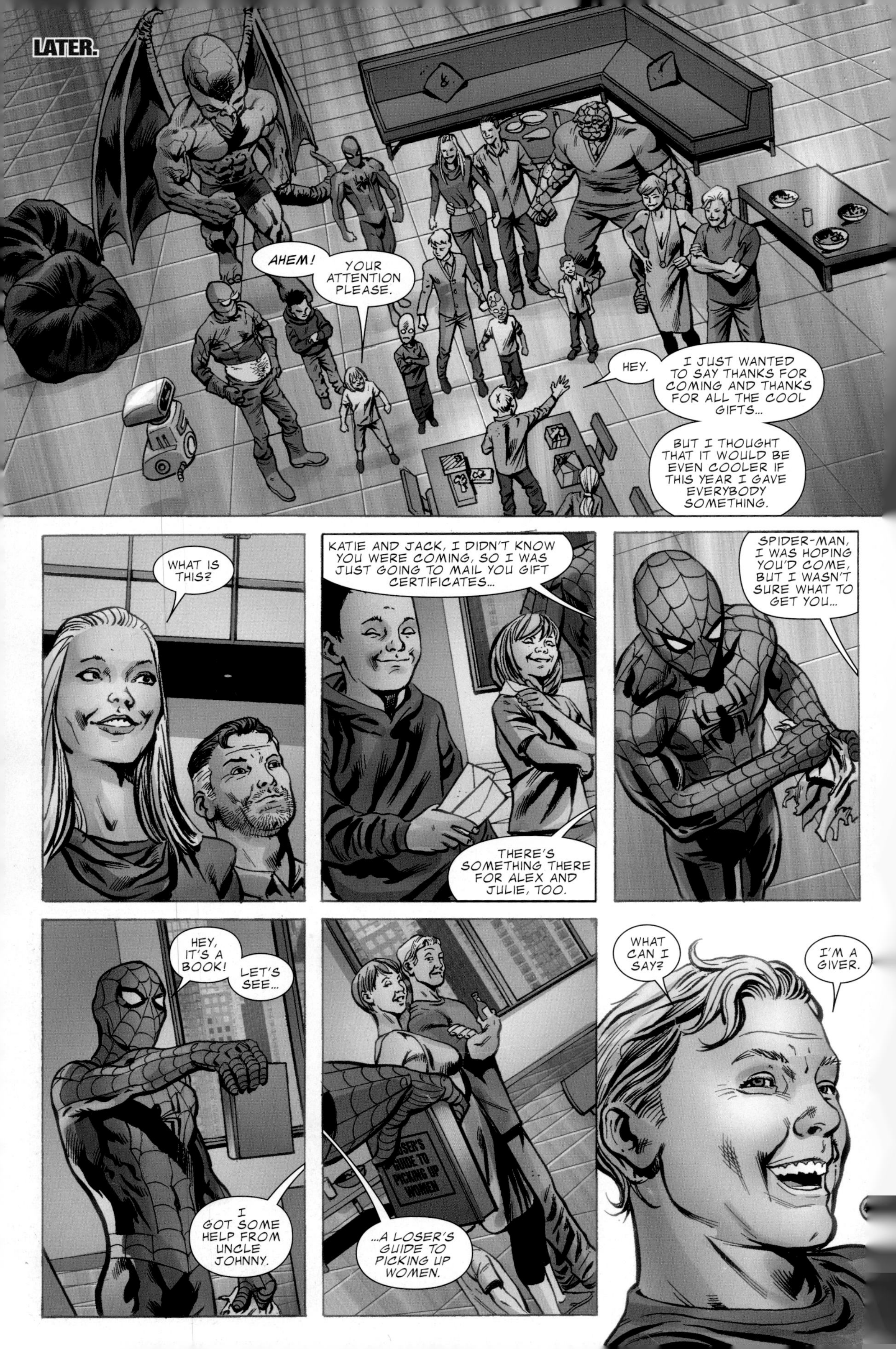
LATER.
AHEM!
YOUR ATTENTION PLEASE.
HEY.
I JUST WANTED TO SAY THANKS FOR COMING AND THANKS FOR ALL THE COOL GIFTS...
BUT I THOUGHT THAT IT WOULD BE EVEN COOLER IF THIS YEAR I GAVE EVERYBODY SOMETHING.
WHAT IS THIS?
KATIE AND JACK, I DIDN'T KNOW YOU WERE COMING, SO I WAS JUST GOING TO MAIL YOU GIFT CERTIFICATES...
THERE'S SOMETHING THERE FOR ALEX AND JULIE, TOO.
SPIDER-MAN, I WAS HOPING YOU'D COME, BUT I WASN'T SURE WHAT TO GET YOU...
HEY, IT'S A BOOK!
LET'S SEE...
I GOT SOME HELP FROM UNCLE JOHNNY.
LOSER'S GUIDE TO PICKING UP WOMEN
...A LOSER'S GUIDE TO PICKING UP WOMEN.
WHAT CAN I SAY?
I'M A GIVER.

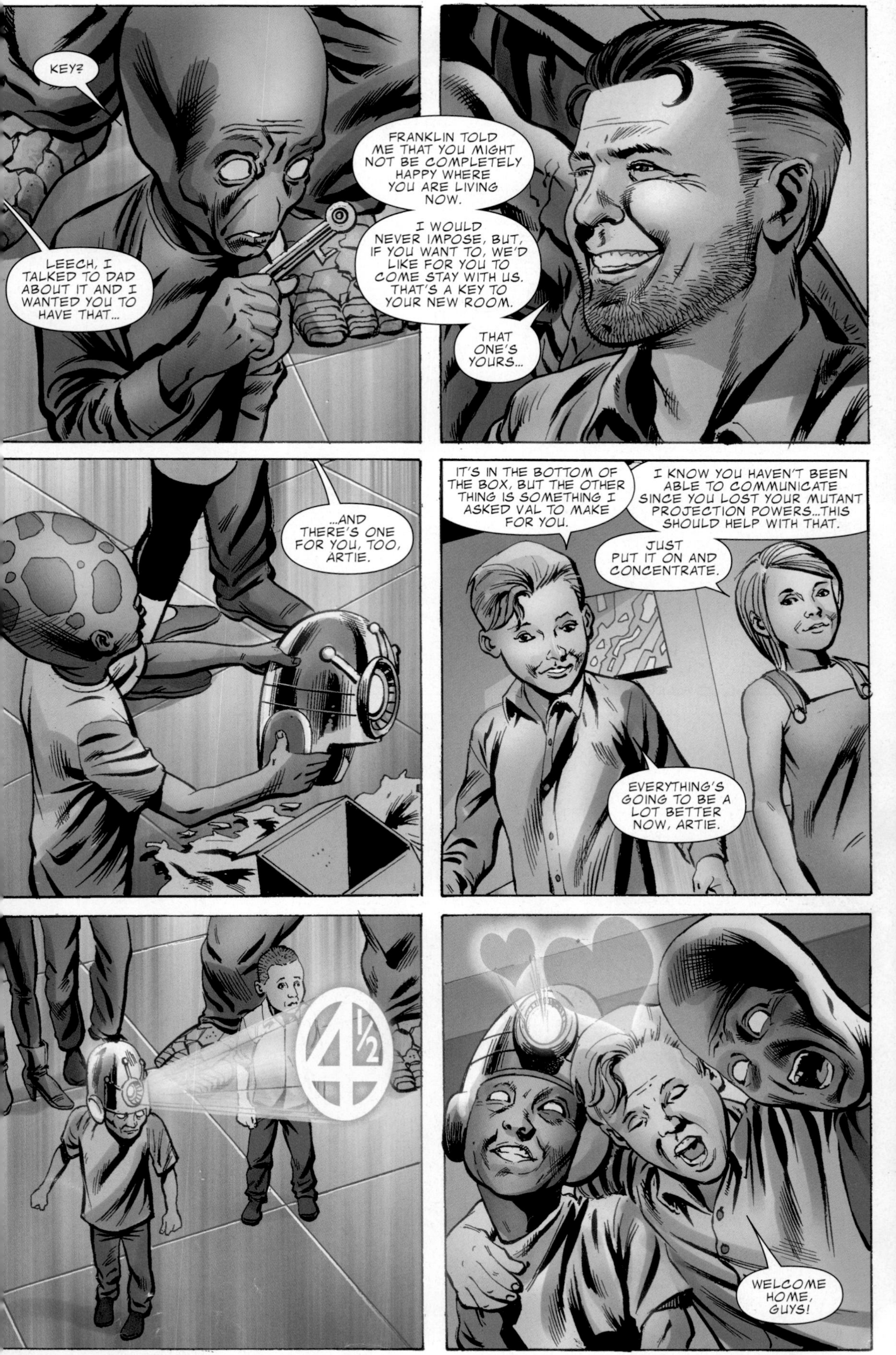
KEY?
LEECH, I TALKED TO DAD ABOUT IT AND I WANTED YOU TO HAVE THAT...
FRANKLIN TOLD ME THAT YOU MIGHT NOT BE COMPLETELY HAPPY WHERE YOU ARE LIVING NOW.
I WOULD NEVER IMPOSE, BUT, IF YOU WANT TO, WE'D LIKE FOR YOU TO COME STAY WITH US. THAT'S A KEY TO YOUR NEW ROOM.
THAT ONE'S YOURS...
...AND THERE'S ONE FOR YOU, TOO, ARTIE.
IT'S IN THE BOTTOM OF THE BOX, BUT THE OTHER THING IS SOMETHING I ASKED VAL TO MAKE FOR YOU.
I KNOW YOU HAVEN'T BEEN ABLE TO COMMUNICATE SINCE YOU LOST YOUR MUTANT PROJECTION POWERS...THIS SHOULD HELP WITH THAT.
JUST PUT IT ON AND CONCENTRATE.
EVERYTHING'S GOING TO BE A LOT BETTER NOW, ARTIE.
4 1/2
WELCOME HOME, GUYS!

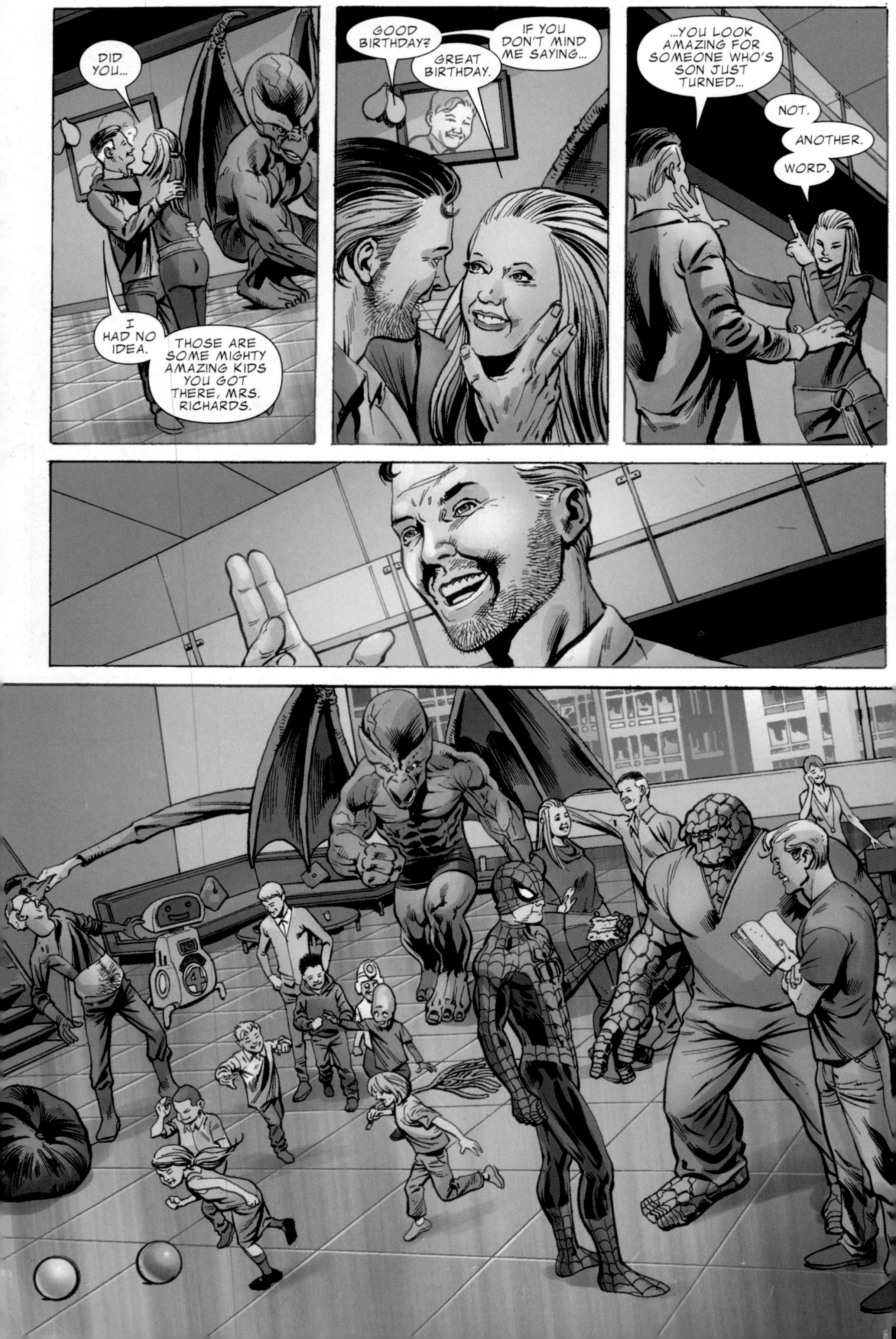
DID YOU...
I HAD NO IDEA.
THOSE ARE SOME MIGHTY AMAZING KIDS YOU GOT THERE, MRS. RICHARDS.
GOOD BIRTHDAY?
GREAT BIRTHDAY.
IF YOU DON'T MIND ME SAYING...
...YOU LOOK AMAZING FOR SOMEONE WHO'S SON JUST TURNED...
NOT.
ANOTHER.
WORD.

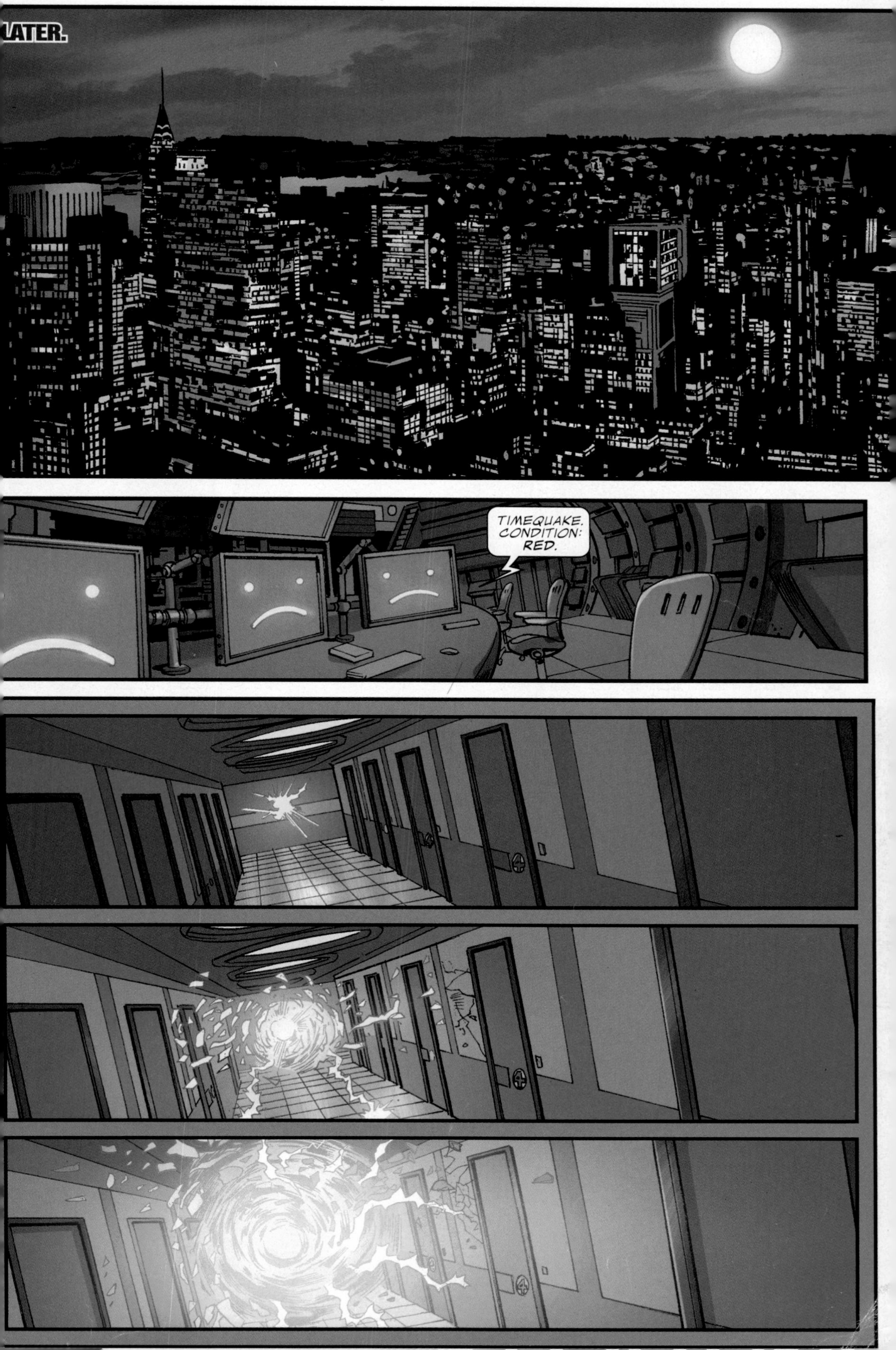
LATER.
TIMEQUAKE. CONDITION: RED.

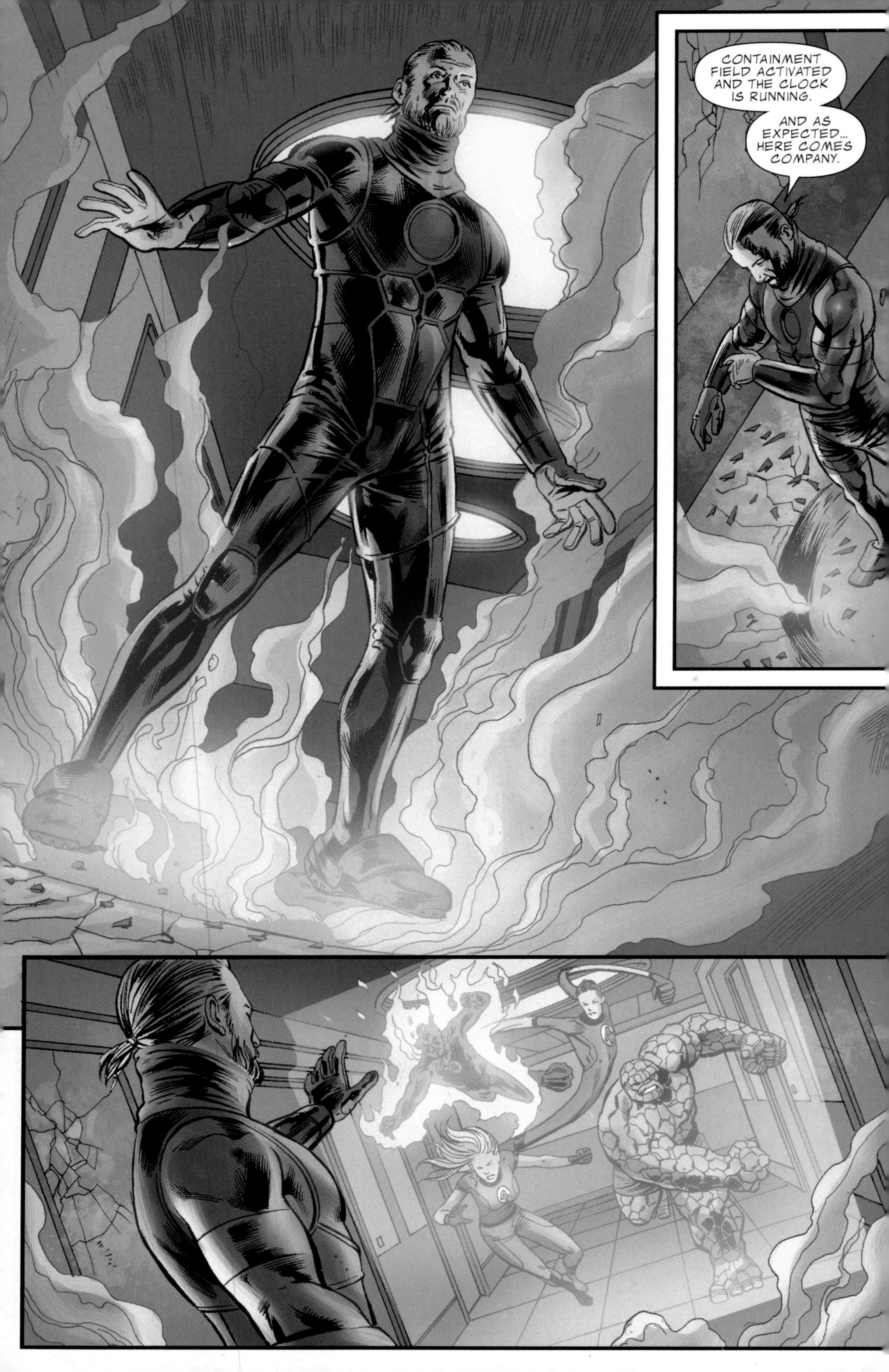
CONTAINMENT FIELD ACTIVATED AND THE CLOCK IS RUNNING.
AND AS EXPECTED... HERE COMES COMPANY.

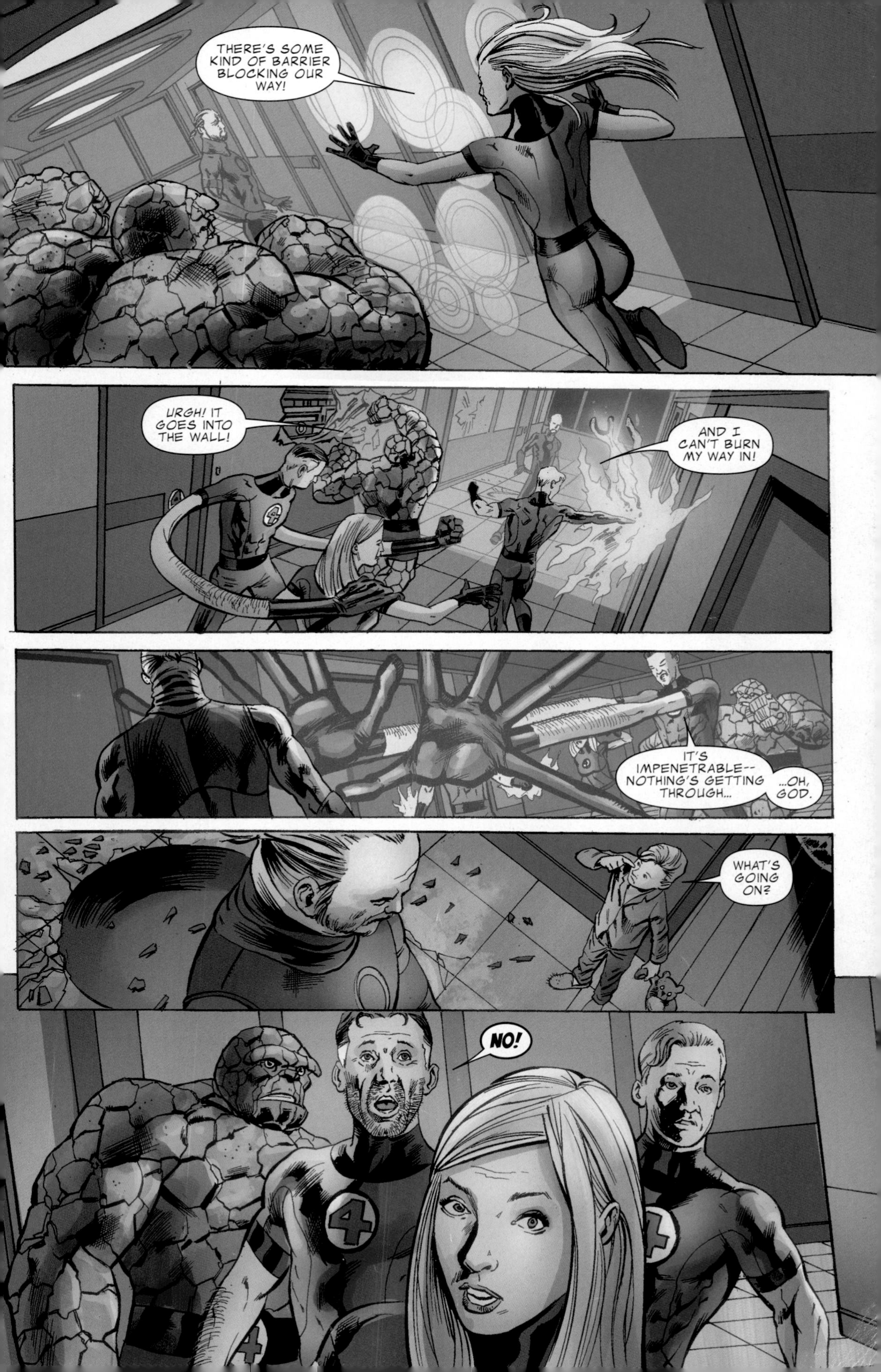
THERE'S SOME KIND OF BARRIER BLOCKING OUR WAY!
URGH! IT GOES INTO THE WALL!
AND I CAN'T BURN MY WAY IN!
IT'S IMPENETRABLE-- NOTHING'S GETTING THROUGH...
...OH, GOD.
WHAT'S GOING ON?
NO!

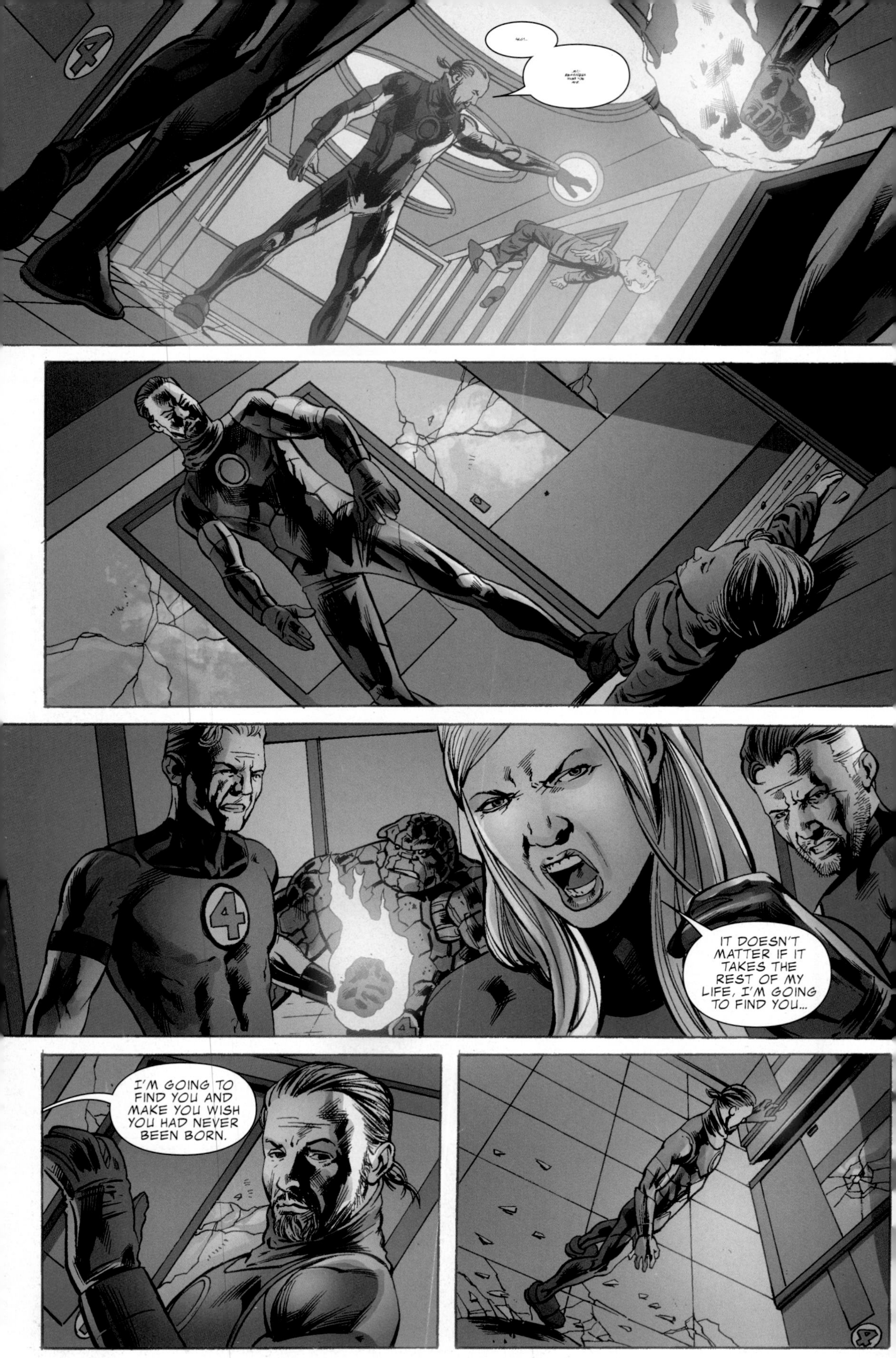
IT DOESN'T MATTER IF IT TAKES THE REST OF MY LIFE, I'M GOING TO FIND YOU...
I'M GOING TO FIND YOU AND MAKE YOU WISH YOU HAD NEVER BEEN BORN.

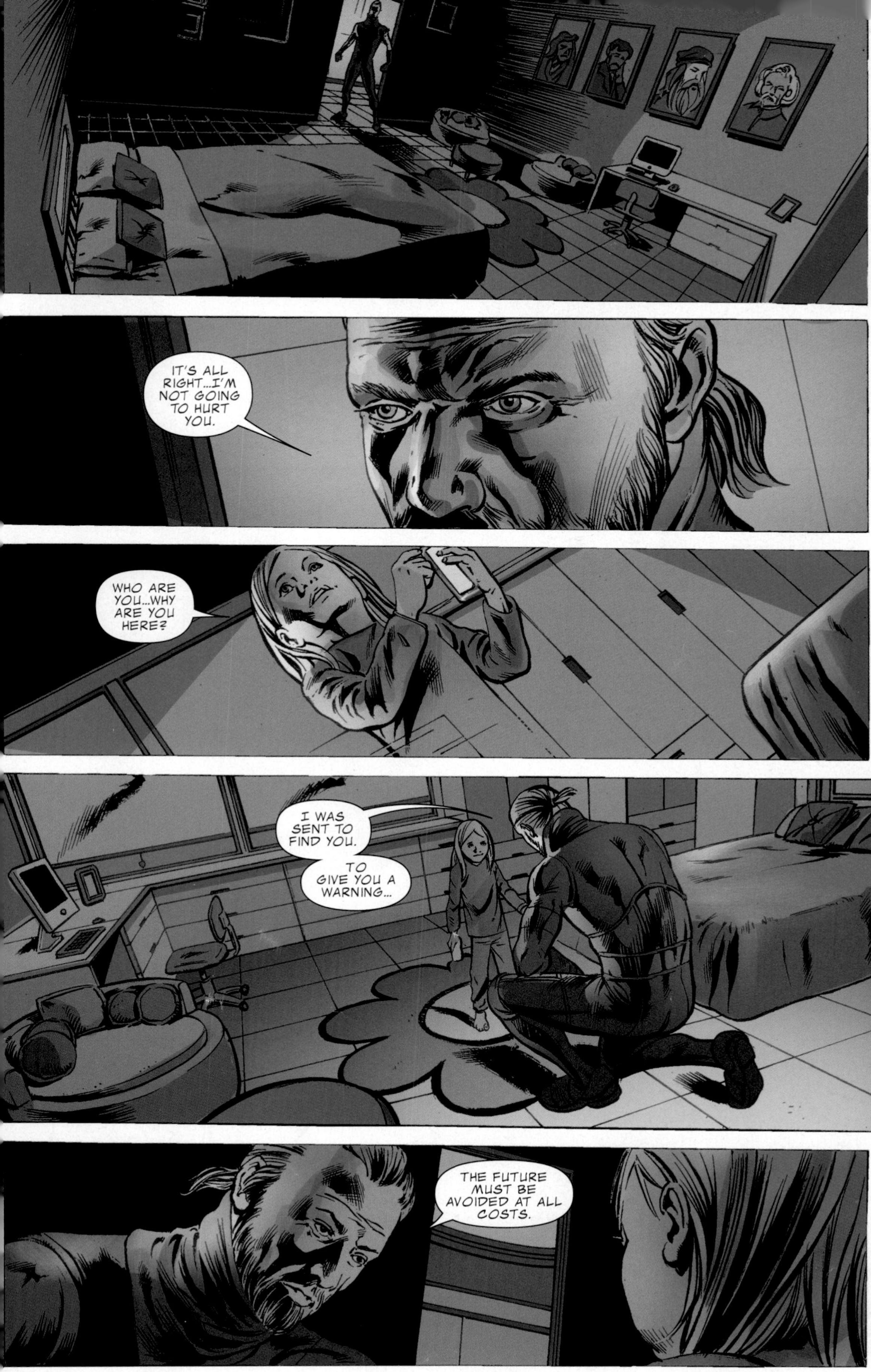
IT'S ALL RIGHT...I'M NOT GOING TO HURT YOU.
WHO ARE YOU...WHY ARE YOU HERE?
I WAS SENT TO FIND YOU.
TO GIVE YOU A WARNING...
THE FUTURE MUST BE AVOIDED AT ALL COSTS.

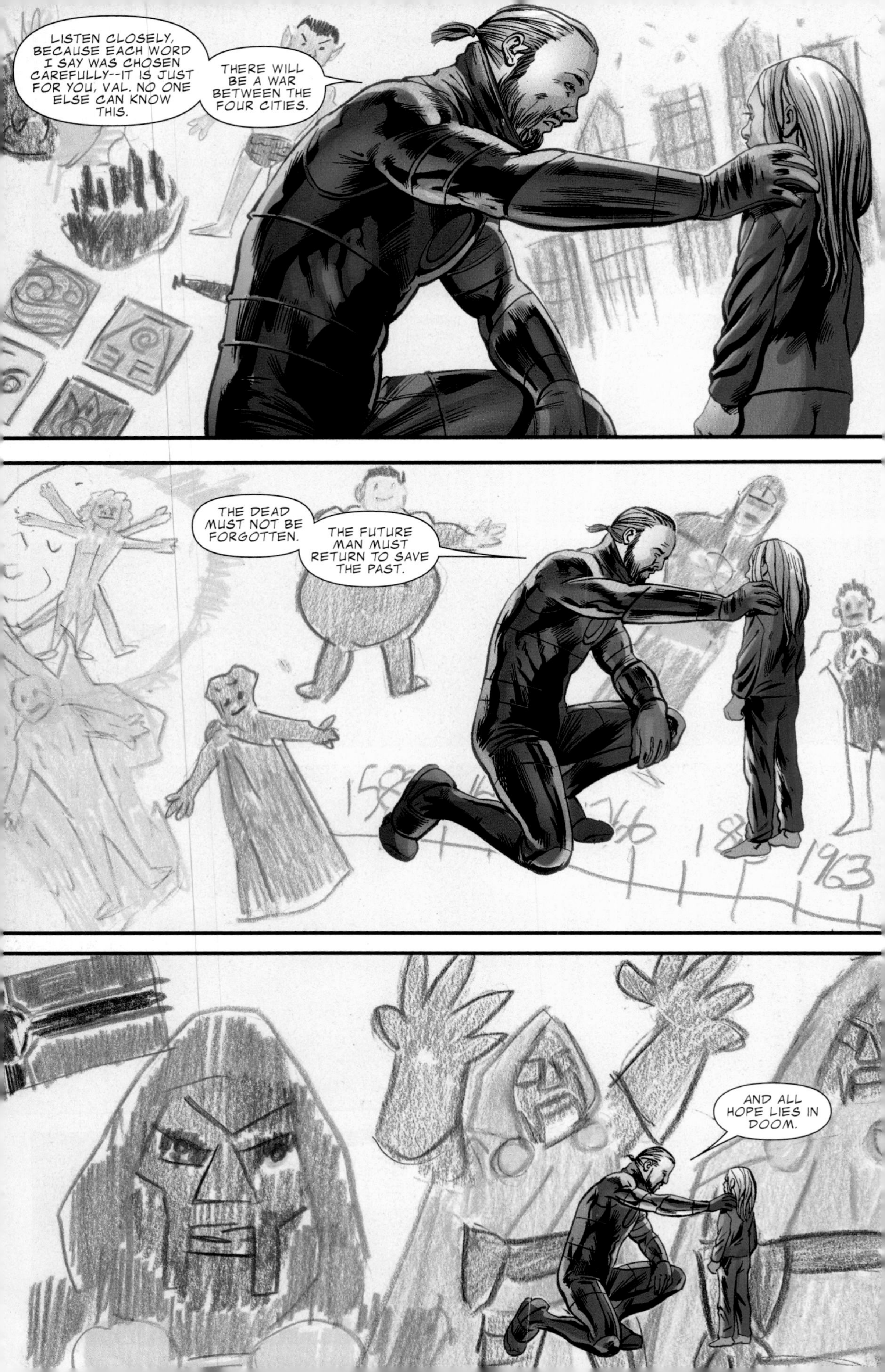
LISTEN CLOSELY, BECAUSE EACH WORD I SAY WAS CHOSEN CAREFULLY--IT IS JUST FOR YOU, VAL. NO ONE ELSE CAN KNOW THIS.
THERE WILL BE A WAR BETWEEN THE FOUR CITIES.
THE DEAD MUST NOT BE FORGOTTEN.
THE FUTURE MAN MUST RETURN TO SAVE THE PAST.
1963
AND ALL HOPE LIES IN DOOM.

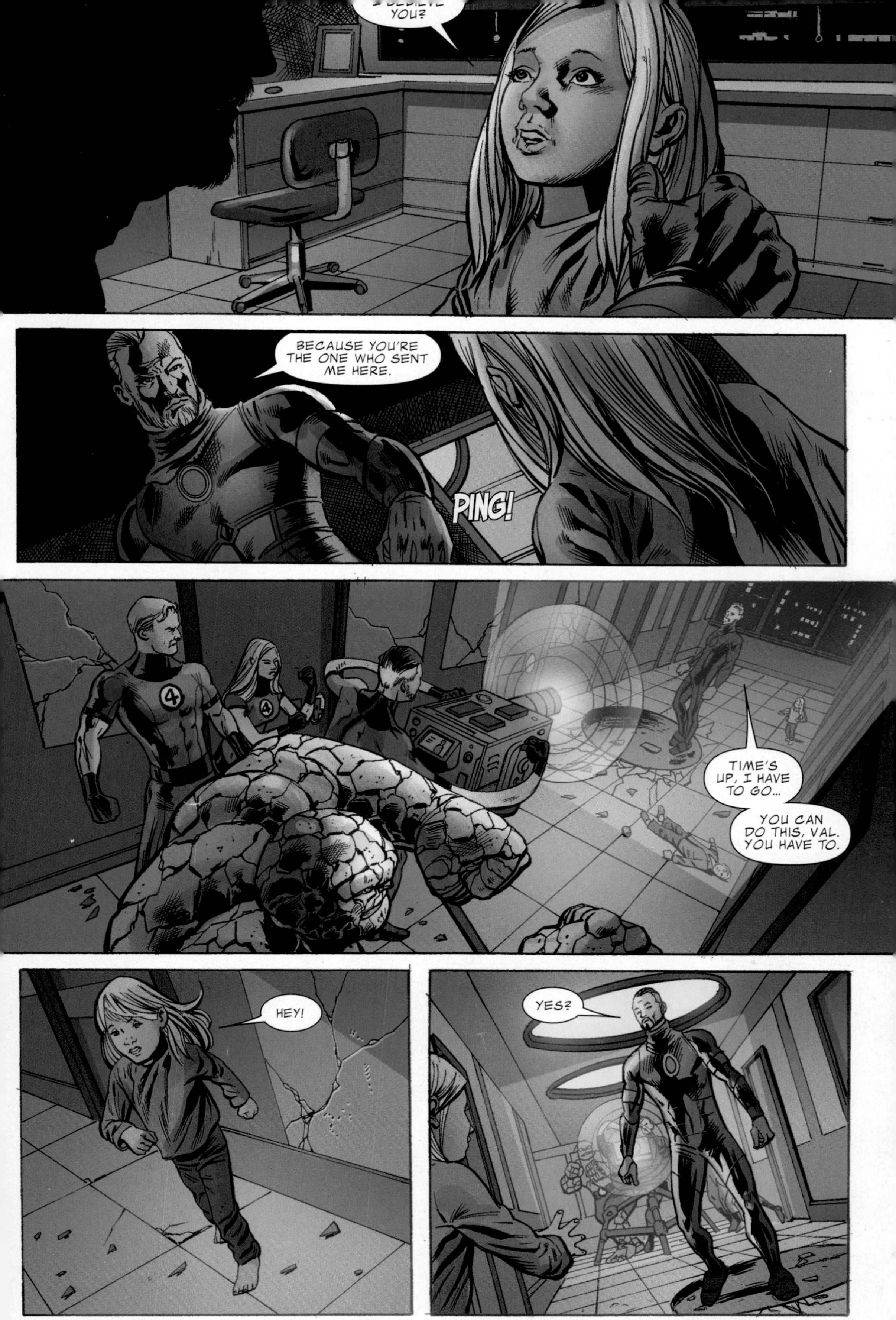
YOU?
BECAUSE YOU'RE THE ONE WHO SENT ME HERE.
PING!
TIME'S UP, I HAVE TO GO...
YOU CAN DO THIS, VAL. YOU HAVE TO.
HEY!
YES?

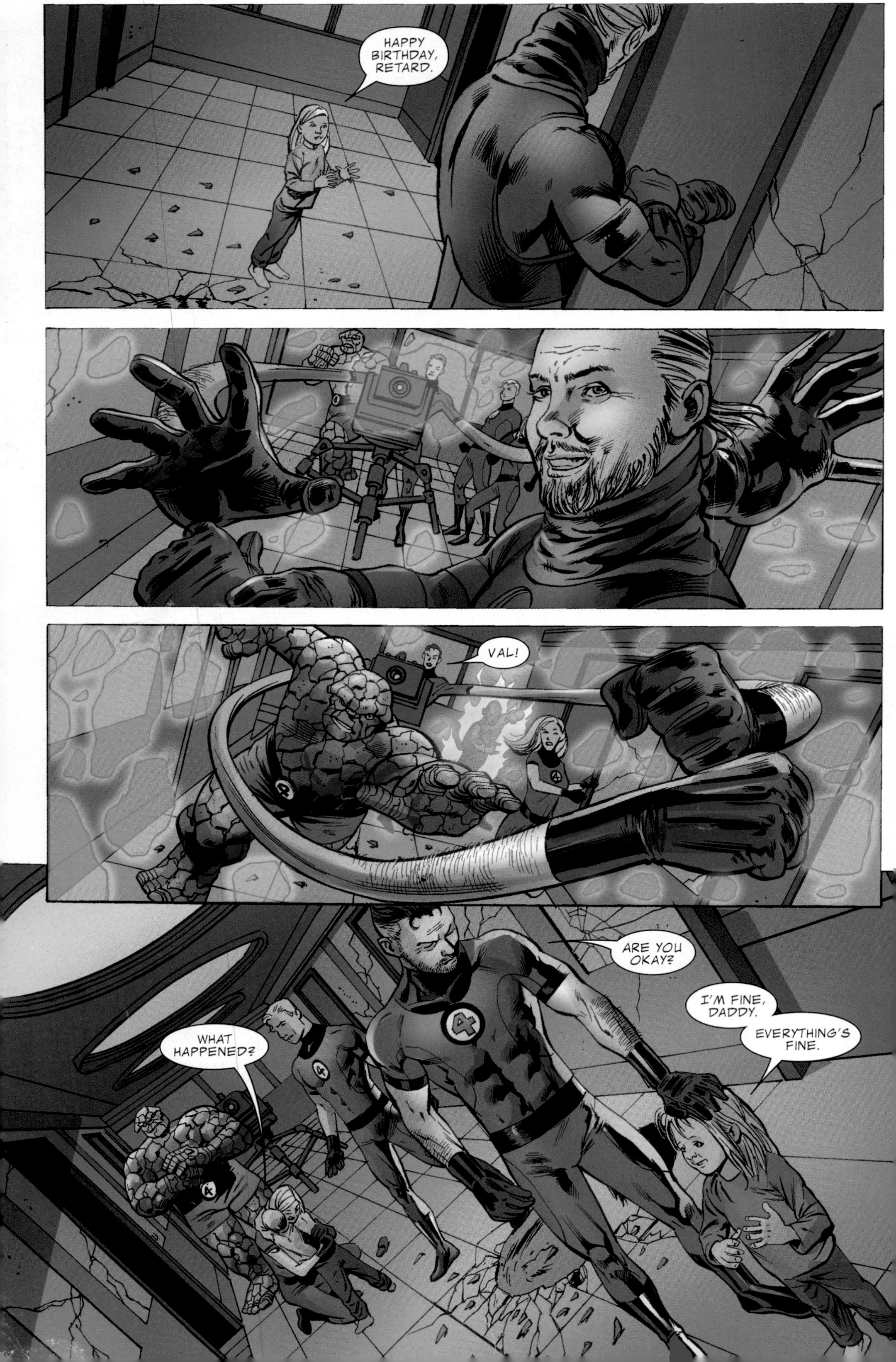
HAPPY BIRTHDAY, RETARD.
VAL!
ARE YOU OKAY?
WHAT HAPPENED?
I'M FINE, DADDY.
EVERYTHING'S FINE.

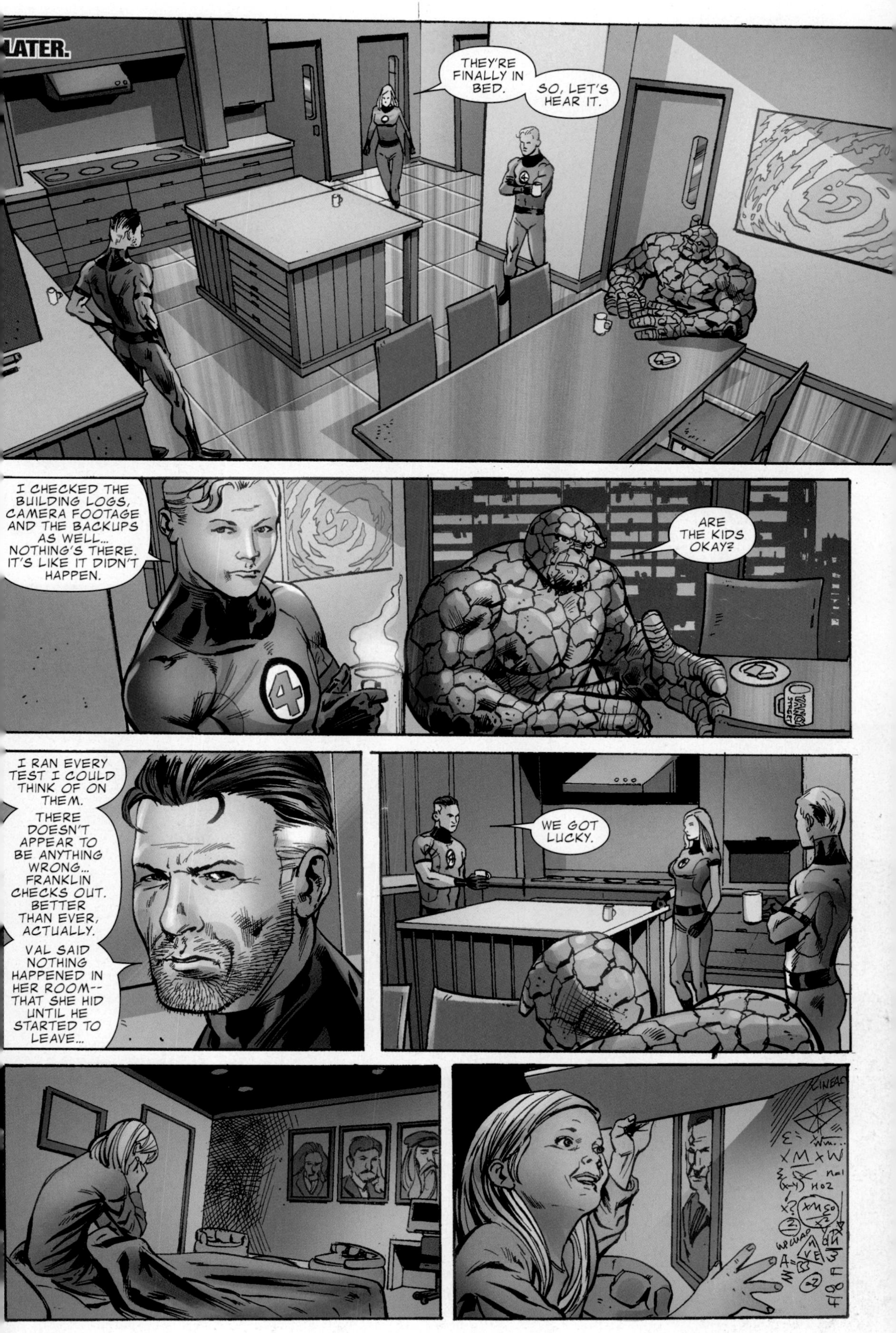
LATER.
THEY'RE FINALLY IN BED.
SO, LET'S HEAR IT.
I CHECKED THE BUILDING LOGS, CAMERA FOOTAGE AND THE BACKUPS AS WELL... NOTHING'S THERE. IT'S LIKE IT DIDN'T HAPPEN.
ARE THE KIDS OKAY?
I RAN EVERY TEST I COULD THINK OF ON THEM.
THERE DOESN'T APPEAR TO BE ANYTHING WRONG... FRANKLIN CHECKS OUT. BETTER THAN EVER, ACTUALLY.
VAL SAID NOTHING HAPPENED IN HER ROOM-- THAT SHE HID UNTIL HE STARTED TO LEAVE...
WE GOT LUCKY.

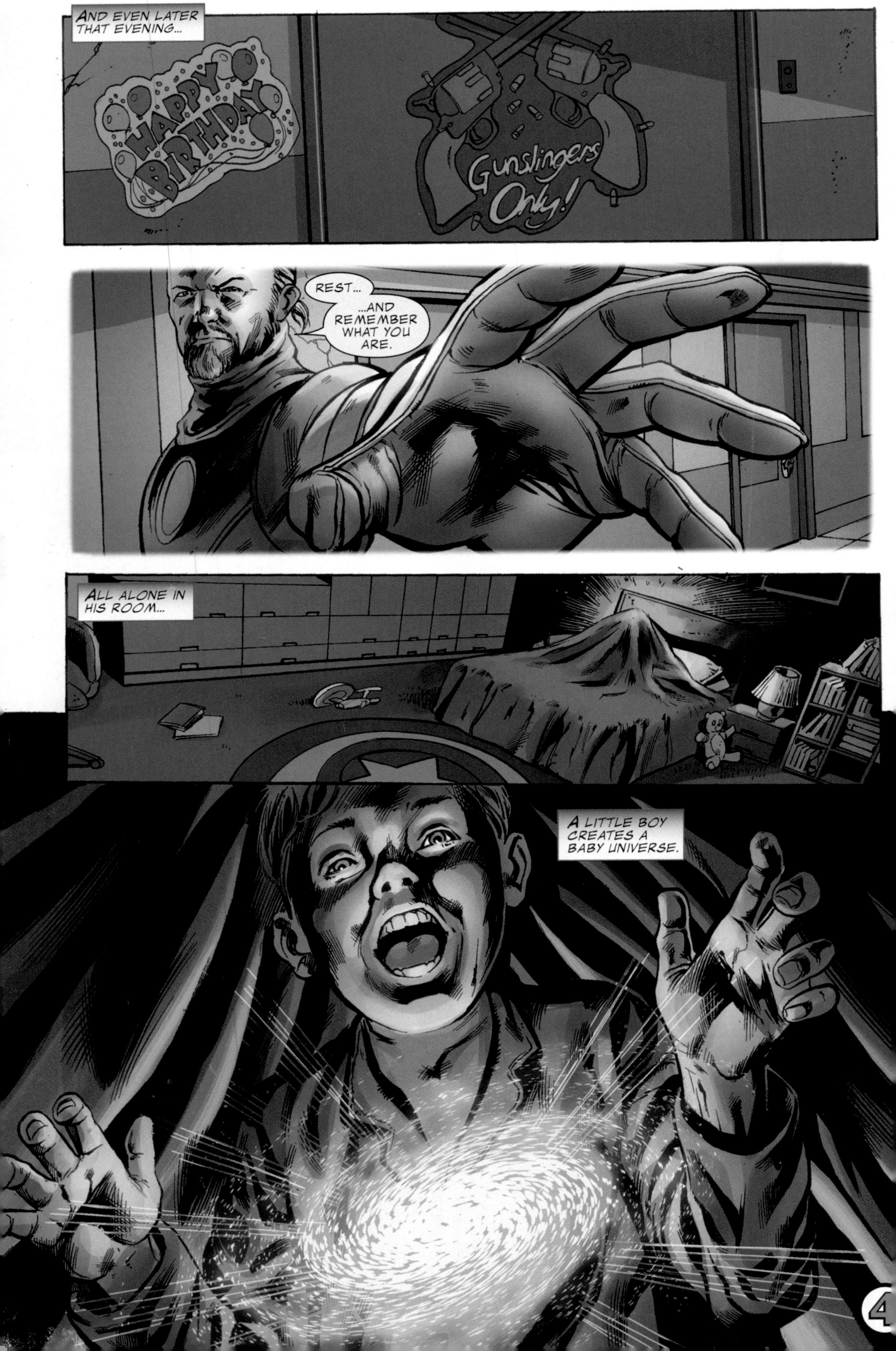
AND EVEN LATER THAT EVENING...
HAPPY BIRTHDAY
Gunslingers Only!
REST...
...AND REMEMBER WHAT YOU ARE.
ALL ALONE IN HIS ROOM...
A LITTLE BOY CREATES A BABY UNIVERSE.
4

COVER GALLERY

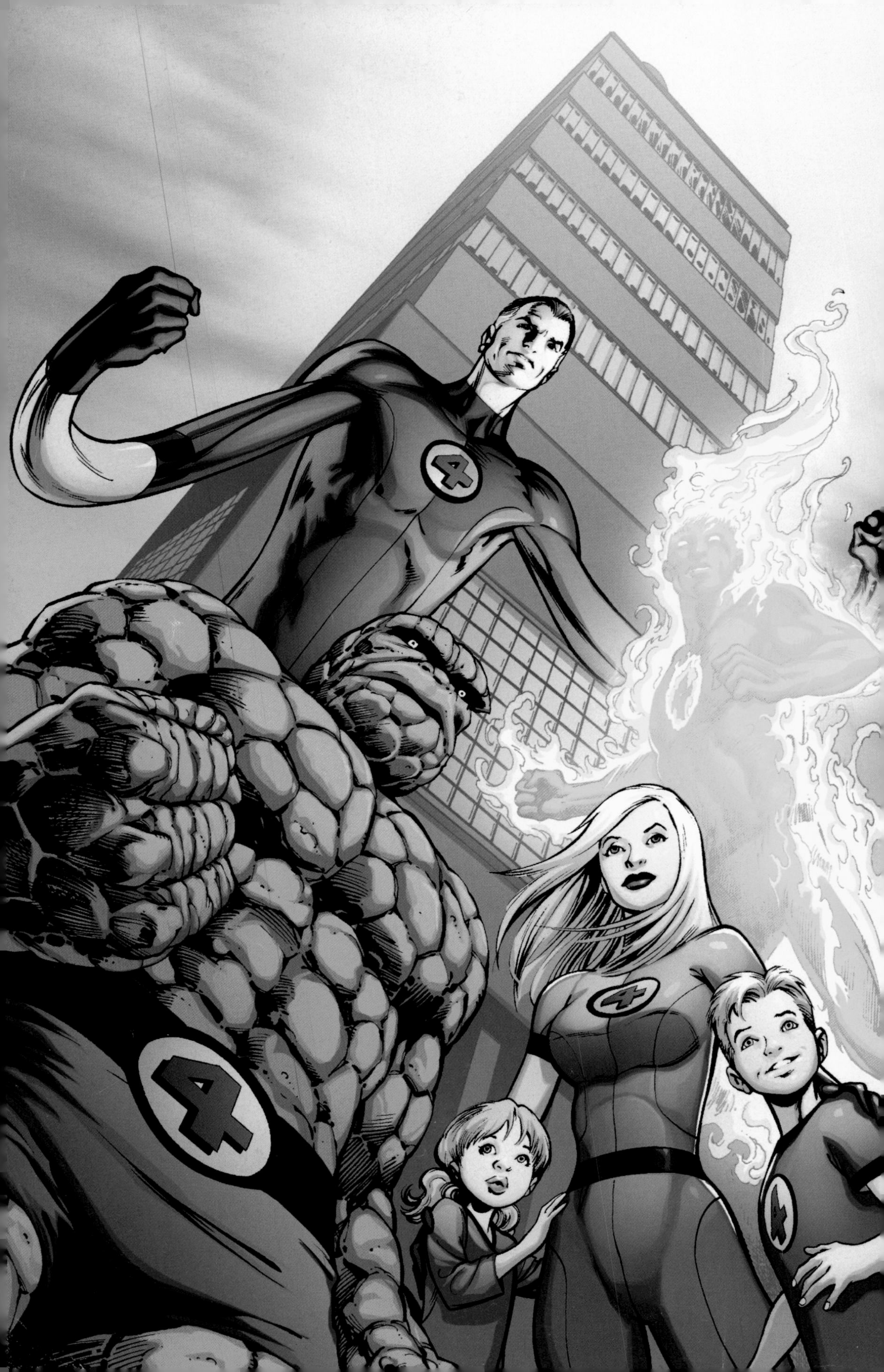

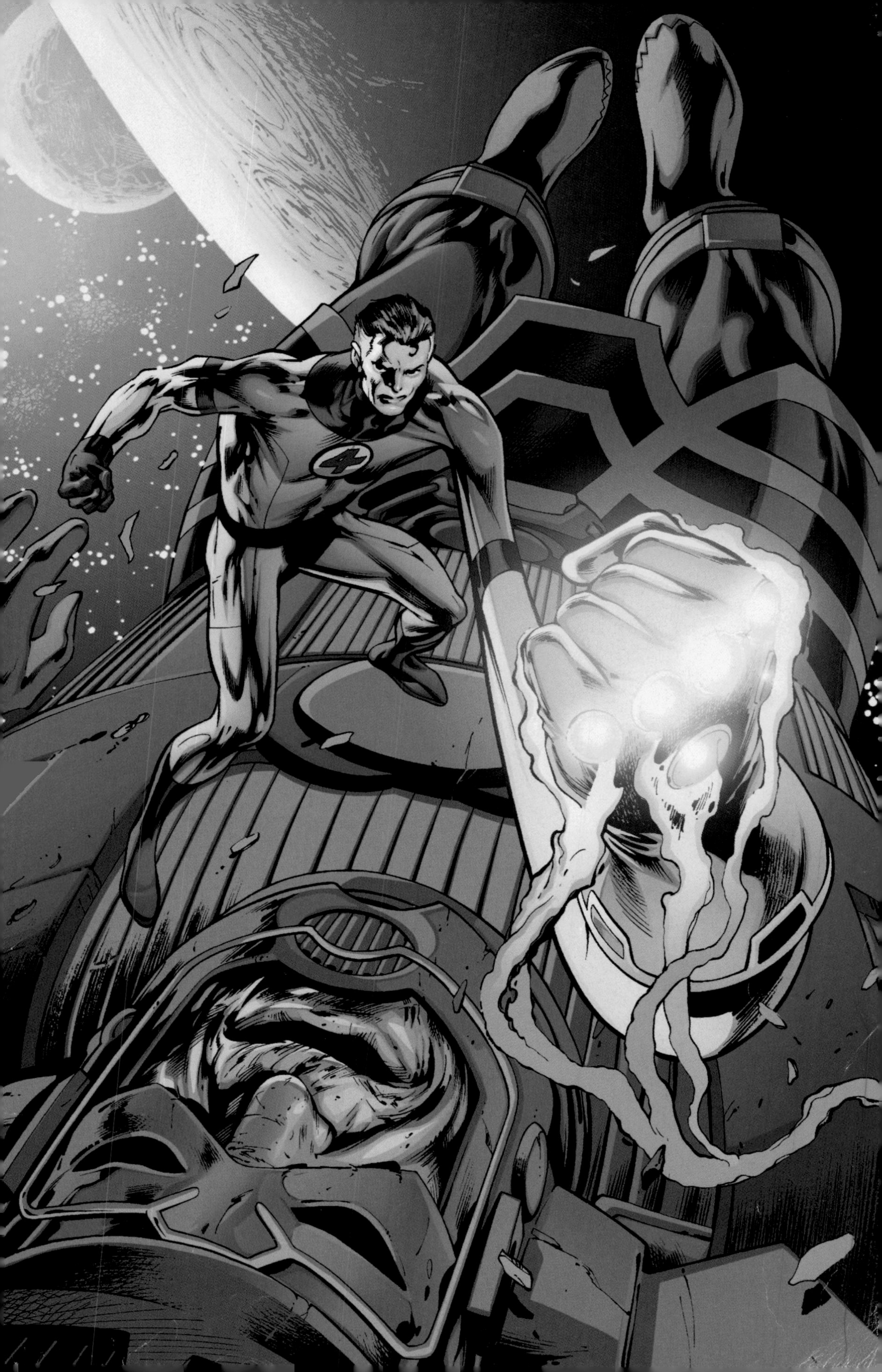

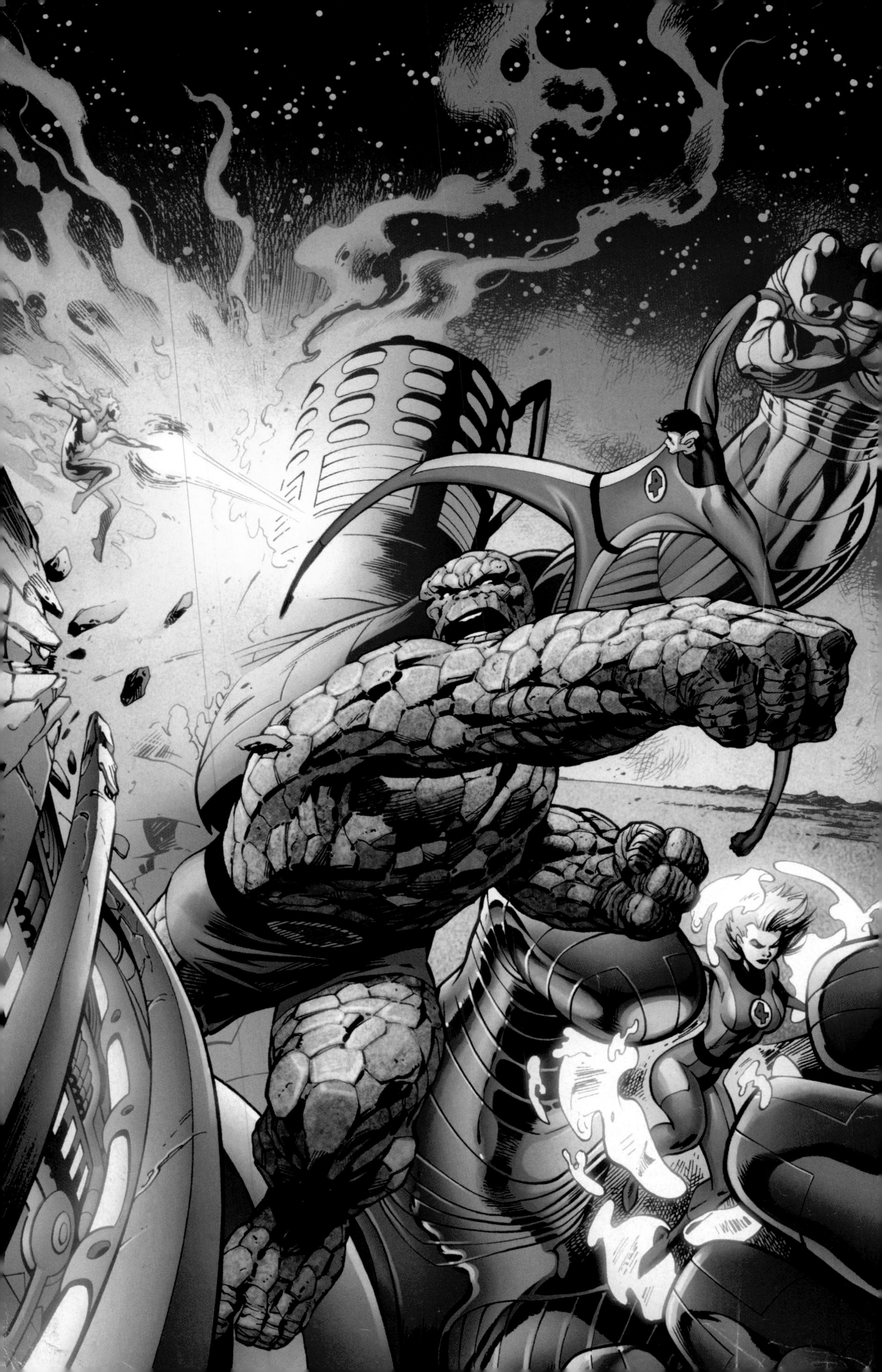

#572 SUPER HERO SQUAD VARIANT: CHRISTOPHER JONES AND SOTOCOLOR

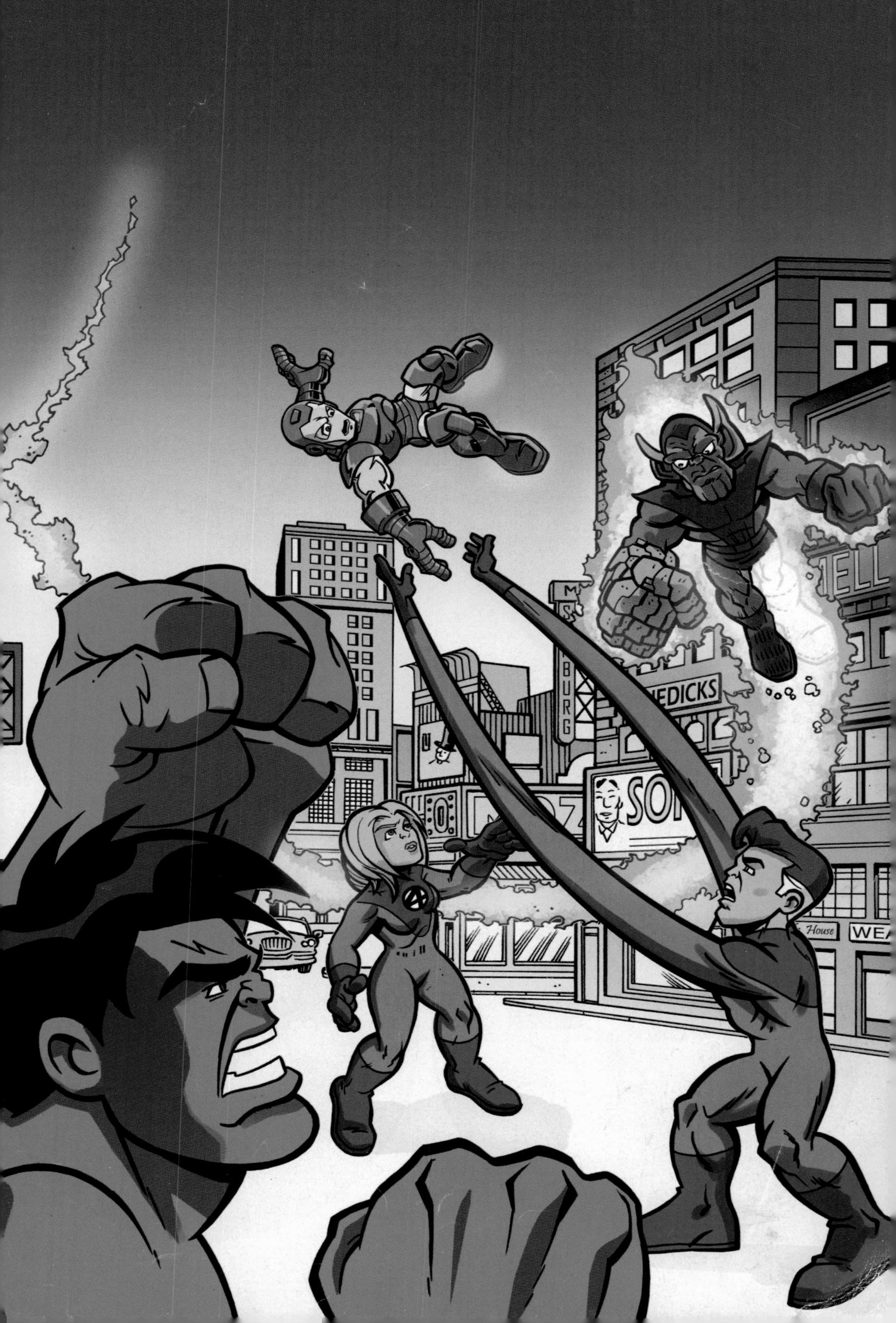
NEDICKS
BURG

#574 VARIANT: DALE EAGLESHAM AND PAUL MOUNTS

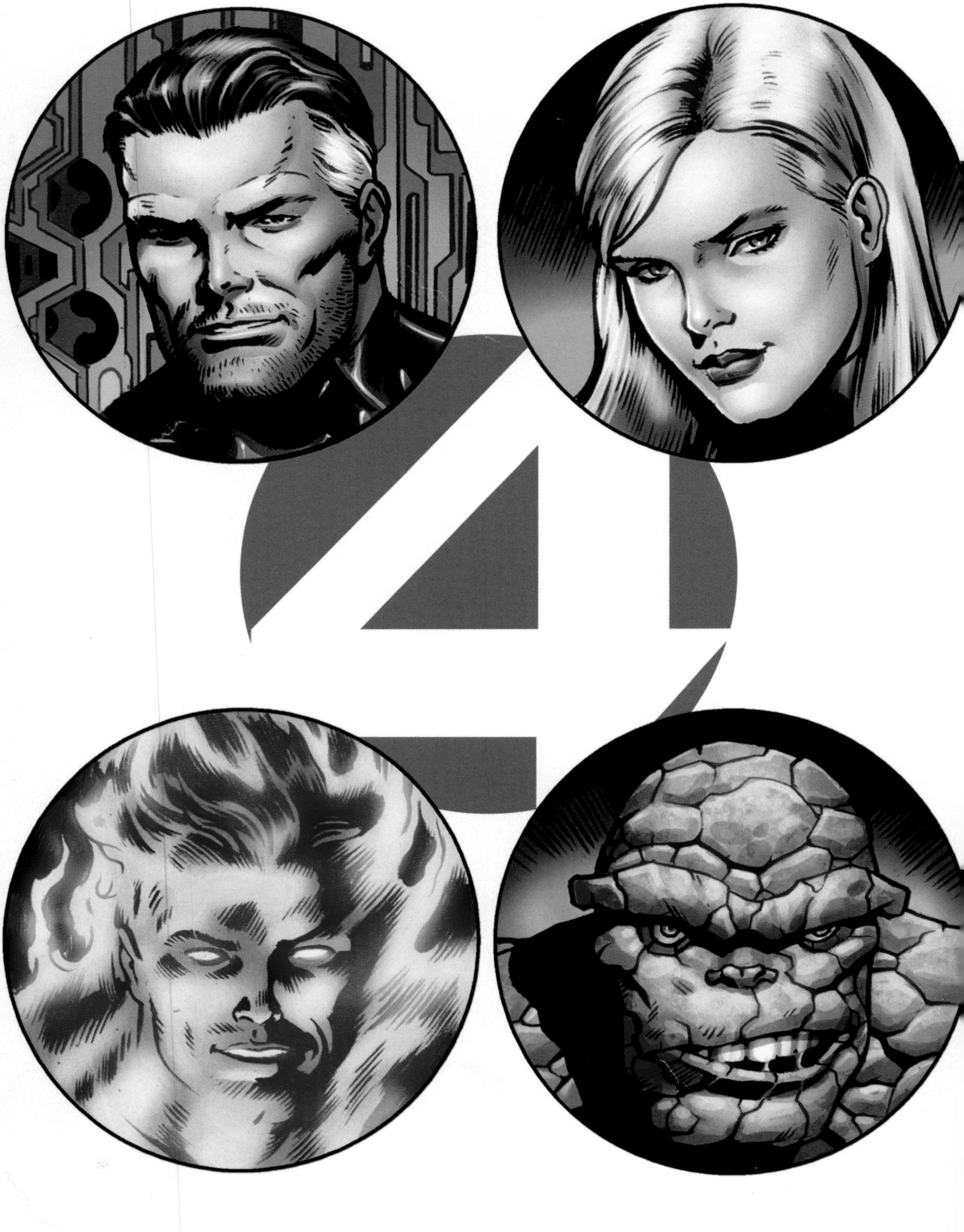